INTERMEDIARIES IN
JUSTIC

Improving commu [...] ble
witnesses an

Joyce Plotnikoff and Ri [...] Woolfson

This book is dedicated to John Thomas and Igor Judge, the current and former Lord Chief Justice, whose leadership has furthered the cause of vulnerable people at court; to the intermediaries themselves, a small group of professionals who 'punch above their weight'; to Barbara Esam, Deborah Turnbull and Kathy Rowe, with whom we worked for longer than any of us care to remember; and to Emily Henderson, who nagged us into embarking on this project, provided the artwork, generously shared her unpublished research and collaborated over many late night and early morning conversations between Hertfordshire and New Zealand.

First published in Great Britain in 2015 by

Policy Press
University of Bristol
1-9 Old Park Hill
Bristol BS2 8BB
UK
t: +44 (0)117 954 5940
pp-info@bristol.ac.uk
www.policypress.co.uk

North America office:
Policy Press
c/o The University of Chicago Press
1427 East 60th Street
Chicago, IL 60637, USA
t: +1 773 702 7700
f: +1 773 702 9756
sales@press.uchicago.edu
www.press.uchicago.edu

Contents

Contents

About the authors

Joyce Plotnikoff and Richard Woolfson have worked together since 1991 and formed Lexicon Limited in 2003. Projects include the *Child Witness Pack* (1993, NSPCC and ChildLine); *Prosecuting Child Abuse* (1995, Blackstone); the judicial training film *A Case for Balance* (1997, NSPCC); *The 'Go-Between', Evaluation of Intermediary Pathfinder Projects* (2007, Ministry of Justice); *Measuring Up? Evaluating Implementation of Government Commitments to Young Witnesses in Criminal Proceedings* (NSPCC and Nuffield Foundation, 2009); and *Registered Intermediaries in Action* (NSPCC and Ministry of Justice, 2011). With Professor Penny Cooper, they are co-founders of www.theadvocatesgateway.org, the Advocacy Training Council's website launched in 2013, and wrote its first 11 toolkits. For over 20 years, they have trained members of overseas judiciary in England and abroad.

Richard holds a doctorate in mathematics from the University of Oxford. He spent six years as an academic before joining the information technology industry. He has been a magistrate, a member of the Access to Justice subgroup of the Civil Justice Council and chaired his local Courts Board and Crown Prosecution Service Local Scrutiny Involvement Panel.

Joyce studied at the Universities of Bristol and Oxford. She has been a social worker and children's guardian. She was a lawyer in the US courts for 10 years. In 1981 she received a US Supreme Court Fellowship and the Justice Tom C Clark award; in 2013, she received an Administration of Justice award from the US Supreme Court Fellows Association. Joyce is a member of the pool of experts advising the Judicial College of England and Wales. In 2015 she received a DBE in the Queen's New Year Honours List.

Relevant guidance is available in toolkit 16, 'Intermediaries: step by step' (www.theadvocatesgateway.org) and in 'Making the most of working with an intermediary' (www.lexiconlimited.co.uk).

The Nuffield Foundation

The Nuffield Foundation is an endowed charitable trust that aims to improve social wellbeing in the widest sense. It funds research and innovation in education and social policy and also works to build capacity in education, science and social science research. The Nuffield Foundation funded this project, but the views expressed are those of the authors and not necessarily those of the Foundation. More information is available at www.nuffieldfoundation.org

Acknowledgements

We are indebted to 20 remarkable intermediaries who shared details of all aspects of their work. Their professional backgrounds span speech and language therapy, psychology, teaching, psychotherapy, occupational therapy and community development with deaf people. Their previous occupations have also included police officer, opera singer and actor; overseas development in Cambodia, Sri Lanka, India and Mozambique; and "the only speech and language therapist in Botswana". A further 45 intermediaries generously provided additional case examples. Our contributors cover every area of relevant specialist skill.

Statistical information was provided by Rachel Surkitt, National Crime Agency; Baljit Wirk and her team at the Ministry of Justice; Lisa McCrindle, NSPCC; and Amanda Naylor, Victim Support. Advice was provided by Karen Bryan and Sally Jones, both of whom have played key roles in independent oversight of the intermediary scheme since its inception. Thanks are also due to the Advocacy Training Council, Bar Standards Board, Criminal Bar Association, Crown Prosecution Service, HM Courts and Tribunals Service, Judicial College, Law Society, Northern Ireland Department of Justice and the Solicitors' Association of Higher Courts Advocates for their patience in responding to our queries.

We received helpful feedback from 138 criminal justice professionals, the largest number yet to comment on the intermediary role: members of the judiciary (obtained with the kind assistance of Patience Lusengo of the Judicial College), lawyers, police officers, Crown Prosecutors and the Witness Service. The National Crime Agency provided access to its database of over 2,000 comments about intermediaries. A representative range of quotes from this database and our respondents are included throughout the book.

Finally, we are grateful to Teresa Williams, Director of Social Research and Policy at the Nuffield Foundation, Sharon Witherspoon MBE, its Director, and to the Foundation's trustees, who have supported our research for many years and awarded the grant for this book.

Foreword

In 2004 Lord Judge warmly welcomed *In Their Own Words,* the seminal study of the giving of evidence by young witnesses written by Dame Joyce Plotnikoff and Dr Richard Woolfson. Following on from that, the implementation of the government's commitment to improve the position of young witnesses giving evidence was the subject of a further study in 2009 by the same authors and entitled *Measuring Up.* I warmly welcomed that further study and added in my foreword that, if we were to have the good fortune of having the benefit of another study by the same authors half a decade hence, I hoped that it would show that real change had been achieved. Half a decade hence we do indeed have the good fortune of a new study directed to one of the commitments – the role of an intermediary.

In writing *Intermediaries in the Criminal Justice System* the authors have produced a work that comprehensively explains the origin of the concept and the way the role of the intermediary has been developed under the provisions of the Youth Justice and Criminal Evidence Act 1999. Its detailed chapters give the invaluable guidance that only these authors can give. Reflecting their characteristic style, the book is accessible and very human. A particularly welcome aspect is the way the role of intermediaries is brought to life in the intermezzo that ends each chapter. It is a book that works on many levels: rigorous and thoughtful enough for those who work in the criminal justice system, yet understandable and engaging for those who have a more general interest.

Besides being a guide it is an incisive and clear evaluation of the practical working of the scheme some 10 years after the scheme was introduced by the Home Office by way of a pilot. It is a truism that change is not just about having a new framework and new legislation in place, but about the change in culture necessary to make the new legislation and framework a reality. It is evident in 2015 that some of the ideas that would have seemed radical at the outset of the intermediary pilot have been absorbed into the culture of criminal proceedings. There have been tangible advances in the way advocates and judges deal with vulnerable witnesses and, while there is much yet to be done, I do believe that we have achieved real change. Good practice needs to continue to be reinforced through training and a willingness to question continually how our system of criminal justice provides a system that is fair to those who are vulnerable.

The case made for the intermediary scheme in the book is compelling, but however compelling a case, the real difficulties, change of culture apart, have to be tackled. That formidable task is made even more difficult by the severe resource constraints currently faced by the criminal justice system. However the care and concern that the authors have demonstrated through their tireless work in improving the position of vulnerable witnesses compels each person interested in the fairness of the criminal justice system to ensure, whatever the difficulties, that the use of intermediaries wherever appropriate becomes an integral part of justice.

I will watch with interest the progress over the next half decade and hope then that either the authors themselves or a further study will be able to demonstrate that the task has finally been achieved.

Lord Thomas of Cwmgiedd
Lord Chief Justice of England and Wales
London, May 2015

ONE

Introduction: a fresh pair of eyes

Picture this.

A police officer is attempting to interview a three-year-old girl to see whether any offence has been committed against her. The person sitting alongside the officer and the child is an intermediary, an independent communication specialist. In an assessment session, the intermediary explores the child's level of communication. The child is invited to draw herself and her mother, also present. The intermediary checks that the drawings have a stable identity in the child's mind by making a deliberate naming error. The child is consistent about 'who is who'. An hour later, in the police interview, the child begins drawing her uncle by marking with her crayon in the middle of the page. She says "uncle's cock" twice, though the intermediary and officer are initially unsure they have heard her correctly. The girl says it again. She continues to draw, adding a little figure between her uncle's legs that she identifies as herself. The police search her uncle's computer which contains thousands of pornographic pictures of young children. He pleads guilty to this and to offences against his niece so she is not required to give evidence at trial.

Officers visit a house and find a young woman who has been kept in virtual slavery. She is deaf and has had no exposure to language or education. An intermediary, deaf himself, works with her over 10 sessions to build rapport and create a method of communicating with her. The police, who are always present, go on to film 14 interviews with the young woman, assisted by the intermediary, in which she gradually discloses rape and other offences. At trial, where her communication is facilitated by the intermediary, she gives evidence over many days. The defendant receives a lengthy sentence.

A 10-year-old girl arrives at school and the teacher sees a bite mark on her upper arm. The child has moderate learning difficulties and poor language skills; she has a low level of understanding, poor articulation and is generally unwilling to speak. When questioned about the bite mark, the girl just says "mummy". An intermediary is asked to assess her. The girl is happy to participate in a variety of play activities and demonstrates her ability to describe situations and simple sequences using small figures, drawings and 'Play-doh' models. At the police interview, the police officer uses the bite mark on the girl's arm as a prompt to explain why he wants to talk to her. With the assistance of the intermediary, the girl shows and tells what happened while she was playing in her garden. She points to her arm and makes a buzzing sound, then uses a figure representing her mother to show mummy's face on her arm. The girl had an insect bite which the mother had sucked out. No police action was required: a happy outcome for a very worried parent.

A young man with Asperger syndrome walks onto a zebra crossing and angers a driver who has to brake suddenly. The driver stabs him; the young man spends weeks in intensive care and even on recovery is afraid to leave home. An intermediary assesses him and assists at the police interview. She recommends that he give evidence over a live link outside the courtroom, but on the day of the trial the young man locks himself in his bathroom. The police persuade him to attend but the live link is not working. He is extremely agitated but agrees to give evidence in court behind a screen, accompanied by the intermediary. The defence advocate follows the intermediary's recommendations by asking short questions and giving the young man plenty of time to respond. The judge asks the intermediary to rephrase some of counsel's questions. The defendant is convicted and receives a custodial sentence. The young man says that, for the first time in 18 months, his life can move on.

A man with schizophrenia is the victim of a violent hate crime. Police officers take a written statement. At his familiarisation visit to the court before the trial, he tells the Witness Service that he has memory problems. This information is relayed to the prosecution and, as a result, an intermediary is asked to assess him. His symptoms include visual and auditory delusions and paranoid thoughts affecting his communication but the intermediary considers that he can give evidence with her assistance. The prosecution's application for the intermediary to be present at trial is contested by the defence but agreed by the judge. The intermediary makes recommendations about how the lawyers should question the witness. These include not muttering, covering their mouths or rustling their papers so as to avoid triggering his paranoid behaviours. During the trial, the man refers to a visual prompt card created by the intermediary, reminding him to listen to the questions and think before answering. The defendant who attacked him is convicted.

Two women with cerebral palsy allege assault by one of their care workers. Intermediaries assess the women's communication and assist them when they are interviewed by the police on film. One witness communicates using an electronic aid with symbols and pictures: the intermediary adds icons for the options 'I don't know', 'I don't understand' and 'not true'. The other can answer only 'yes' and 'no' questions using her eye movements; the intermediary helps identify and document her responses. The questioning takes a lot of time. These filmed interviews are shown to the court but the defence advocate declines to question the women, even with intermediary help. Other witnesses give evidence. The jury convicts the defendant, who receives a custodial sentence.

Intermediaries: new players in the criminal justice system

'The role of registered intermediary is an outstanding tool. Their expertise, enthusiasm and professionalism have been outstanding and played a vital role in the successful outcome of some difficult and protracted enquiries. I am a strong advocate for their use, encouraging my colleagues to employ, where necessary, the outstanding skills they bring to a criminal investigation.' (Senior Crown Prosecutor)

This book celebrates the role of the communication specialists known as intermediaries and describes best practice in their work and that of the professionals who work with them. It follows the criminal justice system's learning curve in the first decade since intermediaries were introduced in a Home Office pilot scheme in 2004; phased national rollout across England and Wales was completed in 2008. A similar scheme is being piloted in Northern Ireland but, to our disappointment as Scots, there is no equivalent provision in Scotland.

Intermediaries have the first active new role at trial for hundreds of years and yet they have almost no public profile. Even so, their impact has been immense. They have helped thousands of children and vulnerable adults, including some who have literally no voice, to be heard by the criminal justice process. Before intermediaries, it was unthinkable that witnesses like those described above would be interviewed by the police, let alone that their evidence would form the basis for criminal charges. The young and vulnerable are targeted precisely because of their vulnerability; for the same reason, they may be denied access to justice. The Court of Appeal, in upholding the conviction in the final example above, said that 'Until recently, there was no possibility of the court even considering the evidence of complainants with serious communication difficulties' (*R v Watts* [2010] EWCA 1824, para 56). Intermediary use is not restricted to extreme cases. They also help improve the quality of evidence from adults with a range of communication needs, many of which are hidden; and from children, at least half of whom, across age groups, do not understand questions asked at court, a figure rising to 90% for those under 10 (Plotnikoff and Woolfson, 2009a). Without assistance, interviewers and questioners are unlikely to address communication problems that are not immediately apparent, and miscommunication is the inevitable result.

Intermediaries are independent and owe their duty to the court, not to either side of the case. Their role is to assist everyone's communication. In a polite but persuasive way, they challenge the traditional criminal justice approach at all levels, advising police officers, lawyers, judges and magistrates, Witness Service supporters and court personnel. Intermediaries represent a range of disciplines; all have years of experience in their chosen field. They bring not only their professional skills but also an outsider's common-sense perspective and lateral thinking to a justice system notoriously resistant to change.

Most of their work is conducted out of public view. Even criminal justice practitioners are likely to have little idea about the full spectrum of intermediary activities, or the creative ways they go about supporting communication. They help police officers plan how to modify questions at investigative interviews and simplify procedures for suspect identification. They identify or create communication aids to clarify a particular line of questioning. They propose ways to modify the surroundings or circumstances in which questioning is conducted in police interview and at trial, negotiating adjustments to maximise the opportunity for people to give their best evidence. No two cases are alike. Some are extraordinary: for example, an intermediary obtained the court's permission for a man with autism spectrum disorder to give evidence wearing a lion's tail, his comfort object in daily life.

Their greatest impact has been on cross-examination at trial. Decades of research have demonstrated that leading questions which suggest the answer, the norm in cross-examination, confuse vulnerable witnesses and are likely to produce unreliable answers. The simple objective of the intermediary role is to ensure that witnesses understand the questions asked, are enabled to give the answers that they wish to give and those in court understand the answers given. Intermediaries use their assessment of the person's communication needs to suggest alternatives to leading and other types of complex question. At trial, they sit alongside witnesses, monitor questions and answers and intervene to alert the court to miscommunication; there is increasing acceptance of their recommendations. In some cases, they change the dynamics of the trial: the intermediary, judge and lawyers on both sides work together to plan how the witness will be questioned, even to the extent of screening cross-examination questions, a degree of collaboration unimaginable when the intermediary scheme was first conceived.

This book is a snapshot of legal culture in transition. Intermediaries have demonstrated the scope for improving interaction with vulnerable witnesses, but only where practitioners are sufficiently skilled and willing to adapt their approach to the witness's needs. The former Lord Chief Justice, Lord Judge (2011, p 16), has observed that intermediaries have 'introduced fresh insights' and 'improved the administration of justice ... without a diminution in the entitlement of the defendant to a fair trial', concluding that we have not yet 'arrived at our final destination' on their use.

Explanations

Intermediaries have identified themselves by pseudonyms.

Most of the book concerns 'registered' intermediaries recruited by the Ministry of Justice to assist vulnerable witnesses. Chapter 13 describes the work of intermediaries for vulnerable defendants; these intermediaries are 'non-registered'.

The term 'vulnerable' as applied to witnesses and defendants is unsatisfactory and may well be rejected by those to whom it is applied. It is, however, the term adopted in legislation, guidance and case law.

The terms 'learning disability' and 'learning difficulty' are sometimes thought to be interchangeable but have different meanings: a learning difficulty (for example dyslexia), unlike learning disability, does not affect intellect.

References to 'the judiciary' include circuit judges and High Court judges, both of whom sit in the Crown Court, and district judges and magistrates, who sit in magistrates' and youth courts. Most rules and procedures applicable to 'judges' apply also to magistrates. The terms 'advocate' and 'lawyer' apply collectively to barristers, solicitor advocates and solicitors.

Examples are drawn from real cases; details have been anonymised and changed. Where case outcomes are known, this information is included for the reader's interest. Outcomes depend on many complex factors, of which intermediary involvement is only one. The government does not collect data about outcomes in intermediary cases.

TWO

The intermediary scheme
in England and Wales

Of all the legislative special measures intended to assist vulnerable witnesses, intermediaries have the greatest potential to help those with a communication need to give their best evidence. In the UK, 1% of people are estimated to have speech, language or communication problems sufficient to affect everyday functioning: this may be an underestimate (Enderby and Davies, 1989; Bryan et al, 1991). More than a million children suffer from speech, language and communication difficulties (Department for Children, Schools and Families, 2008); around 10% have a long-term speech, language and communication need (Law et al, 2000) or a clinically recognisable mental disorder (Office for National Statistics, 2005); and rates of childhood autism are around 1%, far higher than previous estimates (Baird et al, 2006).

The origins of the intermediary role date back to 1955. In that year, Israel introduced the 'youth examiner', a social worker responsible for questioning children (Libai, 1969); South Africa passed legislation in 1977 enabling an intermediary to relay lawyers' questions to children; a few more recent intermediary provisions in other parts of the world are not in active use (Henderson, 2012). Introduction of a scheme is under active consideration in New South Wales and South Australia (communications to the authors, March 2015) and is being piloted in Canada (www.access-to-justice.org).

The intermediary concept was first proposed in England and Wales in 1987. Drawing on the Israeli model, legal scholar Glanville Williams proposed that a 'child examiner' relay lawyers' questions to young witnesses while their evidence

7

was videotaped before trial (Williams, 1987a, 1987b). The idea was quickly taken up by an advisory group chaired by Judge Thomas Pigot QC which recommended capturing all of children's evidence, including cross-examination, before trial and that courts should have discretion to order that the advocate's questions 'be relayed through a person approved by the court who enjoys the child's confidence' (Home Office, 1989, para 2.32). Such use of an 'interlocutor' would be justified where 'it is absolutely impossible for counsel to communicate successfully with a child' (para 2.33).

The Criminal Justice Act 1991 drew on Pigot's recommendations to make some children's police videotaped interviews admissible as their evidence-in-chief, but children still needed to attend trial for cross-examination. Proposals for a child interlocutor and the pre-trial filming of cross-examination were disregarded. However, in 1997 a study of victims with learning disabilities proposed that an 'intermediary questioner' translate the questions of defence and prosecution lawyers (Sanders et al, 1997) and a report the following year recommended that courts be given statutory powers to order intermediary assistance where this would assist vulnerable witnesses to give their best evidence (Home Office, 1998).

The intermediary special measure

'We were unable to communicate at all with the witness. The intermediary assisted us greatly.' (Police officer)

The intermediary is one of a package of special measures in the Youth Justice and Criminal Evidence Act 1999 designed to assist vulnerable witnesses. It provides for examination of eligible witnesses to be conducted through an intermediary whose function is to communicate 'questions put to the witness, and to any persons asking such questions, the answers given by the witness in reply to them, and to explain such questions or answers so far as necessary to enable them to be understood by the witness or person in question' (section 29(2)). The wording of section 29 would allow the intermediary to relay questions and answers as interlocutor, as envisaged by Williams, Pigot and Sanders. In practice, this aspect of the role has developed more restrictively, with intermediaries advising on how best to communicate with the witness, monitoring questioning and alerting questioners when miscommunication occurs or is likely. However, intermediaries are used in many other ways not envisaged by section 29.

Intermediaries are not supporters or expert witnesses: they form an independent new profession owing its duty to the court, not to the witness or either side; the Act requires them to take a formal oath (section 29(5)).

Other special measures

The 1999 Act provides for other special measures: video recorded evidence-in-chief (section 27); giving evidence over a live link from outside the courtroom (section 24; see Figure 2.1 below) or while screened in court (section 23); giving evidence in private (section 25); communication aids to assist witnesses while giving evidence (section 30); and removal of wigs and gowns at Crown Court (section 26). Section 28 provides for pre-recorded cross-examination to be played at trial, as recommended by Judge Pigot. This provision was shelved by successive governments and was not piloted until 2014 (see Chapter Twelve).

Figure 2.1

Eligibility

Section 16 of the 1999 Act sets out the groups eligible for special measures: witnesses with a mental disorder or learning disability; those with a physical disability or physical disorder; and children aged under 17 at the time of the hearing (raised to under 18 by the Coroners and Justice Act 2009, section 98). While children are automatically eligible for special measures, in certain circumstances they may opt out of recorded evidence-in-chief, use of the live link or screens (Coroners and Justice Act 2009, section 100).

The court must determine whether special measures would be likely to improve the quality of an eligible witness's evidence. 'Quality' means more than intelligibility: it encompasses 'completeness, coherence and accuracy' and being able to address the questions put and give answers that can be understood 'both individually and collectively' (section 16(5) of the 1999 Act). The intermediary's primary responsibility is therefore to facilitate 'complete, coherent and accurate communication' when a vulnerable witness is interviewed by the police or questioned at court (Ministry of Justice, 2012, Code of Conduct, para 1); the emphasis on 'accurate' communication has been particularly important in development of the intermediary function. In deciding whether to grant special measures, the court must consider factors including the witness's views and the possibility that special measures might inhibit evidence from being tested effectively (section 17).

Witnesses for both the prosecution and defence are eligible for special measures but, in practice, almost all applications for intermediaries under the Act are made by the prosecution. The lack of applications on behalf of defence witnesses is in part because there are many fewer defence witnesses but also because of an apparent lack of awareness that young or otherwise vulnerable defence witnesses are eligible for special measures (see Chapter Fourteen). This has contributed to a mistaken perception that the intermediary is an arm of the prosecution, particularly as section 17 of the 1999 Act excludes vulnerable defendants from eligibility. (Northern Ireland's pilot scheme, which began in 2013, provides an intermediary for vulnerable defendants but only while giving evidence: Cooper and Wurtzel, 2014; Department of Justice, 2015.)

The judiciary can use its powers to appoint an intermediary for a witness without an application being made (section 19) and has done so, but sometimes not until after the witness started giving evidence, requiring the trial to be adjourned. The Court of Appeal criticised a judge who prevented cross-examination of a child witness without considering additional special measures such as an intermediary 'as he was bound to do' (*R v Lubemba, R v JP* [2014] EWCA Crim 2064, para 24).

Registered intermediaries

> 'Registered intermediaries have gone places that we couldn't.'
> (Police officer)

Section 29 of the 1999 Act, which created the role of intermediary, does not specify who can perform it. Even before the section was implemented, the Court of Appeal accepted the use of a social worker to translate the words at interview of an adult with severe learning difficulties (*R v Duffy* [1999] QB 919). However, the Home Office decided to take forward section 29 by recruiting a cadre of intermediaries with relevant professional skills; registration was subject to passing a training course and a police criminal record check. A Code of Practice, Code of Ethics and guidance manual for registered intermediaries were provided (in the latest version, Ministry of Justice, 2012).

The first intermediaries were recruited in 2003. The Home Office managed the register and responded to requests for an intermediary whose skills most closely matched the needs of the vulnerable witness. The police, Crown Prosecution Service (CPS) and defence lawyers were encouraged to regard the register as the first port of call whenever the need for an intermediary arose. Use of intermediaries from the register is customary for witnesses but is not legally required (*R (OP) v Secretary of State for Justice* [2014] EWHC 1944 (Admin)).

Restricting eligibility for the pilot scheme

> Intermediary use is confined to 'witnesses who have profound communication difficulties who would not be able to give evidence unassisted' and those with 'significant communication difficulty which means evidence could not be given without an intermediary'. (Home Office, 2003, now superseded)

> Intermediaries are available for 'very young' children. (Home Office, 2002, para 2.39, now superseded)

The Home Office pilot scheme operated during 2004 and 2005 in six police force areas. Our two-year evaluation, which aimed to establish a model for national implementation, ended in March 2006 (Plotnikoff and Woolfson, 2007a). At the time of the evaluation, there was little recognition of the extent of miscommunication in the justice process. Poor awareness of special measures and failure to recognise eligibility were fundamental problems (Burton et al, 2006; Cooper and Roberts, 2006).

Section 29 does not prescribe a minimum condition for use of an intermediary. Section 16(5) requires consideration of whether special measures will improve the 'quality' of the witness's evidence. However, initial Home Office guidance imposed a more restrictive interpretation, suggesting that eligibility for intermediary assistance was confined to witnesses with 'profound' or 'significant' communication difficulties who would be unable to give evidence unassisted. As a result, some practitioners in pilot areas believed that the special measure was for those who could communicate only by blinking or otherwise could not speak.

Further confusion was caused by policy messages suggesting intermediaries were only for the youngest witnesses, although at the time few such cases were brought to court (Hansard, 15 April 1999, col 442). Two pilot areas said that they did not prosecute cases involving 'very young' children and one of these did not anticipate applying for intermediaries on behalf of anyone under 17. Thames Valley, which accounted for 41% of all pilot appointments, was the only pilot police force to use intermediaries for significant numbers of children, including some aged four or five. A further dampening effect on requests for intermediaries for children was the tendency of practitioners to apply adult criteria (namely, physical or mental disability or disorder) to those eligible by virtue of age. 'Reading down' eligibility in this way excluded children with no medically diagnosed difficulty but whose communication needs derived from their developmental stage, trauma, poor concentration or challenging behaviour.

Re-launch of the pilot scheme

Problems of interpretation were fed back to the Home Office during the evaluation and the scheme was re-launched in 2005 with fresh guidance explaining accurately the eligibility criteria (Association of Chief Police Officers and Office for Criminal Justice Reform, 2005). This is now expressed as follows:

> An intermediary may be able to help improve the quality of evidence of any vulnerable adult or child witness … who is unable to detect and cope with misunderstanding, or to clearly express their answers to questions, especially in the context of an interview or while giving evidence in court. (Ministry of Justice, 2011a, para 2.194)

Numbers of requests for intermediaries increased after the re-launch but use remained uneven: when the evaluation ended, three areas together accounted for only 13% of appointments. While the revised guidance was generally welcomed, some in both senior and frontline criminal justice roles were uncomfortable with it, or even disagreed with the move towards broader interpretation of eligibility. Defending the fact that his area requested only three intermediary appointments during the pilot period, one Chief Crown Prosecutor responded that "Low intelligence of the victim, or being merely inarticulate, is not in our view enough to engage the intermediary scheme." Overcoming such misconceptions presented a challenge.

The evaluation report recommended national rollout of the intermediary scheme and this was immediately accepted by the

Home Office in 2006. Dr John Reid, then Home Secretary, announced a moratorium on publication in full of all pending research reports, including ours, contributing to criticism from the Centre for Crime and Justice Studies about 'Home Office suppression of criminological research' (Hope and Walters, 2008). After a lengthy delay, an eight-page summary of the evaluation was published by the new Ministry of Justice in June 2007. It was disappointing that the government did not make the practical guidance in the full report available to practitioners; many of the problems it addressed were replicated at national rollout.

Response of practitioners during the pilot stage

Overall, the response of the judiciary, lawyers and police officers who worked directly with intermediaries was highly favourable. Intermediary reports – with assessment findings and recommendations about how best to question a witness and modify arrangements to take their evidence at court – were especially valued as an unprecedented source of advice. A barrister who admitted being "naturally suspicious" acknowledged in hindsight that his cross-examination was "clumsy". He concluded: "As it was, I ended up being the one who was surprised – by the extreme difficulty the complainant had in understanding what I thought were the simplest questions."

Almost all judges in the 12 pilot trials were positive about the experience, for example: "Overall, the intermediary worked very well. She was strong and intervened when questions became too complex. Her interventions did not come that often but they were invaluable." Only one judicial view was negative: a district judge in the youth court who described intermediaries as "a barrier to justice" because "the defence are entitled to lead in cross-examination ... [they] want to attack the witness and they cannot if they have several layers to go through".

His view was mirrored by some in the wider judicial community. At a pilot launch event, an intermediary described strategies she used to facilitate communication. The judge who spoke after her said to the criminal justice audience: "You could use the 'tricks' described by [the intermediary speaker]. We don't need intermediaries to do this. The success [of the intermediary

14

scheme] is not going to be very high." Comments from some judges not involved in pilot trials also downplayed the need: "We do trials with witnesses with minor learning difficulties day in day out"; "You would not have an intermediary for a very young child simply based on age"; and "Cases going through now don't need intermediaries."

Response of witnesses and carers during the pilot stage

It proved difficult to negotiate contact with vulnerable witnesses and their carers following closure of their cases; police officers seldom felt that it was appropriate to ask them to speak to researchers. However, those to whom we spoke were highly positive about the intermediary scheme, for example:

'[She was] brilliant. She helped talk for me.' (14-year-old boy with learning difficulties whose speech was almost unintelligible)

'It went very well. The intermediary was invaluable: she was able to get them to rephrase questions. It was very positive – I can't thank her enough.' (Carer of adult man with severe learning difficulties and speech impediment)

'The intermediary was brilliant – a diamond. I would recommend this to anyone. Without her he wouldn't have coped. He cracked up when he got to court – I was surprised he didn't cry during his evidence. He said there were some questions that he couldn't understand but he turned to her and she helped.' (Mother of an 11-year-old boy with cerebral palsy)

'My five-year-old was physically sick the night before court. The intermediary helped settle him because he was worried about not being able to answer questions. He knew he could tell her if he didn't understand.' (Mother)

'We would thoroughly recommend the intermediary scheme. It's incredible.' (Father of teenagers with significant hearing loss)

National Crime Agency Witness Intermediary Scheme matching service

'I was impressed at the speed with which an intermediary was identified and her ability to conform to the short time frame in which we had to operate.' (Police officer)

Control of the intermediary register passed to the Ministry of Justice in 2008. The Ministry outsourced the Witness Intermediary Scheme matching service in 2009; since 2013, it has been hosted by the National Crime Agency, a non-ministerial government department. Feedback about the quality of service the Agency provides has been very positive.

Almost all requests to the matching service are made by the police or CPS (defence solicitors – in respect of a defence witness – and courts are also entitled to use the service). A Request for Service form is completed by a police officer if the intermediary is sought for the investigative interview, or by the CPS if sought for trial. The form asks questions about the nature of the witness's communication needs. The Agency uses this information to seek an appropriate match to an intermediary with appropriate skills. Almost all requests are for complainants; the majority are for those under 18. Aside from eligibility by virtue of young age, the biggest category of requests is for people with learning disabilities.

Because vulnerable defendants are excluded from the 1999 Act, the government has taken the view that they are not entitled to access registered intermediaries via the matching service when judges exercise their inherent jurisdiction to appoint an intermediary for a defendant. These issues are explored in Chapter Thirteen, which describes the work of non-registered intermediaries with defendants; some of these are, in fact, on the Ministry of Justice register.

On registration, intermediaries are asked to indicate their areas of expertise using the following categories:

- work with children, by age group
- learning disability (mild/moderate, severe)
- attention deficit hyperactivity disorder
- autism spectrum disorder, including Asperger syndrome
- dyspraxia (developmental coordination disorder)
- dysarthria (unclear speech)
- language delay/disorder
- selective/elective mutism
- physical disability
- fluency (stammering and stuttering)
- deafness/hearing impairment
- voice disorders (including tracheotomy and laryngectomy)
- cerebral palsy
- brain or head injury (including stroke)
- neurological and progressive disorders (including Parkinson's disease and motor neurone disease)
- mental health issues (anxiety/depression, bi-polar affective disorder, obsessive compulsive disorder, personality disorder, schizophrenia, dementia)

Registration

'Without the registered intermediary, I simply would not have been able to conduct the interview.' (Police officer)

There were 98 intermediaries on the register at the end of 2014, a year which saw an 86% increase in requests for intermediaries over the previous 12 months. The fluctuation in numbers on the register and the rising level of demand are described in Chapter Fourteen.

Registered intermediaries are self-employed and are paid directly for their services. Most work part time as an intermediary: some are also in paid employment but take on cases in their own time. Most are aged over 40. Three-quarters are speech and language therapists, around 8% are teachers and others are drawn from professions including psychology, occupational therapy, nursing, social work and sign language interpretation.

Speech and language therapy is a predominantly female profession but the number of female intermediaries is striking in the male-dominated Crown Court environment. Women account for only one-third of self-employed barristers (Bar Standards Board, 2013) and one in five circuit judges (Judiciary Diversity Statistics, 2014. Only Azerbaijan and Armenia have a smaller proportion of female judges: European Commission for the Efficiency of Justice, 2014).

The Ministry of Justice's Intermediaries Registration Board oversees recruitment, training, assessment and professional compliance. The lead time from advertisement to registration of trained and police-checked intermediaries can be around six to nine months. Candidates must be graduates or equivalently qualified. The selection process seeks candidates who are not only well qualified and experienced professionally but have the confidence to express themselves and hold their own in a challenging environment: intermediaries draw parallels between the hierarchical culture of the courts and that of the NHS. In order to be registered, candidates must complete a modular training course and a rigorous assessment and accreditation process, consisting of a written examination and role play carried out before a retired judge. All intermediary induction training has been conducted by two barristers, David Wurtzel of City Law School, City University, and Professor Penny Cooper, Kingston Law School, Kingston University.

Wider use of intermediaries

In criminal cases, intermediary use has extended beyond assistance at police interview and trial, for example to facilitating the conduct of suspect identification procedures and the taking of victim personal statements. For the first time, an intermediary has assisted a vulnerable witness give evidence to the Court of Appeal (*R v FA* [2015] EWCA Crim 209); one has recently been requested in extradition proceedings. Their value is such that judges have used their inherent jurisdiction to appoint intermediaries for vulnerable defendants who are excluded from legislative eligibility (see Chapter Thirteen). In the civil jurisdiction, an intermediary has assisted a patient at a Mental Health Tribunal: she facilitated the taking of legal instructions and discussed her report recommendations with the Tribunal in the patient's absence before the hearing. She enabled the patient to say what he wanted to happen; tried to ensure, despite complex medical and legal language, that he understood the proceedings; and alerted the Tribunal when he needed a break.

In family proceedings, particularly in public law, parents as well as children often fall within the criminal law's definition of 'vulnerability'. An intermediary from the Ministry of Justice register can be provided in a family court case only if there is a direct link to a criminal prosecution involving the witness; where one has already been appointed and is available; and where there is no impact on availability of registered intermediaries for witnesses (Judicial College, 2013, chapter 5, para 48). Despite the absence of enabling legislation and formal matching and funding arrangements, judges in the family courts have exercised their inherent jurisdiction to appoint intermediaries for children and for vulnerable parents. (In South Africa, children who are parties or witnesses in family matters must be questioned through an intermediary if courts decide this is in their best interests: Children's Act 38, 2005, section 61(2)).

The use of intermediaries to assist young witnesses was raised by the Supreme Court in a case which removed the presumption that children should not give evidence in family cases except in exceptional circumstances (*Re W (Children) (Family Proceedings: Evidence)* [2010] UKSC 12). As a result, guidance was issued addressing how children's evidence could be taken, including intermediary use (Family Justice Council, 2011). The family courts have adapted the intermediary role as needed: recently, an intermediary acted as an interlocutor for two children, reviewing and simplifying more than 150 questions drafted by advocates. She was then filmed asking the children the questions. The resultant DVDs were submitted as evidence to a fact-finding hearing.

Intermediaries have also been appointed for vulnerable parents. Judges have enabled an intermediary to train and assist counsel in preparing a video recording of a parent's oral evidence (Family

Justice Council, 2014, p 4) and to assist a vulnerable parent to give evidence (*Wiltshire Council v N* [2013] EWHC 3502 (Fam)). The Court of Appeal has highlighted the needs of profoundly deaf participants who require assistance from a professional with 'a sophisticated and to a degree, bespoke understanding' of communication and comprehension (*Re C (A Child)* [2014] EWCA Civ 128, para 18; see also *Re R (Deaf Parents)* [2014] EWCC B41 (Fam)).

While most appointments involve public law cases brought by local authorities, intermediaries have also been used in private law family proceedings. The High Court commended the 'extremely impressive and dedicated involvement' of a registered intermediary who facilitated the evidence of X, a vulnerable 17-year-old witness: without this help, 'in all probability, X would have found it quite simply impossible to say as much as she did' (*Re A (A Child) (Vulnerable Witness: Fact Finding)* [2013] EWHC 2124 (Fam), para 5).

The absence of formal funding and arrangements to source intermediaries is seen as causing 'real obstacles' (*Re X (A Child: Evidence)* [2011] EWHC 3401 (Fam), para 42). 'If access to justice for vulnerable parties is not to be denied it is a matter which requires urgent review and clarification' (Judiciary of England and Wales, 2015, para 20). The Equality Act 2010 means that 'it is simply not an option to fail to afford the right level of regard' to a participant with disabilities (*Re C (A Child)* [2014] EWCA Civ 128, para 35). Funding must be agreed on a case by case basis; the President of the Family Division noted that the court can pay for an intermediary for a vulnerable parent during proceedings but queried how costs should be met where intermediary assistance is needed to assist a parent meeting professionals out of court (*In the matter of D (A Child)* [2014] EWFC 39; see also *Re K and H (Children: unrepresented father: cross-examination of child)* [2015] EWFC 1).

The Children and Vulnerable Witnesses Working Group set up by the President of the Family Division sees a 'pressing need' to address vulnerable people giving evidence in family proceedings, 'something in which the family justice system lags woefully behind the criminal justice system' (Judiciary of England and Wales, 2015, para 1). Its recommendations include enabling 'the direct evidence of children and support for the evidence of children to be heard at the youngest age appropriate for each child' and addressing 'the difficulties encountered when litigants in person seek to cross-examine witnesses who are often vulnerable and victims of abuse' (paras 14 and 35. See also Cooper, 2014; and toolkit 13, *Vulnerable Witnesses and Parties in the Family Courts*, www.theadvocatesgateway.org). The Working Group proposes a new Family Procedure Rule including a provision for 'a party or witness to be questioned through an intermediary' (Judiciary of England and Wales, 2015, para 35).

Intermezzo

Mavis and the disappearing teeth

Kitty (registered intermediary)

Late on a Friday, I received an urgent referral to act as intermediary for Mavis, who was in her 90s and was due to give evidence in a fraud trial the following Monday. I was told I would only be needed for one day. Mavis had hearing difficulties – but no hearing aids – and severe arthritis. Her evidence was to be given over a live link from home as she was too disabled to attend court. I was told that I would be needed to make sure she could hear her police interview when it was played back to her and to ensure that she could hear what was said by the judge and counsel over the live link. I planned to assess Mavis informally before proceedings were underway and report my findings to the judge during the tryout with the live link.

On Monday morning, I met the police officer who was going to drive me to Mavis's house. The officer explained that Mavis would watch the DVD interview in the morning then the BT man would patch us through to the court to test the equipment. On Tuesday, she would be cross-examined – so much for me only being needed for one day.

We arrived at Mavis's house in the cold and wet. Because of her arthritis, it took her 15 minutes to answer the door. The BT man was none too pleased as he had to keep his equipment dry. Mavis apologised for taking so long to get to the door and explained that she couldn't find her false teeth – she'd wrapped them in tissues but couldn't remember where they were. Her speech was nonetheless intelligible. Mavis lived alone; she relished the opportunity to chat and found it difficult to stop. It was apparent that her functional communication skills were good. As long as I raised my voice, she could understand and was completely aware of what was going on.

We started to watch the DVD of her police interview. It was immediately obvious that Mavis could not hear the officer or herself. There was no way I could repeat the interview from the screen. Fortunately the officer had brought the transcript, so I started to read it to her. Mavis quickly interjected: "I never said that. Who said I said that? They're a bloody liar." She was confused by the transcript. I explained again that I was reading what she and the interviewing officer said a year ago. This seemed to help and we started again.

Now Mavis came out with "That's right, that's what happened," only she didn't stop there. Every time I read out a sentence, she added comments; sometimes, she even pre-empted the next chunk of the interview. She was a feisty lady who was keen to see justice done. She did not hold back on her opinion of the defendant.

We had a break for Mavis to have a drink and to test the live link. After some technical hitches, we were patched through to the courtroom. Again, Mavis could hear nothing from the screen, so the judge agreed that I would relay the questions to Mavis word for word the next day. With all of her interjections, and the live link tryout, it had taken over three hours to go through the transcript, and still Mavis was raring to go.

Packing up to leave, I turned to Mavis and, forgetting momentarily, asked in my normal volume, "Can I use your toilet?" She replied, "No thanks love, I can manage myself." Hanging inside the door was her dressing gown, with tissue poking out of the pocket. We are faced with many dilemmas as intermediaries, but this was the first time I had to consider whether to put my hand in a dressing gown pocket to see if it contained missing false teeth. It did and Mavis was delighted to have them back again.

We said we'd return the following morning. A few hours later, my phone rang. It was the officer, to say the defendant had pleaded guilty: "Thanks for your help today. I'm on my way to tell Mavis now."

That ended my involvement. As with many intermediary referrals, there can be a lack of closure. But there is never time to dwell on it before the next referral arrives.

THREE

Behind the scenes: planning to assess the witness

Intermediaries are not like interpreters who can be booked at the last minute to turn up and translate questions and answers. Their work begins with an informal meeting with the witness for the purpose of building rapport and assessing the person's communication skills. This forms the basis of recommendations about how best to communicate with the witness and whether the assistance of an intermediary is required. This chapter describes the preparatory work intermediaries undertake prior to assessment. Even setting up these meetings poses practical challenges. Someone needs to accompany the intermediary, who should never be alone with the witness; it is preferable for this to be the officer who will conduct the interview. Ideally, there is time beforehand to obtain information about the witness from informal and professional sources and to send the witness a personalised letter of introduction. In practice, assessments are often requested at short notice, with little background information; many take place in challenging surroundings.

Contacting the police and obtaining background information

'The intermediary spoke to the witness's teacher and her psychologist. As a result of gaining background knowledge of the witness's learning difficulties, she produced cards which enabled the witness to have a greater understanding of the questions I asked. Due to the assessment, the video interview produced best evidence.' (Police officer)

The assessment cannot take place until the intermediary and the relevant police officer have spoken. Delays are inevitable when officers are hard to contact because of shift patterns or leave and no alternative officer has been identified. Making contact and finding convenient dates to see the witness together often requires perseverance. The police do not provide all the details of the alleged offence but still need to give intermediaries basic information, for example whether the allegation is sexual; involves a family member, carer or teacher; whether the witness has been bereaved; and whether a child is being looked after by the local authority or an adult has been removed to a place of safety. Jeeves assessed P, a young teenager, and enquired about P's support in the classroom: "Fortunately there was only a brief mention of this before the topic moved on, but the police officer confessed afterwards that her heart was in her mouth. The officer hadn't warned me that the suspect was a classroom assistant."

Officers should also provide intermediaries with contact details for key professionals (such as doctors, social workers and others) who can give insights into the witness's communication strengths and weaknesses, social and medical history. These contacts enable the intermediary to check the accuracy of information about the witness's communication needs as described on the Request for Service form. Problems arise where the information on which matching is based is inaccurate. Melissa took on a 'rush job' to assess G, a 10-year-old described as "not speaking, using some 'Makaton' signs and in a special school". The officer accompanying Melissa had not met G. On arrival, she found that little of the assessment material she had prepared was relevant:

> 'You'd want to weep. In fact, G was in mainstream school, receiving a little extra support. He probably had undiagnosed high level autism spectrum disorder. His communication difficulties were combined with sophisticated speech, for example: "You said I was doing okay. I wish to know if you mean that or if you really mean I'm fantastic, extraordinary or superb?" I said "I think you've just had a birthday," trying to get the assessment back on track. G replied: "Why do you want to know? That may be classified

information, and I'd have to consult my mother before divulging it." You certainly have to think on your feet in this job.'

If incorrect information on the Request for Service form results in appointment of an intermediary with the wrong skill set, the case may be returned for reassignment. Tosca was told that E had Asperger syndrome:

'After talking to her, I was pretty sure this wasn't correct. She had cuts indicating self-harm and had been in psychiatric hospital for long periods of time. I finished my assessment, wrote it up and then passed it back to the matching service for them to find an intermediary with mental health experience.'

Intermediaries should obtain information from professional sources before meeting a witness for the first time; this is essential if the witness is known to have mental health problems or other complex needs. Advance information may avoid what Tosca describes as "a bit of a surprise" when a witness said half-way through their first meeting: "Can I take my legs off?" Accessing information from official sources is usually time-consuming and requires consent forms to be signed by witnesses or someone authorised to give consent on their behalf. Officers should negotiate consent on behalf of intermediaries but in practice it often falls to the intermediary to pursue requests directly. Jeeves observes that: "The police often don't really understand care systems enough to know the best people to ask. In many cases, my enquiries before the assessment provide officers with information about the witness's circumstances of which they were unaware."

Lead time before meeting the witness allows the intermediary to send a personalised letter of introduction. This often includes the intermediary's picture and refers to witness interests to be discussed in the assessment. Receipt of this friendly letter can affect the witness's response. Staff in a secure hospital had not passed on Golightly's letter to Y, a teenager with Asperger syndrome and attachment issues:

'Y was very angry and distrusting. When the officer and I turned up for the first meeting, she told us to go away, using several expletives. I then liaised with Y's social worker who worked through my letter with her and she was prepared to meet me a couple of weeks later.'

The assessment location

'There was one dog who bared her teeth at me, three fish tanks, half a dozen parakeets and budgies, seven hamsters and several gerbils.' (Intermediary)

The assessment should take place where the witness feels calm and safe. Paradoxically, from the intermediary's perspective this may be somewhere that is noisy and prone to interruptions. The choice of location is discussed with the police during the first phone call. Assessments have been carried out in schools, hospitals, secure units, supported accommodation and social services departments. Flexibility is the essence: they have also taken place in cafes, at a 'tea party' (for a child with autism spectrum disorder and anxiety, stressed after being taken into care); in an amusement arcade (after the intermediary and officer trawled the town centre for the witness) and at a golf club (for someone in a witness protection programme). Walking was a relaxing activity for Y, a distrusting teenager with complex needs, so Golightly's assessment took place "while we went on a long walk, with the social worker and police officer in tow". Paige was asked to wear protective clothing by L, who had obsessive compulsive disorder and Asperger syndrome. The intermediary donned rubber gloves and plastic shoe covers but even then, L would not let her into the same room:

'I conducted the assessment in the adjoining kitchen. I sat as close to the threshold as L would allow and she came as close as she could. She told me not to make direct eye contact, which I respected. L stopped frequently to do her "repetitions" and then we started again. I was pregnant at the time. The officer was concerned about me sitting on the filthy floor and doused me in disinfecting gel afterwards.'

In a last-minute appointment, Melissa drove for three hours to the home of G, a witness with complex communication needs due to a head injury: "His flat was full of dubious-looking friends so I ended up assessing him sitting on the stairs outside." This intermediary recalled another memorable assessment which began two days before Christmas, in the back of a police car. R had severe learning disabilities and had vanished from hospital where he was being treated for injuries sustained in an attack:

'We toured the back streets in a foot of snow and found R trying to make his way home but lost, confused, cold and ill. We persuaded him to come back to hospital to continue his treatment, and after he had a hot meal I completed my hasty assessment. Two hours later, the officer managed to film a first interview in a hospital room – enough to get names and descriptions of the perpetrators. The officer arrested them, so they spent Christmas in custody and R could be discharged home. Later, I completed my assessment and we carried out a further interview in better surroundings. We made a plan of R's flat and provided wooden manikins so he could show who was where and what they did. He had little speech and a severe stammer, so showing was much easier and clearer for him. The defendants later pleaded guilty after forensic evidence confirmed their presence at the scene of the crime and they were shown the video of R's evidence.'

Many assessments take place in the witness's home, though relatives have to be asked not to answer questions on behalf of the witness. Home visits present other challenges, including cigarette smoke, loud TVs and encounters with animals, many canine (barking, snarling or being "shown undue attention by a large dog"). Roadrunner had to ask for wild rabbits to be removed from the room; Melissa shared an assessment with a three-foot-long iguana. Jeeves paints a graphic picture of assessing D, a man with complex health and other problems, in a room like a mini zoo:

'There was one sofa with me wedged between D and his mother, an aggressive dog, various birds and small animals and an officer chuckling at the sight of me balancing a folder on my knee and trying to talk to D with his mother talking in the other ear. How the police could have decided D showed no signs of vulnerability and had previously taken a written statement from him is beyond me. If nothing else, the graphic tales of what D said could happen to his colostomy bag if he got anxious and the "calming" pills his doctor prescribed should have triggered some kind of concern.'

The police alerted Adrian that K, the female witness, could be "quite stroppy", but that was the limit of the warning. On arrival, Adrian went to shake hands with K and her boyfriend:

'I thought, "Gosh, they are wearing chunky bracelets," and suddenly realised that they had snakes round their wrists. I felt a rather elevated heart rate. They had six baby boas, about two feet long, and said it was important to keep handling them. The boyfriend then brought in their mother, six feet long, round his neck. He started to put it round me, explaining that was the best way to overcome fear. I screamed and quickly back-pedalled into the hall. The assessment didn't go that well; K kept her snake around her throughout, pulling it out and stroking it and putting it down her top. Wanting to end on a good note, I said I'd love to meet their other snakes, including the 10-foot python. It was worth it to see the expression on the officer's face. When we left, the police officer said "Sorry, I forgot about the snakes."'

Given experiences like these, it is perhaps not surprising that some intermediaries prefer to conduct assessments in a structured setting. Day centres attended by adults with a learning disability provide opportunities to observe the person in a familiar location and to discuss issues with staff. Assessment at school allows the intermediary to observe the child in class and discuss with teachers the child's style and level of communication. However, unlike some of her colleagues, Betsey does not favour assessing the witness at home or school because of the risk of 'contaminating' the location for someone unable to rationalise and compartmentalise feelings associated with trauma. Also, in neutral premises like the police suite, it is easier to explain 'rules' such as: "Here, [unlike school] we don't guess."

Assessment at the police interview suite can help 'de-sensitise' an anxious witness, such as someone on the autism spectrum, to the surroundings in preparation for interview. However, the 'witness friendly' quality of police premises varies widely (see Chapter Six).

Carrying out the assessment and interview on the same day

'The intermediary felt that the child was able to communicate to us if she wished, therefore the intermediary facilitated communication in the interview straight after the assessment. This meant that the child did not have to see us more times, which may have caused her distress.' (Police officer)

During the intermediary pilot stage, many assessments were conducted on the same day as the police interview, with knock-on problems for witnesses with limited concentration or who tire easily. These assessments often consisted of little more than getting to know the witness; intermediaries felt pressure to move straight to the interview, sometimes without an opportunity to talk to the officer alone before the interview started. Ten years on, intermediaries will explain the benefits of at least a 24-hour delay between assessment and interview, ensuring that the witness is fresh when the interview starts and allowing time for planning in the interim. Melissa usually resists scheduling both events on the same day:

'I explain that I can't give the police a proper service and they need time to plan their interview once we know how the witness can best communicate. The few I've done on the same day have ranged from disastrous (the witness too tired or fed up being asked questions) to feeling there was no point me being there – I couldn't really contribute without having time to turn my assessment into useful advice, collect or create communication aids and seek additional information about how to best support the communication of that particular witness.'

If the police request that both events are scheduled for the same day and the witness is willing and able to go ahead, the assessment usually takes place at the police interview suite, preferably followed by at least a two-hour break before the interview. Some intermediaries obtain police agreement that the interview can be postponed if this appears necessary in light of the assessment; this also allows for a further assessment session if necessary. Alexa took an urgent referral for a five-year-old in the morning, 'rejigged' her diary, was at the police station by 2 pm and began her assessment at 3.30 pm. After discussing the situation with officers, they agreed to defer the interview to the following day. Betsey has assessed and assisted at interview on the same day but only when there were compelling reasons, as when a five-year-old had been abducted and raped and the offender had not been identified, and when a three-year-old was the sole witness to a murder and suspects were in custody.

Length and number of assessment sessions

'It is often imperative to get the bulk of your assessment material in one session.' (Intermediary)

Intermediaries assess most witnesses in a single session. Duration varies: the meeting may include preliminary discussion with the officer, taking background details from family or staff members and explaining to the witness what is going to happen. Actual time with the witness may be quite short and require breaks.

Where assessment takes place under time pressure, it may be necessary to prioritise the elements in order to focus on key points.

While additional sessions remain unusual, officers are generally sympathetic to requests to see the witness again if intermediaries feel this is necessary before completing their reports. Sometimes extra sessions are needed to build the witness's confidence. The police authorised Bonnie to conduct six preparatory sessions for Y, a young woman whom a psychiatrist described as severely affected by post-traumatic stress disorder. Y needed to build trust and feel safe with the intermediary and officer; in addition to sessions in person, the intermediary built rapport by speaking to Y using 'FaceTime' on the officer's phone. Betsey has seen some children three times, including a young child with trauma-related fear and anxiety who took 40 minutes to come through the door at the first session. If there is a long delay between assessment and trial, further sessions may be needed closer to the trial with a child whose communication may have developed significantly.

Follow-up may also be necessary if someone with mental health concerns is too unwell to be assessed on the intermediary's first visit, where witnesses have limited oral or nonverbal communication, or where the witness's performance at a single session is limited. Alertness and cognitive function may fluctuate. Roadrunner worked with a witness with multiple sclerosis who could not remember carers' names or faces on two occasions but could do so at her third visit. Differences in performance may also be due to temporary ailments such as migraine or infections or the effect of medication; even the time of day can have a significant impact.

Failure to identify the need for an intermediary before the police interview

'We've suggested to the CPS that more vulnerable witnesses should have intermediaries. There is a problem with identifying the level of vulnerability early enough which is why many witnesses don't get one.' (Volunteer, Witness Service)

Failure to identify a witness's need for intermediary assistance in time for the police interview is likely to have adverse consequences for the quality of evidence. A recent inspection of six police force areas found that no intermediary was used in its sample of young witness interviews, even for children under six; 'there was a tendency by some interviewers and their managers to over-estimate their own skill levels and/or underestimate the communication needs of vulnerable witnesses' (Criminal Justice Joint Inspection, 2014a, para 6.3). It recommended that police forces 'promote [intermediary] use and effectiveness at operational level' and officers record 'the rationale and decision for their use or not' (recommendation 4 and paras 1.4, 6.7).

Interviews conducted without an intermediary may be subject to criticism by the defence at trial. An intermediary appointed post-interview may recommend that certain types of question risk unreliable answers from the witness; such questions may have been asked by the police in a filmed interview. Evidential weaknesses are also likely if the police take a written statement from a witness whose communication needs have been overlooked. Written statements do not include the questions asked, so it is not possible to see if these were developmentally appropriate. Officers create statements from the witness's account; they are framed in the first person and are meant to convey the witness's own words. However, intermediaries appointed after the interview sometimes find that the witness is unlikely to have used or understood the language. For example, the statement of a woman with learning disability described a sexual assault as involving 'digital penetration'; the statement of a witness with learning difficulties involved in a traffic accident used the terms 'unobstructed' and 'shown overleaf'. Paige was appointed for Y, who had a learning disability and who had already been interviewed by the police without an intermediary:

> 'The officer paled visibly as my assessment progressed. The police were totally unaware of Y's communication deficits. The prosecution was abandoned following the results of my assessment which showed that Y's written statement was unacceptable. Given that he

had attended a special school, the clues as to Y's difficulties were plain to see.'

Last-minute requests

'I was on my way in 90 minutes.' (Intermediary)

'The intermediary was only given 24 hours' notice as the trial was the next day. She was very proactive and arranged to meet the witness out of office hours. Counsel said the witness gave excellent evidence and the case would not have succeeded without the intermediary.' (CPS)

Police officers in areas with low intermediary usage often complain that "There's no point in requesting an intermediary for the interview because we'd never get one fast enough," but in practice many intermediaries have responded to urgent requests, often within 24 hours. Intermediaries are expected to be flexible in their availability; many work evenings and weekends, with long journeys and overnight stays for assessments, police interviews and court visits across the country. They usually aim to schedule assessments within a week of appointment, though at the time of writing a significant increase in demand has meant that sometimes first meetings take longer to arrange. Unless there are exceptional reasons, there is little point in expediting police interviews if there is insufficient time for assessment and planning beforehand.

Sometimes, the request for an intermediary is received only just before the trial starts. Last-minute requests to assist at interview may be genuinely urgent but late applications for trial are always avoidable. The case will have been in the court system for many months: a prosecution witness's eligibility for special measures should be addressed not only by the police but also by the CPS, for example while completing case management forms for the court. Prosecutors should consider intermediary use in every case involving a child witness (CPS, 2013, paras 37, 85, 86) and the CPS should record decisions, particularly where an intermediary is not used at court (Criminal Justice Joint Inspection, 2014a, recommendation 5, para 6.8).

Trial referrals usually involve the intermediary in various tasks: accompanying witnesses on a pre-trial visit to the court and while their memory is refreshed from their police statements; liaising with police officers, CPS, the court listing office and advocates on both sides; and preparing a report with detailed recommendations. Appointment at short notice does not allow sufficient time for all these tasks and risks important issues being overlooked. Some intermediaries decline last-minute trial appointments: "They don't do our profession any favours and are not in the witness's best interests." Others accept late referrals for trial because they believe that vulnerable witnesses "should not be penalised for others' lack of knowledge" but describe them as very stressful and as "bearing the brunt of bad practice by the criminal justice system".

Melissa accepted an appointment to assess the witness G over a weekend for a trial due to start the following Monday:

> 'G had complex communication difficulties relating to a head injury. He also had a long criminal record and was known to be violent. The assessment was chaotic and, come Monday, I was in the witness box giving a verbal report and recommendations which included a request for a security guard to sit outside the live link room in case of difficulty. The ensuing cross-examination was a disaster. Never again.'

Intermezzo

Helping Chris manage her stress while giving evidence

Evelyn (registered intermediary)

I was appointed as intermediary for Chris, a lady with significant mental health difficulties, who alleged historical sexual abuse by a relative. She had borderline personality disorder, post-traumatic stress disorder and had been detained in hospital under the Mental Health Act 1983. Chris was suicidal and was extremely anxious about being a witness. It was hoped she would give evidence to court via live link from her hospital ward.

Chris agreed to let me assess her and to speak to her medical professionals. We had to postpone the assessment due to a blizzard – not a good start, given her anxiety. I finally made it to her hospital and met her, the police officer, psychiatric social worker and her nurse. The assessment went well. I was able to reassure her that nothing that she said was going to shock me. We built rapport quickly and could discuss my findings and recommendations. I'd been told how difficult she found it to trust people, so I was relieved when she agreed for me to be involved.

Her language skills appeared good but she had difficulty with complex sentences, some time-related questions (particularly those involving numerical calculations) and spatial words. She also required additional time to process questions and compose herself before answering. She thought it would be more difficult for her to ask for clarification or to say when she didn't know or couldn't remember if she felt pressured to answer. I therefore suggested that she had visual aids in front of her to use for these responses.

The most critical issue was the impact of increased stress on her mental health. Beyond a certain point, she would withdraw totally, be unable to process anything anyone said and be unable to speak. She didn't always appear as stressed as she actually felt, partly due to having relatively flat affect and limited nonverbal communication. For example, during the assessment she looked relatively relaxed but when asked how she was feeling, she said she was "extremely worried and confused" and was thinking about self-harm and suicide.

When I watched Chris's police interviews, it was evident that as she became more stressed, her body language became even less expressive and her eye contact reduced. I therefore devised a 1 to 10 rating scale she could use to indicate her level of stress. If she indicated between 4 and 7 on the scale, I would keep checking with her whether it was okay to carry on safely and would request regular breaks. By '7', I would request an immediate break. At that stress level, we would check whether she needed a private talk with her nurse or medication.

At a special measures meeting at the hospital, we confirmed which room was to be used as the live link room; the first place suggested was inappropriate. I helped the CPS and police officer to explain the trial process to Chris. We used the scale to gauge her stress levels and the effect on her communication, as well as ensuring the effectiveness of the action taken. At the subsequent ground rules hearing, the prosecutor told the judge about the usefulness of the scale.

I was asked to assist at trial for three days, with Chris due to give evidence on day two. On day one, I went to see her and check the live link had been installed. Her mental health had unfortunately deteriorated. She was extremely stressed, didn't want to see me and told the nurses that she wasn't sure she could go ahead with giving evidence. I then went on to the ground rules hearing. I explained my role and findings to the judge; he agreed to all my recommendations. He warned the defence barrister to change his style of questioning; apparently he was known for asking multi-part questions in the form of statements. I explained my concerns for Chris's mental health and that in order for her to communicate at all, we needed to do everything possible to reduce her stress. The judge agreed that I could tap the stress scale during Chris's evidence to get her to point to where she was on the scale. A nurse was permitted to be with us in the live link room as a safety precaution. It was agreed that Chris could watch her police interviews at a different time from the jury.

On day two, the police officer and I were unsure whether Chris would give evidence. She agreed to meet me, but was reluctant to go into the live link room. It took a lot of persuasion for her to try it one step at a time. Initially she agreed to sit in the chair, then to say hello to the judge, and then to listen to the first question. From then on she did amazingly well. A confidence I had not seen in her before emerged and she answered the questions clearly and firmly. At one point, she said to the defence barrister, "I know what you're doing – you're trying to say I'm lying, but I'm not." I intervened a few times to alert the court to sound problems or to reduce the complexity of the question and to ask for a break when her stress levels increased, but Chris did herself proud. (The defendant was found guilty and given a long prison sentence.)

FOUR

Assessment methods
and involvement of the interviewer

Unlike health settings, intermediaries have no standard approach to assessments for justice system purposes. It depends on the intermediary, the requirements of the case and the capabilities of the witness. The intermediary may conclude that the witness simply does not have the ability to give evidence, even with assistance.

Assessment is not always straightforward: some people are willing to discuss with the intermediary issues that affect them (one witness described herself as having "that bipolar bear thingy where you go up and down") but many others have spent a lifetime covering up their communication and literacy difficulties, especially to anyone in authority. However, it is unusual for the offer of intermediary assistance to be declined.

Police officers, lawyers and judges often change in the course of a single case but, continuity of intermediary through assessment, interview and trial is important to ensure familiarity with the witness's communication and establish trust. Assessment underpins intermediary recommendations about adapting questioning techniques and procedures at the police interview and at court. If a recommendation is challenged, intermediaries must be able to justify it based on their assessment findings. Intermediaries are not expert witnesses and their report is not part of the evidence, but they must keep notes of their assessment which could be disclosed at trial. In certain circumstances the assessment may be filmed, for example where a young child may make a spontaneous disclosure about the alleged offence or if the witness uses a communication method that must be demonstrated to be transparent.

This is how one intermediary who works with children explains her assessments in her court reports. The principles are of general application:

> 'The activities are designed to quickly assess the witness's communication, vocabulary and attention; her ability to understand language and question forms and to use language to describe and clarify; whether she is aware that others have knowledge that she does not have; and her ability to refute inaccurate suggestions. I also assess her ability to concentrate, attend and to manage her arousal [anxiety] levels; I try out approaches for keeping her calm and engaged and introduce "talking rules", such as "don't guess".'

If the person accompanying the intermediary is a police officer, it avoids any concern that the intermediary has coached the witness. In addition, the officer can record any remarks from the witness that may be evidentially relevant and if necessary give evidence about what was said. This protects the intermediary from having to give evidence.

This chapter describes innovative ways in which intermediaries approach assessment. It explains the benefits of the police interviewer's involvement in the assessment and how this contributes to planning and communication at the interview itself.

Creative assessment methods

> 'I've never watched "EastEnders", but as a result of countless assessments I've developed a pretty good knowledge of their doings.' (Intermediary)

Most registered intermediaries are speech and language therapists. When the pilot scheme began, they often assessed a witness's communication abilities using formal tools from their professional repertoire, such as the Renfrew Action Picture Test and British Picture Vocabulary Scale. The ability to include formal test results in their reports, providing standardised age levels for comprehension and expression, helped validate their recommendations and probably contributed to their credibility with judges and lawyers. Over time, however, intermediaries found that formal tests alone were inadequate to reveal the adjustments needed to enable vulnerable people to give their best evidence. Assessments are now entirely or largely informal, based on a wide range of materials (some home made), created to support the requirements of forensic questioning.

Intermediaries describe this approach as "finding a subject that the person really wants to tell you about"; assessing "functional communication skills through observation, conversation and practical table-top activities appropriate for the age and skill-set of the individual"; and trying to make it "feel like an exploration of what a witness can do, rather than focusing on what they can't do". Exchanging experiences about assessment methods is a 'hot topic' whenever intermediaries get together. Many have accumulated so much material that it can be "backbreaking wheeling large bags filled with equipment".

Rapport building

The first essential is to establish rapport quickly. For children, this means building confidence through play. Intermediaries try to find out about the child's particular interests and bring relevant pictures, stickers, toys and games. Maria, for example, has wind-up toys so that young children can have races with "robots, witches, snails, 'Sonic the Hedgehog' and so on". She goes prepared to talk about "anything from 'Peppa Pig', 'Ben 10' and 'Playstation' to fishing" – whatever is the child's interest.

The same principles apply in identifying what will engage the interest of adults whose language skills are poor. Hermione found that anything Japanese, particularly artwork, interested a witness with a diagnosis of learning disability and autism. Lucia uses teenage magazines, asking girls to "find a certain page number – this itself is revealing"; she tests their response to leading questions relating to fashion items. Jeeves is such a habitué of the local newsagent that the staff "must have a very odd view of me". This intermediary too buys teen magazines but also those about TV soap operas, sports and music, finding that even the reaction to the magazine indicates a lot about the person's social and emotional maturity. For C, an emotionally damaged teenager, Jeeves found out about her favourite pop stars and put together an ingenious quiz:

> 'C and the police officer accompanying us both answered the questions. Of course, C won. I could then test out how confident she was about her answers, using an illustrated "True or False?" prompt sheet. Pleasingly, C refused to tick some boxes, saying "I don't know" – just what we wanted her to do, as she had a long-term history of guessing.'

Sometimes the intermediary can engage a witness on a subject of mutual interest or relevance. For James, building rapport usually starts with a conversation with the witness about their shared experience of deafness: "We then move on to talk about special interests or general topics such as holidays, football or the weather. This conversation allows me to assess the person's signing skills and ability to understand questions and respond appropriately."

Finding the right subject often pushes intermediaries beyond their comfort zone. Jeeves self-confessedly "hates musicals" but swotted up on 'Cats' (the musical) in preparing a picture quiz for J, who had learning difficulties: "As soon as J saw the picture from 'Cats' in the letter I'd sent him, he was 'sold'." Ramiro asks about hobbies and favourite television programmes: "Nine times out of ten, the answer is 'EastEnders'. This gives me an excuse to ask 'Oh, what happened in last night's episode? I missed it.'"

But even an intermediary has her limits. Tosca described herself as "a bit thrown" when asking about the interests of B, a young man with autism. The reply was "pornography". She concluded, with some degree of understatement, that she "might not be able to incorporate B's primary interest into her assessment":

> 'I asked about his other interests and was told "Flies, especially killing them with fly spray." I set to work

downloading pictures of different kinds of flies, putting in wasps and bees as well, and all sorts of fly sprays. These formed the first part of my assessment and generated quite a bit of conversation.'

Even with this kind of advance preparation, it is not always possible to motivate witnesses to participate. Tosca had carefully worked out plans for assessing T, a woman with Asperger syndrome:

'The minute I walked into T's house I realised I'd have to abandon them. Even questioning was difficult. When I asked about schooling she asked "Why are you interrogating me about my childhood?" I asked if she would like to meet the judge and barristers, to which she said "No. I don't know how you've got the fucking audacity to ask me if I would want to meet that fucking low life who is going to protect that man."'

Golightly has also abandoned planned parts of her assessment with volatile or challenging witnesses, and has focused instead on avoiding confrontation. Even though she eventually "gets somewhere" in forming rapport, "It is still difficult to write up my report with lots of areas that were not explored." Hazeley found that R, a witness with selective mutism and a possible learning disability, was unable to cope with assessment at home – the scene of the alleged crime. Hazeley used the home visit to build rapport and obtained R's agreement to meet again; the assessment then took place in the police interview suite.

Serving the needs of the criminal justice process

'Without intermediary assistance, we would not have got to the stage of conducting a video interview.' (Police officer)

'The intermediary (who is herself deaf) ensured that the complainant could understand questions asked of her by the sign language interpreter. This involved the advocate asking a question which was translated into sign language and then modified slightly by the intermediary to aid the complainant's more limited understanding. This worked extremely well and the complainant was able to provide her clearest account to date of the sexual abuse she had suffered. The intermediary provided the complainant with a voice. Without her assistance, the complainant would have been denied justice.' (Senior CPS prosecutor)

Certain questions routinely arise in a criminal trial. These include the timing of events, the sequence in which they occurred and the identification of individuals by name and sometimes by appearance. Intermediaries have such matters in mind during assessment. They must consider the witness's ability to understand questions on these topics and capacity to respond in a way that can be understood by the court. In many cases, the vulnerable witness's usual communication will be inadequate to convey the quality of information required by the criminal justice process. In these circumstances, intermediaries often find imaginative ways of facilitating communication, improving the quality of evidence and, for some witnesses, enabling them to access a justice process from which they were previously excluded.

Determining receptive communication skills

Intermediaries assess the witness's ability to understand others in terms of question length, complexity and vocabulary, taking account of the types of question often used in the police interview and at trial. Complex language, sentence structure and the use of negatives make questions more difficult to process (Chapter Eleven).

'Do you remember …?' questions are complex, particularly where vulnerable witnesses are asked not about an event, but about what they told someone else. Intermediaries must assess a witness's abilities to disentangle the meaning of such questions. They must also determine the witness's ability to cope with figures of speech and idiom. These are common features of questioning both in police interviews and at court, but they confuse and obstruct communication with those whose understanding of language is literal. If the alleged offence is sexual, the intermediary will check the words used by the witness for parts of the body and will consider whether an aid would assist the witness to 'show and tell' at interview or trial (see Chapter Five).

Assessments usually explore understanding of time concepts. Charges against the defendant and the indictment at court must specify dates or time periods. Intermediaries will report any difficulties the witness has with time or numbers. Where possible, intermediaries try to fix time by relating it to other neutral events (development of timelines for this purpose is discussed in Chapter Five).

Witnesses are often asked *why* something happened. 'Why' questions are generally abstract and involve understanding concepts, not just reporting facts; thus the intermediary will report on the ability to understand motivation (one's own or someone else's), known as 'theory of mind'. Someone with a learning disability is likely to have difficulty with identifying emotions or intentions, and those on the autism spectrum may see no reason to explain events because of a lack of awareness that not everyone experiences the world as they do. 'The ability to respond reliably to questions that ask for inferences about the internal processes or behaviour of others is not well established until children are 10 to 13 years old' (Graffam Walker, 2013, pp 71–72); lawyers often seem unaware that questions about motivation are developmentally inappropriate for a young child (Krähenbühl, 2011) and should therefore be avoided.

Witnesses known to have communication difficulties are routinely invited to say if they do not understand a question. This request is not as reasonable as it seems. It requires that witnesses have both the ability to recognise something they do not understand and the confidence to say so to someone in a position of authority. Intermediaries will also advise on the person's short-term or 'working' memory, namely, the ability to 'hold' what is asked long enough to process the question and answer it (as distinct from commenting on the accuracy of a witness's recall, which is beyond the scope of the intermediary function). These matters are checked as part of the assessment, as is reliable use of 'yes' and 'no', guessing even when told not to, and how the witness makes use of 'don't know', 'don't remember' and 'not sure' responses.

Leading questions suggesting the answer are the norm in cross-examination (see Chapter Ten). It is therefore essential to check whether the witness is able to understand this type of question and answer reliably. By suggesting the wrong answer, intermediaries check the extent to which the witness may acquiesce, for example "asking 'I came here on the bus, didn't I?', when they don't know if I did or not". Depending on the findings, intermediaries may recommend that certain forms of leading question be avoided. They also check the effect on accuracy of repeating the question. Repetition by an authority figure may cause a compliant witness to conclude that the first answer was wrong, even if correct, and change it (see Chapter Eight).

Determining expressive communication skills

In interview, the police invite the witness to say what happened. A key feature of assessment is therefore to explore the way the person answers questions, often by inviting a narrative description (with or without visual aids – see Chapter Five) of an event that is nothing to do with the alleged offence. This gives insights into someone's ability to recall past events and explain them in the appropriate order. If the police interviewer needs a description of the perpetrator, the intermediary will check whether the witness can describe physical features and may develop aids to help with communicating details.

In Hazeley's assessment of M, a young man with Down syndrome, they agreed to use his smart phone. This helped the intermediary to establish not only if he understood days and dates but, by discussing an event in his phone diary, Hazeley could assess M's ability to give an account of names and places and express his feelings. Hermione has devised a narrative task using cut-out models of a child's pets. Maria asks children to give her five bits of information about something they enjoyed in the past few days or a TV programme they like. This also familiarises the child with providing the level of detail they may be asked for in forensic questioning:

'I hold up my fingers and put them down as each
bit of information is given. Then I do the same again
and ask for five details about a couple of the items.
They look carefully at my hands while they talk and
think it is quite fun. I often draw pictures of what
they say on five cards and then ask them to sequence
them. Similarly, using photo-cards that tell a story, I
ask what happened "first", "last", "before" and "after"
using the pictures. You get a lot of information from
this activity about their language in the past tense and
knowledge of time; their vocabulary and expressive
language; how the child remembers and sequences
the story; and how they think people in the pictures
are feeling.'

Assessment of expression takes account of clarity of speech, how
words are spoken (intonation, emphasis and pauses) and whether
the person has a stammer or stutter. Where speech is apparently
unintelligible, the intermediary will need more time and is likely
to require assistance from someone familiar with the witness's
communication. Those with the voice disorder aphonia or who
have undergone laryngectomy or tracheostomy can 'speak' but
without sound; lip-reading skills are then necessary but are
only partially reliable, so other means of communication must
be considered. Hearing, sight and other health needs will also
be addressed.

The intermediary must consider the witness's use of nonverbal
communication – facial expression, gesture and body language
– and how best to capture this in the police interview DVD
and at trial, where many vulnerable witnesses are viewed by the
court over a live link screen. It may also be necessary to check
literacy, as some witnesses prefer to write answers by hand or
on a computer. For those who have already given the police a
written statement, it is important to know whether they will
be able to read and understand it for memory-refreshing before
trial (see chapter 9).

Assessing someone who is deaf requires specific strategies. For
example, James always assesses ability to recall names: "This can
be difficult for some deaf people as they have never heard the

name said. They may use 'sign names' and I need to check out who they are talking about."

Presence of the interviewer at the assessment

'The intermediary was very professional and knowledgeable. I was grateful for her advice. The child seemed to love the activities she was doing and had no idea she was being assessed, which came as a surprise to me. I thought the procedure would be quite clinical.' (Police officer)

Best practice requires that the officer who will conduct the interview accompany the intermediary at assessment. (Intermediaries occasionally encounter difficulty in arranging for any officer to be present. A resourceful intermediary has even resorted to calling '111' to obtain a replacement officer for one who failed to turn up.)

Officer continuity contributes to building rapport, regarded as essential prior to formal questioning (Ministry of Justice, 2011a, para 2.87), and helps the officer 'tune in' to the witness's communication. Interviewers often describe their first intermediary assessment as an 'eye-opener'. Even experienced interviewers sometimes express surprise at ways in which the assessment can expose the limits of a witness's abilities: many vulnerable witnesses are adept at masking their problems with learned responses and small talk. Interviewers present at the assessment are almost always positive about the concrete benefits. Those who do not attend may have no opportunity to gain insight into the needs of the witness and fail to see how the intermediary can help with communication. Melissa worked with S, an elderly woman with learning difficulties, dementia and hearing impairment, whose interviewing officer was allocated at the last minute and who began the interview without knowledge of S or the intermediary's advice. The officer said, "It's okay, I'll wing it." S walked out of the interview after a few minutes: "Why is this person I don't know asking me all these questions? I don't know what she wants or who she is. I want to go home."

Engaging the interviewer in the assessment

Intermediaries often try to engage interviewers in their activities with the witness. Hazeley assessed T, a man with a severe physical disability:

> 'T didn't have the energy to complete an assessment in one session. Observation helped the officer understand the need to complete T's assessment at a second session and to do so at a slow pace. I enlisted her help in presenting material, holding pictures at different angles to accommodate T's awkward body posture and writing down his answers. It was a real joint effort. She commented afterwards that she had learned so much by participating.'

Betsey explains to officers that the assessment will give them a chance to practise communicating with the child before the interview, asking questions about neutral topics. She also wants to check if the prospective interviewer is able to adapt communication to the child's needs or whether to ask for a switch of interviewer, which she has done on occasion:

> '"Do you think Keith can draw a picture of Keith while you draw a picture of you?" When I get it right, children are engaged within moments of arrival and perceive the assessment as a collaborative series of fun jobs including putting things "on", "under", "in" and "beside"; hiding and finding small objects; and drawing pictures. They are given a photo list of their "jobs" (actually, the assessment tasks) to tick off. Teaching by doing is essential. I use my communication with the officer to share information with the child, using simple language: "Oh, are there rules in this room? Let's practise the rules." It's almost impossible for children of two or three to comply with the rule "Say if you don't know." It needs to be actively taught and modelled.'

The interviewer's observation of the assessment almost always helps in planning the interview and is likely to save time. Golightly lists other advantages:

> 'Planning together how to approach questioning while the witness's needs are fresh in the officer's mind is more useful than any written report I could write. For officers who could be a little wary of the intermediary as an intruder in their interview, this can be useful. The officer gets used to interacting with the witness and the intermediary through the informal environment of the assessment and vice versa. It also creates consistency for anxious witnesses.'

The presence of the interviewer at assessment of a deaf witness

The involvement of the interviewer at assessment of a deaf witness is different. James describes the interviewer at this stage as totally reliant on James and the interpreter to relay what the witness says:

> 'The interviewer is usually present at the assessment but at this stage I need to build rapport and "tune in" to the person's signing. For the majority of my cases, the deaf person is not a clear and fluent signer because they have additional needs, for example learning disability, minimal language skills or mental health problems. The interpreter, whose second language is British Sign Language, quite often cannot accurately voice over into English because the communication is not clear. I talk about general topics and the interpreter voices to the police officer the topics that are being discussed. If any issues arise in relation to the offence then this is conveyed to the police officer but if I relayed everything that is said at this point, it would interrupt my assessment and probably interfere with rapport. I then discuss the deaf person's communication needs with the police officer and formalise this in the report. At that stage,

I explain how questions should be framed. In the interview, because there is often a lot of "cultural" (deaf) adaptation, I tend to reframe the questions in ways that do not change meaning but that the deaf person can understand, given their level of communication. So communication in the interview is usually (but not always) relayed in the following sequence: Questioner → Interpreter → Intermediary → Deaf person. This is also how it works in reverse. I normally tell the interpreter to wait until I relay back the answer to the question. This is less confusing as I am only putting the same question that the police officer has asked and it would just be duplication if the interpreter voices everything.'

James observes that this may feel disempowering for an interviewer who cannot follow the language and exchanges directly. He has encountered some police officers who cannot perceive how a deaf person can act as intermediary and have insisted that they want a hearing intermediary: "They fail to understand that I share the same language as the deaf person and that I am therefore well placed to assess their language and adapt any questions that may be asked, as British Sign Language is my first language."

A change of officer between assessment and interview

Changing an officer who has already established rapport with a vulnerable witness can have an adverse effect. Jeeves was concerned about the impact of last-minute changes on T, a six-year-old boy who was nonverbal. The intermediary included the original officer's details in the letter of introduction to T. Just before the assessment was due to start, the police allocated a second officer to attend the assessment and a third to conduct the interview:

'They thought an officer who had never met T was a good idea to interview a little boy who doesn't speak, signs and uses a communication aid. I finally heard back from a cheery officer who didn't seem to consider it a problem that the only thing she knew about T was his name – and would we need long to plan? Kept calm. Hastily rewrote my letter to introduce yet another "friend" to see T with me on Friday. I sent the interviewer my advice but despite my best efforts, most of my recommendations were ignored. The interview was a perfect example of how not to do it. The officers said that they never get much time for building rapport with any child.'

Roadrunner observes that if an interviewer who has not met the witness has to take time to build rapport before the interview starts, this can drain the energy of the witness, with an adverse effect on questioning:

'D had severe multiple sclerosis, with good cognitive function but impaired and hard-to-follow speech. The interviewing officer only met D on the day of the interview and had to spend precious time getting familiar with her speech before the interview. D fatigued so quickly that she needed rests every 15–20 minutes. Possibly she could have used the energy required for rapport building to give more evidential information.'

Just occasionally a change of interviewer is justified. Betsey worked with G, a girl of four believed to have witnessed a serious offence and to have experienced serious, sustained violence. G had already been interviewed by the police without an intermediary. Betsey watched G's DVD interview and considered that G was "highly compliant" to the male officer throughout. Betsey recommended that the interviewer shift his approach. The officer attended her assessment and was responsive to her guidance but G "could not shift her expectations with him and persisted with actively submissive behaviours". They switched to a female officer for the interview and G "was very different, able to assert herself more and to give considerable information".

Intermezzo

Jim: a sense of humour despite a catastrophic brain injury

Bonnie (registered intermediary)

Jim, aged 20, was attacked on the street by a man who stabbed him in the face. This penetrated his brain close to the eye socket, causing severe brain damage. Shortly after he came out of a coma, the police asked me to assist with communication. Jim could not move or speak, was unable to swallow and was fed through a tube. I visited him in hospital with the investigating officer and assessed his communication from his bedside. His understanding was good but his communication was restricted to blinking once for 'yes' and twice for 'no'.

Jim could point with his index finger, so over several assessment sessions I introduced him to an alphabet spelling chart and a 'Talking Mat' offering sets of picture communication symbols. This allowed us to select pictures relevant to his interests and enabled him to communicate by choosing symbol options. He was relieved to have something to communicate with. He could indicate his likes and dislikes by pushing, extremely slowly, the symbol under the appropriate column (for example, headings for 'yes', 'ok-ish' and 'no') on the 'Talking Mat'. This gradual process overcame another barrier to communication: Jim had been suspicious of the police and made the officer and me laugh by indicating that the symbol for 'the police' should be 'out of the door' and not even on the Mat. He learned to trust the officer; it was deeply touching when Jim very slowly indicated when he wanted to shake hands with the police officer to say 'goodbye'. In due course, I introduced Jim to the use of a voice synthesis app on an iPad to indicate 'yes' or 'no'.

My assessments showed that Jim could communicate and that his responses were consistent. The process was slow and laboured but he showed great determination. The officer concluded that, with my assistance, Jim could use these methods in interview. The officer then devised the questions and alternative 'routes' the answers might take to the next question. I helped simplify questions and developed symbols for the 'Talking Mat', providing a range of possible answers so that Jim could demonstrate he was making his own choice freely. For example, in respect of the weapon, pictures were offered of a hammer, gun, scissors, screwdriver and a knife. He used finger-pointing on an alphabet chart where it was necessary to clarify names or other matters.

Each interview required careful preparation and had to be scripted in advance. I assisted the police in filming four interviews with Jim, each one clarifying and developing information he had provided previously. He also took part in a suspect identification procedure using a photo 'line-up' after I adapted the standard formal script for use with 'yes and 'no' on the iPad. I was present at all interactions with the police to assist Jim's communication. After approximately eight months, Jim began to swallow and eat and then gradually his ability to speak was restored: it became apparent that he was an eloquent young man. The police filmed a further two interviews to clarify the facts of the assault. Jim began to regain his mobility and was using a wheelchair by the time his case came to trial.

The defendant's lawyer opposed my appointment to assist Jim's communication at trial. I attended court to explain my role and why an intermediary was necessary. The defence also challenged Jim's filmed police interviews as his evidence-in-chief. After much discussion, a selection of the interviews was admitted as evidence to be shown to the jury. My recommendation was accepted that Jim be cross-examined over a remote live link between the rehabilitation centre where he lived and the trial court. On the day he was due to give evidence, after many hours of waiting, we learned that the defendant had pleaded guilty. Months later, Jim came to the Registered Intermediary Continuing Professional Development training day and walked onto the platform to speak about his experience and read one of his poems. It was a moving occasion for all concerned.

FIVE

Communication aids and stress reduction strategies

The justice system has improved physical accessibility, for example through providing ramps for wheelchairs in court buildings, but it still has much to learn about communication 'ramps' – visual tools like pictures, symbols and figures to support communication (see, for example, Schalling, 2009). While few people rely on 'augmentative and alternative communication' in their daily lives, many in the justice system can benefit from aids to improve the quality and effectiveness of communication, reduce challenging behaviour and increase assertiveness (Communication Matters, 2013). Visual aids are less taxing to auditory working memory and provide concrete reminders to those with limited understanding of spoken language.

Section 30 of the Youth Justice and Criminal Evidence Act 1999 enables a vulnerable witness to be 'provided with such device as the court considers appropriate with a view to enable questions or answers to be communicated' (see also Ministry of Justice, 2011a, paras 3.103–122; and Judicial College, 2013, chapter 5, para 53). This is a separate special measure from the section 29 intermediary provision; in practice, applications for communication aids seem to be confined to cases in which intermediaries are appointed.

This chapter describes a range of aids and the way they are used. These include aids to reinforce 'rules' when being questioned, such as 'Don't guess', as well as stress reduction strategies. Being questioned in the police interview or at court inevitably heightens anxiety, sometimes to the point where the witness is unable to continue. Stress is likely to impair accurate communication. Vulnerable witnesses with access to visual tools are often more confident and reliable communicators. Exploring the need for communication aids and stress reduction strategies is a key element of the intermediary's assessment process. Development of the appropriate tools requires preparation time and may involve a second assessment appointment. Their use can mean additional time is needed for questioning but they can also shorten the questioning process by keeping the witness calm and focused.

Recognising the value of communication aids

'She provided excellent advice on how best to communicate with the witness and also provided useful props for the assessment and interview process. I learned hugely from the experience.' (Police officer)

During the pilot phase, intermediaries contributed communication aids to the majority of police interviews despite the anxiety of some officers about introducing anything visual. Claire recalls working with two girls aged under three, who had done well in assessment using simple visual aids to identify rooms, parts of the body and clothing, but were unable to cooperate in their interviews because toys, dolls or colouring crayons were not allowed.

Before the interview, it is essential to discuss with the officer the purpose of each potential prop, where they will be placed and when they may be introduced. Other good practice principles include considering how to 'capture' use of the aid for evidential purposes, for example using an additional camera to record the computer screen and the hands of a witness who typed his responses. Prior CPS approval of aids is not required but is helpful. Jeeves recommended showing P, a witness with severe learning disabilities, photos of bites on P's arm to help 'signpost' the topic at the start of the interview. This was discussed with the CPS, which approved the strategy because of the extent of P's learning disabilities: "This produced her best account, which was to mime being bitten on her arm and naming who did it."

If the witness is offered a choice of visual options, such as faces showing expressions from 'happy' to 'sad', the range must be limited to the number the witness can cope with – generally no more than five or six. Whatever the number, the options must be balanced and, like all communication aids, used in a neutral manner.

It is now unusual for the police or courts to refuse the use of aids, though explanations of their purpose will be needed. Judges generally approve retrospectively aids employed at the police interview and approve most of those applied for at trial. Copies may be provided to jurors and intermediaries asked to explain their purpose. Although formal objections to the use of aids at trial are infrequent, a lawyer may withdraw a question rather than have the witness answer it with the support of a visual aid. A ground rule was agreed for Golightly to introduce a 'word body map' (allowing the witness to point to a word instead of a picture) to reduce the anxiety of Y, a teenager with Asperger syndrome who was acutely embarrassed about saying the words. Nevertheless, defence counsel objected to its use at trial when asking Y where she had been touched:

> 'Defence counsel insisted that I come to the courtroom to discuss this, arguing that I was "shielding" Y from cross-examination. I referred to the ground rules document which included my recommendation and the judge's ruling. Defence counsel then opted to withdraw her question, rather than let Y answer using the body map.'

Many aids are simple – paper, pens, symbol cards and figures. Some are more sophisticated: an increasing number of relevant computer applications support communication and also the assessment process. For example, interactive 'apps' are available to assess sequencing skills (what happened 'first', 'next' and 'last') and understanding of prepositions (such as 'in', 'under'). Computer graphics illustrate contrasting concepts such as 'wet/dry', 'in/out' and 'hard/soft'. One intermediary's comment is typical: "My communication aids are evolving all the time, as I meet new witnesses with different needs and as I get better at anticipating what might work."

Representations, parts of the body, positioning and penetration

'The use of figures as props was invaluable, due to the witness being unable to offer the information unprompted. The evidence would not have been available had we not used an intermediary.' (Police officer)

Drawings, figures or models can represent the witness and others, as well as relevant physical surroundings. If the witness can use such aids consistently and constructively, they can be employed at interview and trial. Checking the witness's ability to draw – even rudimentary stick figures or diagrams – can provide important support to communication. These can be annotated by the officer or intermediary with what the witness says the drawing represents. If the witness's drawings are not sufficiently developed for the purpose of representation, figures or models may be used. A judge was initially unhappy with Strider's recommendation that P, an anxious 10-year-old, be allowed to use dolls' house furniture and figures to describe positions in bed:

'The judge said: "These are toys and we are not here to use imagination and play." I asked her what she would be happy with and she said: "We usually use drawing." The defence suggested that a rectangle be drawn to represent the bed. I explained that an abstract concept from an aerial view was inappropriate for a child and that it was unfair to ask a child to have artistic, spatial awareness and mapping skills. I believed P would not see use of a model bed and figures to represent people as "playing". It would be much easier for her to *show* what happened. The judge accepted my recommendation and agreed to allow the furniture and figures.'

Jeeves worked with a T, a man with learning difficulties who was easily distracted while drawing. Instead, the intermediary provided cut-out figures of people and a car for him to personalise at interview. T selected from these to act out what he had previously conveyed in single words and phrases. He took the hand of a card figure and brought it down on the roof of the car, while bringing the foot firmly up against the side of the car, "confirming and clarifying his previous verbal account".

Maria assessed B, aged 10, who had a learning disability and was on the autism spectrum. B coloured in a cardboard cut-out of himself and used it to show what happened; he also used the school's dolls' house and its model people: "He could understand simple questions, and was able to show and tell what happened and who did it."

Pipe cleaner figures

Figures can be created: Hazeley worked with N, a three-year-old with delayed language skills, who the police believed had witnessed a serious assault upon a baby. N only spoke in single words but had good attention skills and was cooperative. Hazeley helped N make a family of people with pipe cleaners, with N choosing the colours and naming the people. He proceeded to demonstrate clearly what had happened: "This was done in several different ways and he repeated the same action each time. It was startlingly and horrifyingly clear." In a different case, Hazeley worked with G, a young woman with a moderate learning disability who had made an allegation of historical rape. G was acutely embarrassed, refused to use any body part words and could not describe positions or actions: "However, she responded enthusiastically to two pipe cleaner figures and chose one to represent herself. Without prompting, she placed the figures in the position she had been unable to describe in words."

Identifying parts of the body

The witness's difficulties may be due not just to embarrassment but to a lack of – or confusion about – vocabulary. To avoid misinterpretation, intermediaries must check what words the individual uses and their meanings. If the allegation is sexual, intermediaries have different ways of finding out how the witness names parts of the body: "It's always surprising the expressions some people use to refer to genitals." C, a 40-year-old woman with learning difficulties and cerebral palsy, had already been interviewed by the police regarding a rape allegation. The CPS requested a second interview involving an intermediary because of C's confused terminology. Poppy found that C's "language skills in relation to body parts and sexual acts were underdeveloped and inconsistent. She sometimes called the penis a 'vagina' or a 'thing'." At the second interview, Poppy provided pictures with male and female body parts to which C could point in order to clarify her verbal descriptions. These aids were used again at the trial.

Intermediaries are surprised by the absence of basic communication tools in police video suites, particularly for identifying parts of the body. Although some witnesses may spontaneously try to 'show' what happened to them, they should never be asked to demonstrate intimate touching on their own body. This is abusive, particularly when asked by an authority figure, and is contrary to guidance (most recently, Criminal Practice Direction 3E.6, 2015). Despite this, over the years we have encountered instances of such requests during cross-examination in all of our young witness studies. In 2013, the Court of Appeal criticised failure to take up an intermediary's recommendation to provide a nonverbal witness with an alternative to pointing to her own body to clarify questions about touching (*R v F* [2013] EWCA Crim 424). The witness can point to 'a doll, model or drawing'; at trial 'the judge's agreement should be sought on the use of an alternative method before the question arises' (Ministry of Justice, 2011a, para 4.74). Golightly has created life-size body maps "where we have drawn around the outline of a child on a large roll of paper". Betsey routinely asks children to draw themselves in order to assess their symbolic representation, but she does not usually ask a child to draw adults until filming the interview starts "as they often helpfully annotate the drawing or start with genitals and you need this recorded".

Anatomical dolls

All intermediaries include in their repertoire toys, dolls or cut-out people with removable clothing. However, they differ in their use of anatomically detailed dolls. Guidance warns that these can produce 'distortions and inaccuracies'; can be upsetting and are not appropriate for very young children; and should only be used in children's interviews to demonstrate the meaning of terms or to clarify verbal statements (Ministry of Justice, 2011a, paras 3.106, 3.122). Some intermediaries suggest anatomically detailed dolls where their use accords with the guidance.

Penetration is a key element of certain sexual offences. It is therefore crucial to understand what the witness alleges has happened. Some vulnerable witnesses are unable to describe this in words. Finding a way to demonstrate penetration is not simple: one intermediary who tried to find a model vagina on the internet found herself in dialogue with a Chinese supplier of sex toys. Another has borrowed a medical model, costing hundreds of pounds; others have made their own. Jeeves provided dolls for the interview of a teenager who was able to use them to clarify questions about whether sexual assault was penetrative: "It was not. Use of the dolls allowed her to speak more about what happened." Heathcliff assisted at three interviews over a four-year period with B, a 10-year-old with learning difficulties. These related to allegations of sexual assault when B was six. The trial collapsed and a retrial was ordered. In the first three interviews it had not been possible to establish if the assault involved penetration. The judge asked Heathcliff to assist at a further interview to try to clarify what had happened to B. Betsey, an intermediary colleague, provided the following advice to Heathcliff:

> 'You need to assess understanding of "in", "out", "on" and "under" using small objects. Make sure these don't all go in and out easily. Dropping a ball into a box is not anywhere near akin to the kind of "in" you need to ask about. I have a collection of little things that have to be pushed quite hard in and out of soft things; sorry to be graphic. I have tiny fish, marbles, buttons and fat little crayons that fit into little

tight containers (doll's house shelves and drawers, a baby's sock and a tiny drawstring bag). Then, if she is confident receptively with "in", "out", "on" and "under" you need to assess her ability to use those words. I do this is with little photo cards showing the same objects in different positions, for example, a little fish under a doll's house chair. Where the mother has accompanied the child, I say "Look at this picture. Don't *show* mummy – *tell* mummy how to do this." Then I prompt if needed ("So mummy needs to find ..."). Most children love this game. It reveals that many who are absolutely confident receptively will struggle to use those same words to explain positions, and end up pointing and showing. If this is the case, you need to provide "scaffolds" [resources which support communication, thinking and recall: Maybin et al, 1992; Lamb et al, 2013] for questions about the words at trial. These need not be anatomically correct dolls; they need to be things that she understands can go "on" or "in". It's crucial to remember that it's not "on" *or* "in", it's usually "on" or "on" *and* "in". It's also not only "in", it's usually "in and out and in and out again and again", as one two-year-old explained clearly at interview last week.'

Based on this advice, Heathcliff carried out a further assessment, established that B understood the concept of in and out, and assisted at a fourth interview at which three questions were asked which had been agreed by the judge and both advocates. The intermediary also used a visual aid with symbolised faces and a numerical scale, which enable B to indicate the level of pain. This further interview was played at trial and the child was not required to attend for questioning.

Timelines

'The intermediary was able to aid the interview extremely well with her use of timelines and keeping the witness focused on the task at hand.' (Police officer)

Intermediaries are frequently asked to assist with questions about offences over a period of time. Locating in time events that may have happened months or years previously, or describing them chronologically, is daunting even for those with excellent recall and communication. For vulnerable people coping with the stress of a police interview or giving evidence, it is almost impossible without assistance. Intermediaries have been creative in developing ways to support this area of questioning.

Sometimes the task is straightforward, such as drawing various events on a series of blank postcards as they are discussed and asking the witness to put the cards in order, but it is often more complex. M was a vulnerable woman who alleged that assaults had taken place in different hotels over a period of years. When questioned by the police, M could describe each hotel accurately, but mixed up the locations and dates. The interviewing officer tried various strategies to help M's recollection, without obviously leading her: she showed M maps, elicited more detailed descriptions of the locations, and eventually showed her the hotel receipts, with the dates clearly described. M looked at these items, agreed they were correct, then went back to her original confusion about places and dates. Laurel was appointed to facilitate communication with M in the third and fourth interviews:

'Having witnessed M's confusion in the third interview, I suggested we provide a timeline that M could complete herself and keep in front of her while being questioned to help fix the information in her mind. We wrote out the years in chronological order, from left to right, and put in other significant but neutral events to help her understanding. She was then shown the hotel receipts again, and asked if she could write on the timeline – the name of the hotel, the relevant resort, and the months of stay – under the appropriate year heading. Once she had put the information in order herself, she was able to refer to this timeline, and could then provide the correct information when questioned. At court she was allowed to keep it in front of her to support her understanding. She was fully able to answer questions put to her in cross-examination.' (The trial resulted in a conviction.)

Following an unclear first interview with S, a teenager with global developmental delay, at a second interview Betsey used 'sticky notes' to label events in S's own words, for example "the time in the basement" and "the time he took me for ice cream". The interview isolated different events and multiple offences, all of which were eventually the subject of charges by the police. Golightly worked with W, who had a significant learning disability. The intermediary and interviewing officer planned carefully to identify props, pictures and gestures to help W understand and communicate:

'After W's initial free recall, during a break we produced a cartoon strip as a framework to represent what W had already said and shown about an alleged sexual assault. When questioning resumed, the strip was annotated to add new information. The officer then used gesture and simple, slowed language to ask direct questions. W was able to make a coherent disclosure which supported CCTV evidence in the prosecution's possession.'

Photographs

'I was asked how big the playground was [where the assault took place] and when I couldn't say, they asked how many tennis courts would fit into it. I thought about it and said two but my dad says it was probably four. If it was important, why didn't they have a picture?' (14-year-old witness: Plotnikoff and Woolfson, 2009a, p 114)

During the pilot phase, an intermediary recommended that the police use photos of the alleged crime scene to interview a teenager with learning disabilities because "pictures helped this witness focus and keep going". The police declined the suggestion in case it was seen as "leading the witness". Since then, photos have been increasingly employed as interview props when suggested by intermediaries but otherwise their use does not appear to be routine. For example, much time is wasted in asking witnesses to describe locations where reference to a photo could help provide a clear answer.

Tess worked on an urgent call-out concerning L, a three-year-old who was the only witness to the death of another child. The interviewing officer attended the assessment. L was able to communicate while engaged in various activities and remained focused for around five to eight minutes at a time. Afterwards, the officer and intermediary spent two hours planning the interview. Tess reworded complex questions, simplified the vocabulary and proposed the use of photos of the locations and other props, such as a toy ambulance, to introduce questions relating to where something had happened. L's interview took place the following day:

> 'We "signposted" specific topics using the visual prompts. My assessment showed that L had the ability to answer open-ended "What happened?" type questions. This detailed planning resulted in a highly structured and successful interview in which L was able to give clear, detailed evidence.'

The police took a written statement from J, a woman with learning difficulties. Before the trial, Alexa was appointed to assess J and concluded that she would have difficulty answering questions "about positions, directions and distances" on the street where the offence was alleged to have occurred. Alexa recommended that crime scene photos be provided for J. This was done, and at trial, J was able to use them to answer questions.

Modifying suspect identification procedures

Intermediaries can assist when witnesses participate in a video identification parade electronic recording (VIPER), a replacement for old-style line-ups of suspects. (There are a few other methods, such as 'E-fit'.) The police assemble a DVD showing the suspect alongside a selection of similar images from a large database. This can be played in a police station or at the witness's home. The process must be conducted in compliance with the Police and Criminal Evidence Act 1984, Code D, as amended. In consultation with the police identification officer, the steps and formal wording can be modified to accommodate a witness's needs. Adjustments must be fair and reasonable and reasons for changing the formal process must be documented.

Adaptations recommended by intermediaries have included paraphrasing the formal script; allowing the witness to practise using non-evidential images; requesting use of symbols instead of numbers (a witness able to make a successful identification may be unable to count reliably to 10); allowing the witness to use 'yes'/'no' cards after viewing each image; reducing the number of images presented at one time; and changing the pace of their presentation. Betsey worked with C, an eight-year-old, during a VIPER process and obtained permission for C to draw what was 'not right' about an image of a suspect to which C kept returning. This showed the suspect with spiky hair; C drew someone with a smoothed-down fringe. The suspect was charged and convicted. He had apparently changed his usual hairstyle prior to the attack.

Jeeves received an urgent referral concerning E and S, two teenagers with moderate learning disabilities. The police sought information relevant to the next stages of an operation in which a number of suspects had already been arrested. Jeeves immediately assessed E and S in their special school; police interviews were conducted the following day. The intermediary then researched what was involved in VIPER, liaising closely with the identification officer who managed the process and prepared visual materials to explain how it works: for example, the witness sees an image of the same person four times, looking straight ahead, to the left and right and then straight ahead again. Each image has the same number. Jeeves recalled: "Both girls were able to make positive identifications and named the suspects. I had little need to intervene when the process was underway but the preparation and planning was crucial to enabling this outcome."

Sometimes an intermediary is not used at the VIPER process, to save money. This can be short-sighted: in at least one trial, an element of the defence case was that a witness with learning disability did not understand the instructions used during the VIPER identification.

Other aids to communication

'We acted out exactly what had happened during the crime using some complex role play.' (Intermediary)

James uses pictures and other visual aids to facilitate communication with deaf people but one of his main tools is role play. He worked with M, a deaf man, who had been attacked with weapons by men who had approached him from different angles. M had no language other than idiosyncratic signs and gestures that he had created with his family. The police were unable to establish what had happened using an interpreter. With assistance from James and by demonstrating in role play, M was able to give a detailed account of events.

Poppy worked with N, a man in his 50s who had had a stroke and was a selective mute. He was attacked in the street but could not describe in words the route he had followed. Poppy asked for 'Google Map' printouts which helped him identify the route. N was able to mutter a couple of responses to questions but these could not be picked up by the microphone in the room. Poppy therefore gave him a notebook in which to write down his responses and she read these back to the officer and for the record during the interview. N made a 'thumbs up' or 'thumbs down' gesture to confirm if her repetition was correct.

Visual aids can be helpful when alleged offences are financial in nature. In an investigation as to whether M, a man in his 60s with learning disabilities, had been defrauded, Poppy and the interviewing officer discussed how to use neutral visual symbols to structure questions about his understanding of financial matters. Poppy prepared pictures of a TV, a loaf of bread, a pint of beer and a pair of trousers which M could be asked to rank in order of cost; he could not do this accurately. She also put together visual aids to help the police establish if M could attach meanings to words such as 'cash', 'cheque', 'credit card' and 'bank'; she provided 'yes', 'no' and 'don't know' cards to help him respond. M demonstrated limited understanding of these financial concepts. On the morning of the trial, the defendants pleaded guilty. In a similar context, Rebus produced a board with pictures to represent different bank accounts to help a witness in a fraud trial follow the topic areas of cross-examination. Melissa prepared visual aids for places to keep money (including 'under the mattress') and recalls that these were challenged by the defence as "leading". The judge replied "I can't think of anywhere else to keep your money, so how are they leading?"

Use of prompt cards

Police officers are expected to explain the 'rules' to a vulnerable witness at the start of the interview, for example that it is permissible to say "I don't know," "I don't understand," "I can't remember" and "That's wrong" or "That's not true." However, officers are inconsistent in providing these explanations (Criminal Justice Joint Inspection, 2014a). Intermediaries assist by offering a range of visual methods to explain and reinforce such rules for answering questions in interview or at trial. Cards using pictures and words remind the person about telling the truth and not guessing the answer. Other cards have 'listen', 'think' and 'speak' symbols, for use with impulsive witnesses prone to rush to answer. Practice with cards such as 'completely sure', 'quite sure' and 'not sure' can encourage vulnerable witnesses to monitor their own comprehension. Such visual prompts can be particularly helpful if the witness has limited spoken language or a mental disorder. These techniques seem to be most effective where witnesses help select or make appropriate cards, choose the images and decide whether pictures or symbols should be combined with words. Rebus made an illustrated reminder card for a pop fan: 'Lady Gaga says ... Just remember, Tanya, say when you don't understand; take your time when you answer – don't rush!' Melissa assisted a man with a head injury that caused a constant flow of irrelevant speech. She asked him what sort of prompt card would help him be quiet and listen to the questions. He replied, "A card with 'Fucking shut up' would do nicely." This was not the way Melissa styled the card for court.

Intermediaries are expected to alert the court when the witness needs a break. The witness may signal to the intermediary using cards with the words 'toilet' or 'break', or, increasingly, the symbols for 'play', 'pause' and 'stop'. 'Stop' cards are usually red (sometimes red for an immediate break and amber if the need is imminent), but the meaning of the colour must be checked with the individual: Roadrunner worked with a witness whose 'stop' card was coloured green. Cards signalling the need for a break are usually agreed without comment, although a judge turned down Claire's recommendation for use of a red card to indicate the need for an urgent break:

> 'I was in the live link room with a man who had an explosive personality disorder and was a drug user. I am afraid I just put the card on my knee and told the witness to point to it or touch it if he felt he needed a break. He appeared to be calmed by the fact that it was there and he could have used it if necessary.'

Helping the witness to focus and to manage stress

> 'The judge agreed to let an anxious witness hold a "fidget ball" to help him concentrate, but only after the judge insisted on examining it to assess its capacity as a possible missile.' (Intermediary)

Communication aids are often a significant benefit to anxious witnesses: one told the intermediary: "I'll be fine so long as I know my cards are there". Aids can also help manage the questioning process. Harriet uses counters as a visual reminder of the number of questions or groups of questions to be be asked; as each question is asked and answered, the witness puts a counter in the box:

> 'I raise this at the ground rules hearing. When an advocate seemed to want to ask a lot of questions, I helped her group them so that we ended up with only 10 topics. That allowed the advocate to keep

the number of questions she wanted but kept it manageable for the child.'

Aids can contribute to communication by helping manage the witness's stress. During the assessment intermediaries explore the calming effect of witness activities, for example folding paper, playing with stickers, doodling, colouring and fiddling with 'stress' toys. Objects used for this purpose include 'Koosh' balls and moulding material like 'Play-doh'. A visual schedule, with stickers to attach as each activity is completed, can make anxious witnesses feel more in control and comfortable, as can allowing a child to return to a parent or carer at will.

There are different ways to enable witnesses to monitor their own stress levels, which help them indicate any increase to the intermediary who can then request a break. These include 'thermometer' cards, 'traffic lights' or a scale of numbers to which the intermediary and witness add personalised stress indicators. For those with mental health problems, Bonnie asks about psycho-social history, experience of flashbacks and what may trigger them, and whether witnesses have their own strategies to help manage stress:

> 'Emotional containment is the first requisite for any type of communication to take place. We discuss breathing techniques. A relaxation app may be helpful at court; some people like to watch a slow-moving image to help contain their emotions. I check sensory sensitivity and whether certain smells can calm them. S, a young woman with mental health issues, sometimes dissociated (that is, became detached from reality). She could identify what helped to bring her back to the present moment: calling her name, tapping her arm, ice, water and certain smells. We avoided use of lavender, a scent many people find relaxing, because S had been pushed into a lavender bush full of bees by the abuser.'

During assessment, Bonnie also checks witnesses' response to touch. Someone with autism spectrum disorder, for example, usually dislikes being touched but others may find it helpful if the intermediary gently touches their arm. Kelly saw that T, a traumatised adult witness, was calmer and reassured when stroking her placid dog and arranged for T to bring the dog to the police interview: "The dog normalised the whole procedure and without it, the interview wouldn't have gone ahead." T stroked the dog's fur throughout, and when her thoughts became disconnected, Kelly helped her refocus by talking to her about the dog.

Intermezzo

The helpful fire alarm and Tammy, a selective mute witness

Lucia (registered intermediary)

I was appointed to assess Tammy, aged 21, who had made an allegation of rape. The referral said she communicated in an odd way and that she had had a laryngectomy. This was incorrect but her presentation was strange; it emerged that she had mental health problems and learning disabilities but had never received services and had little contact with her GP. She was difficult to engage. She talked in single words, often looked blank when asked a question and appeared highly anxious, even with the officer who knew her quite well. Tammy could write single words and even if spelled incorrectly, the intended word was usually clear. Following the assessment, I gave the officer written guidance and we came up with a plan for the interview.

At the interview, however, Tammy declined to speak or to consent to being filmed answering questions. Instead, the officer took a written statement by asking a question, then repeating it and simplifying it if I suggested this was needed. If Tammy didn't reply (as was often the case) we offered her either a piece of paper with 'yes/no/don't know' on it or a blank piece of paper. She could either point to the answer or write her own word down. Her response to more open questions was usually a blank look and silence. A number of times she 'froze', unable to communicate in any way. When this happened we took a break. She had a tremor that seemed to be exacerbated by stress. It was difficult to get any information about this, either from Tammy or anyone else. It's hard to work with a witness about whose background so little is known. Completing her statement required a second day, when I was unavailable. The officer continued without me, working in the way we'd established the day before. The CPS was reluctant to request my appointment for trial but the officer was quite assertive and this eventually happened.

While I was waiting at court to find out about the ground rules hearing, there was a fire alarm evacuation. When we filed back in I overheard a barrister talking about my case so I investigated and discovered that the ground rules hearing was about to be called. This was the best ground rules hearing I have attended – apart from not being informed it was due to start. The judge addressed me directly. He was thorough: we went through each of my recommendations, coming up with definite answers or potential solutions to all the issues, with the proviso that if they did not work an urgent second ground rules hearing would be held.

We talked through Tammy either writing answers, which I would read out, or pointing to the sheet of paper with 'yes'/'no'/'don't know' alternatives. I explained use of a 'traffic light' stress chart so that she could point to the red, amber or green symbol according to how she felt. I also introduced a card that Tammy had drawn herself to use when she felt nervous and could not speak. We would need to be prescriptive about breaks because she wouldn't volunteer that she needed one. We discussed how Tammy should take the oath. I felt that if the court insisted that she say it aloud, it wouldn't be a good start to her evidence. It was proposed that she should try to repeat it back but if necessary she could write it down. I was to explain this to her. This was a concern because, although she could write simple words, the words of the oath were not easy and might have been a stumbling block.

As agreed with the judge, I assisted Tammy to refresh her memory from her written statement prepared by the police. This contained words that she wouldn't understand; I wrote those down and asked the officer to explain what they meant.

I made a list of words that she had not understood, along with the officer's explanations, which was given to both barristers.

At the trial, the judge and barristers came to meet Tammy. She spoke the oath verbally, which was a good start. Questioning followed the same order as at interview, namely: the question; the question repeated at my request (she needed to hear virtually all questions twice); pause, in case she could respond verbally; then the offer of plain paper (for her to write on and for me to say the words for the court) or the 'yes'/'no'/'don't know' card on which she could point to her preferred answer. Breaks were taken about every 15 minutes. After two rounds of questioning there was concern that I was 'leading' in offering her the blank paper to write on or the card with alternatives answers on it. A further ground rules hearing took place, which culminated in the barristers coming to the live link room to see the layout. As a result, we placed the card and blank paper on a table to allow Tammy to choose which to use. However, unless prompted, she neither touched the card nor wrote on the paper. We then agreed that I should try to have her write her answer and only offer her the 'yes'/'no'/'don't know' card as a last resort. Overall, this worked. Tammy's evidence continued for three days with regular breaks. Everyone got into the swing of this unusual form of communication.

Someone with whom Tammy was familiar acted as her supporter but was deemed a witness halfway through the proceedings (in the end he did not give evidence). As he played a vital role, it was agreed that he could continue supporting her during breaks. The prosecution should have checked his status in advance because if he had been unable to support Tammy it would have been devastating. At one point she had a severe panic attack, collapsed completely and was almost unrousable. The supporter played an important role in getting her back on track and enabling her to resume giving evidence.

The defendant was acquitted, but I felt that the court had been very flexible in allowing Tammy to communicate to the best of her ability.

SIX

Contributing to the effectiveness of the police interview

It is a police responsibility when planning a witness interview to identify 'vulnerability', encompassing communication needs by virtue of age or other factor (see toolkit 10, *Identifying vulnerability of witnesses and defendants*, www.theadvocatesgateway.org). When someone is recognised as vulnerable, special procedures come into play. *Achieving Best Evidence in Criminal Proceedings: Guidance on interviewing victims and witnesses and guidance on using special measures* (Ministry of Justice, 2011a), known as 'ABE', governs how the witness should be questioned by an 'ABE-trained' interviewer. Failure to observe ABE guidance and the lack of refresher training has been criticised (Criminal Justice Joint Inspection, 2014a; *Re M (a child: failure to comply with Achieving Best Evidence)* [2014] EWFC B141).

ABE interviews are filmed; the prosecution can apply to the court to play the recording, edited if necessary, as the witness's evidence-in-chief (Youth Justice and Criminal Evidence Act, 1999, section 27; this special measure is also open to vulnerable defence witnesses but is rarely used). Interviews facilitated by an intermediary are filmed unless the witness objects, as in the intermezzo at the end of the previous chapter. Taking part in a filmed ABE interview does not relieve the witness of all further questioning, although sometimes witnesses mistakenly believe that having made the recording, they will not have to go to court at all. Officers should advise witnesses that the ABE recording is admissible as evidence-in-chief where the witness is available for cross-examination; only in exceptional situations can it be played without calling the witness (Ministry of Justice, 2011a, para 2.12).

The police should request an intermediary where this would help improve the quality of evidence of a vulnerable witness (Ministry of Justice, 2011a, para 2.44, Box 2.1), especially if the witness is of primary school age (Criminal Practice Direction 3F.3, 2015; Association of Chief Police Officers et al, 2015, para 4.4). The intermediary is independent, not part of the police or prosecution team, and is neither a witness nor joint interviewer. Conduct and management of the interview are police responsibilities. Officers in police specialist units should be trained in working with an intermediary (Ministry of Justice, 2011a, para 1.30) but intermediaries suggest that there are still parts of the country where there is no routine intermediary input to training.

This chapter examines how the interviewing officer and intermediary can best work together to plan the interview: whether the room may need to be modified or portable equipment used to conduct the interview elsewhere; what rules or boundaries may be necessary; how the witness's understanding of truth and lies can be tested; and whether the interview requires extra time. Issues concerning young children include interviews where no prior disclosure has been made and requests for an intermediary's assistance when an initial interview was unsatisfactory. The chapter finishes by considering the value of interviews where no offence is identified.

Joint planning

The evidential importance of the ABE interview cannot be overstated; this is often the key element underpinning a prosecution ... it is vital that there is a quality product because it invariably forms the evidence-in-chief of the witness ... The absence of effective planning was the root of the many failings observed ... (Criminal Justice Joint Inspection, 2014a, paras 1.4, 1.7)

'The intermediary's knowledge and experience were a huge advantage in dealing with the complainant. We went through the interview beforehand in great depth, formulating how I was going to conduct my questioning.' (Police officer)

When first introduced, intermediaries played only a marginal role at interview, describing themselves as "very conservative about getting involved". Over time it became clear that collaborative advance planning with the police interviewer is the key to maximising intermediary usefulness (intermediaries described 'the benefit of taking time to prepare for the interview with officers' as 'the biggest learning point' from the Northern Ireland pilot scheme: Department of Justice, 205, para 49). Intermediaries observe that much depends on interviewers' receptiveness to trying something new, such as using non-speech-based methods of communication. Officers are reassured if intermediaries are able to say, when recommending a particular step, that they have done this with officers in other forces, or that the techniques in question have been used successfully at trial.

Allocating planning time

If the interviewer attends the assessment, planning the interview may start immediately afterwards, but if the situation is not urgent some intermediaries prefer to take time to formulate their advice and produce an interim report. Additional time also allows for the development of communication aids. Planning may include phone calls and emails, with officers sending the intermediary their interview plan; typically, at least an hour is then needed for face-to-face discussion.

Advice from the intermediary about the witness's concentration span can assist the interviewing officer to prioritise the content of the interview. In the case of C, who had learning disability, attention deficit disorder and temper management issues, Hermione recommended breaks every 15 minutes. C had difficulty retelling an event in sequence. He frequently went off the subject and "happily talked without stopping" unless brought back to the topic in hand: "If the interviewer had had a clearer idea of what she wanted from the interview, she could have limited the number of her questions."

Scripting the interview

The interviewer should give the intermediary the sequence of interview topics and at least some of the questions to be asked. Clarifying what the interviewer wants to find out helps to focus the advice provided, for example whether a witness may have problems with time concepts or 'position' words. Many well-conducted interviews are almost all scripted in consultation. Interviewing officers who plan and write down their questions find it easier to modify their language: "Clearly, the questioner has to react to what the witness says, but even so the interview goes more smoothly."

Simplifying the questions seldom reduces their overall number. Hermione recalls receiving the interviewer's list of 17 questions which, after discussion, increased to over 100 much simpler, shorter questions. Together with photos, drawings, 'Talking Mats', dolls and toy furniture, the interview was conducted over three half-hour sessions: "The witness was able to respond to the questions asked." Lucia engaged in joint planning for an interview with P, a teenager with learning disabilities and mental health issues. Using the intermediary's written advice, the officer created an A4 ring-binder containing questions, pictures and timelines in a clear format: "The officer stuck to the strategies that we'd planned. Seeing the materials helped P to understand the interview process and follow its likely length."

Where the witness is nonverbal, it is essential to agree written questions in advance and plan how to enable the witness to respond. K, who had good comprehension but was nonverbal because of a stroke, alleged assault by a driver. Bonnie created communication aids to support questions with words such as 'seatbelt' and 'taxi'. Melissa assessed F, a man with a laryngectomy who could speak but made no sound. His mouth was hidden by a lot of facial hair, making lip-reading difficult. Melissa requested his carers, with his permission, "to prune things a bit" so she could see his lips. At interview, questions for F were printed out in advance and read out by the interviewer; F wrote his answers underneath. Melissa then read out F's answers for the camera, or lip-read his 'spoken' answers, and asked F to nod or shake his head to indicate whether she had repeated his answer correctly.

The interview location

'The waiting room has nothing in it apart from a chair and table, and worst of all, the doors lock when closed, so they're locked in. It's a dismal and embarrassing place to have to bring a witness.' (Intermediary)

'There's a lovely police house where volunteers maintain a beautiful garden, the fridge is full of snacks and drinks and the décor is relaxed and friendly.' (Intermediary)

The Criminal Justice Act 1991 introduced the playing of children's video interviews as their evidence-in-chief at court. This measure resulted in police forces setting up interview suites with wall-mounted video cameras operated by an officer in an adjoining room. The first priority is that the equipment works. Intermediaries encounter frequent instances when it does not and interviews have to be moved not just to an adjoining suite but to locations miles away, inconvenient for them but distressing for the witness; one was car-sick on the way. Surprisingly, given the purpose of recording evidence for trial, suites are not always soundproof. Golightly was present at a challenging interview with K, a three-year-old with a passion for trains, in a suite beside a railway station: "We 'lost' K for several minutes every time a train came in."

The accommodation's comfort can be a significant factor in alleviating tension for vulnerable witnesses. Intermediaries report that relatively few interview suites are of a high standard; many are in need of a major overhaul. They describe facilities that are "forbidding", "shabby", "dirty" and as "having an 'empty house' feel"; some seating is unsuitable, especially for children – particularly oversized sofas, "so deep that only a six-foot person could reach the floor". They may be unwelcoming in other ways; some lack ventilation or are too hot or cold. Intermediaries want police officers to look at these environments through the witness's eyes: the lack of attention to detail sends the wrong message about the importance of the interview. However, they stress that "The most important feature is a team who want to facilitate in a kind way. This makes up for a multitude of shortcomings."

Modifying the interview room

Intermediaries sometimes familiarise witnesses with the interview room by showing them pictures beforehand; they may also recommend adjustments to the room layout to accommodate the witness's needs, the interview plan and the recording. Communication between the intermediary and witness must be clear to the interviewer and anyone watching the DVD; camera positions may be altered or an additional camera employed to capture facial expression, gesture, signing or communication aids. A practice run with the equipment is advisable to check the quality of sound and picture. Where a witness communicates by 'eye pointing' (gazing at double-sided symbols including 'yes', 'no' and 'don't know' on a transparent plastic frame) the intermediary will ensure that the witness's face and the frame are clearly shown; the intermediary speaks the witness's answers for the record and checks with the witness that they are correct.

Some suites have an additional camera for use with a sign-language interpreter to record the signer's face, upper body and hand movements, as well as those of the witness (Ministry of Justice, 2011a, para 2.192). James, who works with deaf witnesses, always changes the seating arrangement "as it needs to be a deaf-friendly environment with the witness, interpreter and intermediary 'on camera'"; the interviewer can be heard on the recording but need not appear on screen. However, if positioning needs to accommodate someone who lip-reads, the intermediary will advise that witnesses must be able to see faces when viewing the recording to refresh their memory before the trial.

Where witnesses are soft-spoken, microphones must be positioned to pick up their responses, otherwise the intermediary should repeat answers for the record. S, a teenager with cerebral palsy, had a quiet voice and struggled to maintain her body temperature. Poppy positioned S's wheelchair close to a wall-mounted microphone on one side and on the other arranged a floor-mounted fan to regulate body temperature. Maria found that C, an eight-year-old girl with a middle ear infection, could not hear well or speak at volume: the position of microphones and where both C and the questioner faced while talking were therefore crucial.

The interviewing officer needs to engage the witness; the intermediary usually wants eye contact with the interviewer and to be able to observe the witness. It is helpful if seating is flexible, allowing it to be brought closer together for a small child or further apart to provide personal space for a witness who is touch averse. Positioning furniture in this way maximises the witness's comfort and control. Golightly assessed a teenager with Asperger syndrome in the interview room. She observed that he frequently chose to avert his gaze and look out of the window: "This seemed to have a calming and focusing effect on him, so we replicated that for the interview." Laurel places 'sun' symbols on the walls and explains to fearful young witnesses that this is a reminder they are safe in the witness suite.

Some intermediaries bring their own small tables and chairs for children. Claire arranged for a set of nursery furniture for the interview with C, aged three:

> 'We allocated different spaces in the interview room according to C's activities. She had three "stations" – one was a little table where she answered the police officer's questions. The second was a little table for drawing and games and the third was a spot marked on the floor for hopping about.'

Intermediaries may suggest that everyone sits on the floor for the interview. Bonnie encourages "even the biggest of officers" to do this. She brings a red circular rug that the child may choose to sit on to answer questions. This is used in combination with picture symbols for 'sit on mat', 'listen', 'question' and 'play': "The child can roll onto her back, stretch out and sit up when she wants to: some children need to move to think." She has recently found 'ears' which she places on either side of the rug to help remind the child to listen.

Sometimes paper and pens are lacking in the interview suite. Intermediaries always have a supply and where necessary will bring a table, board or tray suitable for display of visual aids or a table cloth to ensure that aids and drawings show up on camera. Some interview rooms may be distracting or over-stimulating to the witness. At a "lovely suite with lots of flowers and knickknacks", Tosca cleared them all away for a distractible, hyperactive child of six: "We left only a free-standing bookcase and yes, the small witness climbed up that." Golightly removed objects that could be thrown by a volatile witness and ensured there were "clear exit points and an adequate distance" between the interviewer, herself and a witness "known to be unpredictable in her tendency to slap faces. All went well, but my spare glasses were packed that day." At some facilities, including Triangle's purpose-built interview suite in Brighton, the intermediary can give young witnesses some control over the process by involving them in setting up the interview room and choosing the furniture, communication aids and calming play materials. This approach can be adopted elsewhere.

Interviews using mobile equipment

Enabling vulnerable witnesses to participate in a filmed interview in their own setting requires additional work but is a helpful strategy for witnesses who cannot easily be brought to an interview suite or for whom this would be too stressful. Tess recommended interviewing in a special school because bringing young witnesses to police premises would have "heightened their anxiety and made them feel they were 'in trouble'". Hazeley assisted at an interview in the witness's local pub:

> 'His home was unsuitable and the pub was his preference as he could get there on his mobility scooter. The police officer arranged to use the main room of the pub just before opening hours and she brought a mobile camera. It worked perfectly.'

Conducting a police interview in medical or social care facilities requires privacy and careful negotiation. Poppy assessed M, a man with motor neurone disease, in hospital on three occasions over a nine-day period because he could not tolerate more than

20 minutes of interaction at a time. His interview was filmed in a side room of the ward. His speech, which was impaired, was affected by his muscle tone when he tried to speak; his communication deteriorated quickly due to fatigue. He was unable to sit out of bed and required frequent changes of position by a nurse. Planning included asking staff to monitor when M's medication had an optimal effect on his muscle tone.

Filming an interview with someone in bed presents its own challenges. Bonnie brings a high stool so that she can sit at the right level next to a hospital bed, and a 'writing wedge' to display symbols to witnesses lying down. Melissa assisted at the interview of F, an elderly woman who could not sit up and who had "a tiny whispered voice, some hearing loss and no hearing aid". The interview was carried out with the intermediary half-lying on the bed, repeating questions into F's ear and relaying her whispered answers: "Highly detailed, accurate evidence resulted." In rare cases it may be appropriate to conduct the interview in the place where the alleged offence occurred. Melissa helped at the interview of G, an elderly man who was too frail to leave his house:

> 'It was difficult as we were all squashed into a tiny room, but well worth it. G was able to "show" graphically how the intruder had pinned him against the wall. His speech was difficult to understand as he had Parkinson's but with his demonstrations it was all was very clear.'

A witness in a secure hospital should always be interviewed on site using mobile equipment. Unfortunately, technical problems are as common as with equipment in video suites. Jeeves was appointed as intermediary for Y, a woman with learning disabilities and mental health concerns who was detained in a secure hospital where she was assaulted. When mobile equipment broke down, a planned interview at the hospital was moved to a police suite. During a break, the control officer stepped out of the observation room and while unobserved, Y pulled a camera off the wall. When forcibly removed from the police station, she damaged a car and ended up being handcuffed and returned to the secure hospital. Jeeves concluded: "This could all have been so different if the mobile equipment had worked."

Several of the problems highlighted by intermediaries – problems of poor quality interview suites, unreliability of fixed and portable recording equipment and lack of interview props and communication aids – were highlighted by a Criminal Justice Joint Inspection (2014a, recommendation 3).

Setting rules for the interview

> 'He will need consistent boundaries that are confidently maintained with clear, non-negotiable rules alongside a calm and tolerant response to low-level challenging behaviours (swearing, shouting) in order to minimise the risk of more extreme behaviours (violence and running away).' (Intermediary)

Before investigative questioning gets underway, rules such as 'Tell the truth', 'Don't guess' and so on should be explained to the witness (communication aids to reinforce these rules are described in Chapter Five). Other types of rules may also be necessary. Lucia assessed P, a teenager with learning disabilities and mental health issues. P wanted to hold hands with Lucia or the police officer during the interview: "We managed to put in some rules at the start which everyone was happy with, so that P did not hold hands with us."

George was asked to assess H, a woman with a diagnosis of borderline personality disorder. Having done so, he recommended that H be assigned a female intermediary, but none was available with the requisite skill set. The interview was imminent and H and the interviewer were content to proceed with George in the role. In what he described as "a very unusual situation", he, the interviewer and H agreed rules for his participation at the interview:

> 'My presence appeared to help reduce H's distress but we agreed that if H was about to disclose anything about "women's parts", I would leave the room. This seemed to work. On two occasions, after initial disclosures, I was invited back in and, using drawings

and wooden mannequins, I was able to help H to clarify what happened.'

Similar rules were adopted by Jim, appointed to facilitate communication with N, a 19-year-old woman with mental health problems who would not reveal key details of sexual assaults or the perpetrator's identity. There was a concern that N was still at significant risk. In this case, the strategy went a step further:

'The information came out eventually, achieved mainly through letting N do it in her own time (it took four ABE interviews); my leaving the interview room sometimes and watching from the control room (my gender made it more difficult for her); letting her write information down instead of speaking; and both the interviewing officer and I leaving the room and letting her speak on her own to camera for brief periods, then returning to the room to ask questions.'

Sometimes rules are required to manage a disturbed child. Betsey assessed W, a five-year-old with extremely challenging behaviour who was "particularly resistant to adult direction". Betsey advised about the boundaries needed in order for W to participate in an interview:

'We got away with no kicking, biting, hitting, spitting or throwing in the room, but it was difficult: "Why do I have to tell you my sex secret … I don't want to. It's none of your business … I not talking about it … You're so stupid, you're so dumb, you can't even hear properly. Mind your own business, mate. I not telling you, whatever. If I don't want to, I don't want to, simple. Why you asking stupid questions, oh for fuck's sake …" By the end of the interview, at least we knew enough about this five-year-old's "sex secret" to keep him safe.'

The intermediary's contribution during the interview

'With the intermediary's assistance, a video interview was conducted where very good evidence was gleaned which was a big surprise to us all.' (Police officer)

The officer agreed when it was put to her in cross-examination that the first suggestion that the bin was where he [the child] could see something going on came from the RI [registered intermediary]. (Wurtzel, 2014, p 897)

Intermediaries are not joint interviewers; their status in the interview room can be unclear. Many intermediaries feel that it is harder to intervene during interview than at court, "perhaps because we're aware everything is being video'd and we're reluctant to disrupt the interview in case it contaminates evidence". Once the cameras are running, the intermediary may appear to be a silent bystander. This is open to misinterpretation. Criminal justice professionals may conclude when watching the recording that the intermediary had no role to play. This is sometimes put forward to support an argument that an intermediary is not required at trial, but judicial guidance points out that a lack of intervention is more likely to be due to the interviewer following the intermediary's advice; in any event, an intermediary may be needed because questioning at court is more challenging and stressful (Judicial College, 2013, chapter 5, para 47).

In some cases the intermediary plays an active part to facilitate communication, speaking alongside the interviewer – for example, to a very young or developmentally delayed child who finds one-to-one questioning stressful or where the witness uses 'Makaton' signs not understood by the interviewer. This more active participation is not without risk: one judge observed in court that "In the videos, I couldn't work out who was the interviewer and who the intermediary." Intermediaries may be legitimately subject to challenge if it appears they have introduced forensic details in interview (Wurtzel, 2014).

Whichever approach is adopted, it is important that intermediaries explain the rationale in their reports for court.

Cases can be jeopardised where there is a lack of understanding of the intermediary's contribution. When Paige was appointed to assist T, a four-year-old, the intermediary regarded it as "one of the best interviews with which I've ever been involved". Planning was thorough: "The officer made every attempt to follow my advice in wording her questions about the alleged sexual assault at the correct developmental level." T's mother was anxious and cooperated because of the intermediary's involvement. Building on all the work done beforehand, the interview went smoothly. However, the CPS decided, after viewing the interview, that T would not need intermediary assistance at court. T was unable to cope with cross-examination, became very distressed, curled up in the foetal position and could not continue. (The defendant was acquitted.)

Testing understanding of 'truth and lies'

Children under 14 do not take an oath to tell the truth at court; they give their evidence unsworn. However, at the police interview and at trial they, and some vulnerable adult witnesses, will be asked to demonstrate their understanding of the difference between truth and lies 'where there is likely to be an issue as to whether they understand the value and importance of telling the truth in court' (Ministry of Justice, 2011a, paras 3.17–21). Police interviewers are expected to employ examples suitable to the child's age, experience and understanding', focusing on 'the intention to deceive rather than mere mistakes' (paras 3.19, 3.22). Children gain an understanding of the difference between truth and lies earlier than was previously thought, but the way officers carry out the test is often confusing, particularly for young children or those with learning disabilities, autism or other impairments of communication (Marchant, 2013b). The example should be simple; it should not invite the child to imagine or pretend; and it should not involve the child directly. Betsey observed the following explanation by a police officer to a young child, which failed all these tests:

> 'I have to check with you that you know the difference between telling the truth and telling a lie.

I'm going to give you an example. If I took this pen,
and wrote on the wall in big letters, and I said "My
boss is stupid," imagine I've done that; now my boss
comes here and says to me "Who wrote that on the
wall?" and I say "It was you," would that be a lie?'

The bemused child answered "Maybe? Yes? No?"

The intermediary will consider how best to present the 'truth
and lies' test to the witness. In a constructive development,
the children's organisation 'Triangle', led by an intermediary
contributing to this book, has developed 20 filmed scenarios
(10–15 seconds in length), available as a DVD and app, to illustrate
'truth and lies'; the people shown in the scenarios range from
small children to young adults. These short films have been used
successfully in interview and at trial.

Interviews that require more time

'The witness had cerebral palsy and used a "Vantage Lite"
communication device that shows a range of symbols and speaks
the word when a symbol is pressed. Due to the time it took
him to communicate, he was interviewed over four days with
each of four separate allegations discussed on each day. Each
interview lasted around two hours.' (Intermediary)

Sometimes it is simply not possible to shorten the interview
process. Melissa describes as a 'baptism of fire' the first interview
she attended as an intermediary. It involved D, a young woman
who was paralysed and could not speak but could finger-spell.
She was ill, so had to have frequent breaks. Melissa helped
structure questions as D also had comprehension problems. She
spoke the sound that D signed and wrote it down if D nodded.
D was dyslexic so her spelling was sometimes inaccurate. As
the interview progressed, Melissa made keyword charts using
words D had already spelled out such as names, verbs and parts
of the body, so that if D needed them again she could point to
the whole word:

'All this took many hours over two days. At the end, the interviewer said that it was one of the most complete and compelling interviews she had ever achieved. D was delighted that she had been able to tell what happened. The defendant pleaded guilty after he was shown her video interview. According to his counsel, the defendant realised that the mute woman he had raped because she wouldn't be able to tell could in fact tell her story in great detail.'

Interviewing young children

'The child was very young and the intermediary's incorporation of play and the use of a doll assisted us in obtaining information that was extremely useful to the investigation.' (Police officer)

In the 18th century, judge and legal scholar William Blackstone (1769, book 4, chapter 15) considered that 'Infants of very tender years often give the clearest and truest testimony.' In the mid-20th century, however, the Court of Appeal's reluctance to rely on little children's evidence had a dampening effect on police attitudes. In 1958, the court found it 'ridiculous' to consider that juries could attach any value to the evidence of a child of five (R v Wallwork [1958] 42 CAR 153); 'quite exceptional circumstances' were required to justify calling a child of six (R v Wright and Ormerod [1990] 90 CAR 91); a five-year-old would 'very rarely satisfy' statutory requirements as a witness (R v Z [1990] 2 WB 355).

The Criminal Justice Act 1991 abolished the competency requirement for child witnesses, with the effect that there would be no lower age limit, but there was no apparent increase in prosecutions involving pre-school children (Plotnikoff and Woolfson, 1995). A shift of approach was signalled in 2010 when a child of four was accepted as a competent witness (R v Barker [2010] EWCA Crim 4; see Chapter Ten). The Court of Appeal confirmed: 'Many accreted suspicions and misunderstandings about children ... have been swept away' (para 33). This decision affected practice slowly, with some police areas post-Barker reporting no interviews with under-fives (Marchant, 2013a).

However, numbers eventually increased and in 2014 the National Crime Agency appointed intermediaries for 406 children aged four or under (communication to the authors).

Intermediaries report that, with careful planning and use of appropriate communication aids, interviews with very young children can be of evidential value. Hazeley assessed two girls (A aged three and R aged five) over two sessions. The interviewing officer had already made several visits to gain the girls' trust because of concern that they were too traumatised to speak about what had happened. The next step was to familiarise them with the interview environment. On the day before the interview, they were taken to play in a park near the police suite; they also explored the interview room. At the interview, Hazeley felt that they were in "a familiar place where they had previously had a good time". Both children had poor language skills and R had regressed significantly, so Hazeley proposed strategies to support their communication and ensure sensitivity to their feelings:

> 'They needed to speak about what happened in two different houses, so we made drawings with each girl and identified each location with the names they used. Their interviews followed similar lines, the common theme being extensive use of narrative sheets depicting in simple line drawings what the girls were saying. Lots of breaks with games and drinks were built in. It was important to us all that they went home as happy as possible. The reaction of those investigating the offence was incredulity that such young and troubled children had been successfully interviewed. It would have been impossible without careful planning and a sensitive interviewing officer.'

If there has been no disclosure before the interview

The objective of an ABE interview is to obtain a 'free-narrative' account from the witness in response to open-ended questions. Questions implying the answer are asked only 'as a last resort' (Ministry of Justice, 2011a, para 3.44). Avoidance of suggestive questioning is so engrained in police training that Betsey finds that "interviewers often produce complex questions as they fall over backwards not to 'mention the war'. The guidance is clear – the younger the child, the more likely you will need to 'mention the war.'" This ABE guidance acknowledges that someone with a learning disability or a young child may be reluctant to respond to open invitations ("Tell me everything that happened") and require prompting to disclose that an offence has been committed (Ministry of Justice, 2011a, Appendix F.2.3).

Interviewers need to be actively supportive, rather than leading, when interviewing unforthcoming witnesses, for example, "What do you do with daddy?" or "You said he touched you there. Tell me about the touching" (Maybin et al, 1992; Lamb et al, 2013). Reluctance should be identified and addressed at the outset, before negative dynamics emerge (Lamb et al, 2013). Where no disclosure has been made, intermediaries can help officers plan how best to approach discussion of the alleged offence and build rapport. Melissa was appointed for K, a five-year-old with learning difficulties. K was terrified that the defendant would come to 'get' him and his mother if he told what happened. Two interviews were conducted at which K would not tell what happened. Before the third attempt to interview him, Melissa "borrowed a big uniformed policeman":

> 'We brought him into the interview room where he talked to K about his job to protect children and their families, walking round the streets looking out for anyone who might harm people. It worked like magic. K could not tell in words what happened but showed by drawing an erect penis and a picture of himself. When he was asked what happened with the penis, he pointed to his mouth. He was then able to give other information verbally. The same uniformed policeman saw him again just before the trial, to reassure him. The drawings were accepted in court, so he didn't have to tell the "yukky" bits, as he put it. By then, K had enough confidence to tell defence counsel: "You need to make that easier for me, mister," and "You're not giving me time to

think" – saving me from doing so.' (The defendant was found guilty.)

Interviewers have to avoid the temptation to push on too fast. Intermediaries may recommend letting a child leave the interview room to see the carer and to return when they like. Betsey makes a point of practising basic instructions before the interview, for example: "Go out if you need to," "Come back when you're ready," "Can you find the toilet and come back?" and "Can you find your foster carer and come back?" We observed a graphic example of the effectiveness of this strategy during the interview of E, a seven-year-old with attention deficit hyperactivity disorder. The intermediary helped E take three short breaks, going out of the interview room to see his mother. When he came back and closed the door, which he had not done previously, he was finally ready. The interviewer then asked: "Tell me what happened on your way home from the park." E replied: "Allan touched my willy." E went on to give a clear account of what happened, interspersed with several more exits to see his carer.

This strategy has to be talked through and agreed with the officer before the interview. In a different case, an officer complained to us that "by allowing the child to come and go from the interview room" rather than utilising planned breaks, "the interviewing officer can easily lose their train of thought and miss important points".

When the witness is desperate to tell

The intermediary's assessment avoids any discussion of the alleged offence but some witnesses arrive at the assessment desperate to tell about what has happened to them. If this situation is anticipated, it is easiest to respond if the interviewing officer is present and the interview suite is close by. Kitty had this experience with V, a chatty girl of two-and-a-half, who spontaneously named the alleged perpetrator and disclosed other information about the offence while still in the assessment. Betsey has conducted a number of short assessments with children unable to hold back. The shortest – seven minutes – was with H, a bright, typically developing and securely attached three-year-old, the victim of a single incident of attempted sexual assault:

> 'On arrival at the assessment H said to us: "Do you know John asked me to lick his willy?" I said, "We'll talk about that later." I managed to do a very rapid language-processing assessment before H said it again: "He did ask me to lick his willy and I did say 'No, naughty.'" I was working with an officer I know well, so we did the quickest planning ever and were interviewing on film within 11 minutes of H arriving in the building.'

Appointment of an intermediary for a further interview

'The level of communication was far greater than it had been on previous occasions without an intermediary.' (Police officer)

It is relatively common for an intermediary to be appointed only when one or more interviews have proved unsatisfactory; sometimes the request is triggered by review by a CPS lawyer. Reasons for not using an intermediary at the first interview include a perceived need for speed (though an intermediary can often assist quickly, and some 'urgent' cases are not, and would benefit from more planning), concern about cost (misplaced, given the cost of a failed interview) and lack of previous experience with the intermediary scheme. Conducting a further interview with intermediary assistance is often worthwhile. One officer said:

> 'An interview was carried out with the same child two years ago without an intermediary. No disclosures were made. The intermediary's assessment and report helped me prepare my interview plan and carry out the interview in the most appropriate way. Without the intermediary's input, it is likely that we would've been in the same situation as before. The child has now disclosed that she has been abused by six individuals and identified a further child who

may be at risk. The intermediary was fundamental in achieving the environment that allowed the child to feel safe enough to disclose the offences.'

The assessment may suggest alternative strategies for a further interview. Poppy was appointed for M, a man of 64 with learning disabilities and an acquired brain injury who had been interviewed but failed to disclose details of the alleged offence. Her assessment established that M's listening skills were poor and he was slow to process information; he was repetitive to the point of obsession when certain topics were mentioned, including football. At the first interview, the police officer had used football to build rapport with M before formal questioning began. Poppy considered that when M went into the interview suite, he was probably unable to switch away from the football discussion. She and a new interviewing officer planned a second interview avoiding any talk about subjects of obsessional interest to M. In the interview, he went on to disclose what had happened to him. Using pen and paper, M drew the layout of the room where the assault took place, something he had difficulty describing in words.

Interviews that do not disclose an offence

'The officer allowed the witness to work through the apparent allegations in his own convoluted way. We produced written bullet points of key details or flow charts when the officer paused periodically to summarise what had been said. N's account, although tortuous, indicated that no crime had been committed and the suspect was released.' (Intermediary)

A police interview does not invariably result in disclosure of a crime. It is equally valuable when the interview reveals that no crime has been committed; intermediaries can assist in ensuring that a full and accurate picture emerges. In several instances, interviews facilitated by an intermediary have revealed that a suspect in custody was not the assailant. V, a girl with Down syndrome, was placed into emergency foster care after her school noticed a mark on her face and V used the words "Mum" and "iron". Following assessment, Ashley stressed the need to check the meanings of M's vocabulary. During the interview, using pictures and gesture to support verbal communication, it became apparent that V's use of "iron" related to a curling iron used to curl her hair that had touched her cheek. No further action was taken and the child was returned to her mother's care.

Intermezzo

Upma and a breakdown in communication
Ashley (registered intermediary)

At a district judge's request, I was appointed to assist Upma, a girl of 12, at a magistrates' court trial. She had been interviewed without an intermediary about sexual touching by a stranger. This was a last-minute referral: I was told she had no known communication difficulties other than her age, so I agreed (contrary to usual practice) to combine my assessment with her court familiarisation visit. Upma's family didn't want her to give evidence. They had concerns about the shame this would cause to her community. It was hoped that the court visit would address their concerns but Upma and her family failed to attend. Despite Upma's age, the judge issued a witness summons for her to attend trial. I therefore agreed to attend court on the day of trial, assess Upma and report my findings orally at the ground rules hearing, with her evidence to follow in the afternoon.

I was told to attend court at 9 am; this meant leaving home by 6:30 am. The day before, I came home to find that our dog had eaten boxes of Christmas chocolates. My daughter panicked as chocolate is poisonous to dogs and we couldn't contact a vet. I thought that if the dog died overnight, I'd have no option but to hide the body as I wouldn't be able to tell my daughter. Without question I had to be at court by 9 am: ringing the court to explain the story was not a possibility.

At court, Upma and her father were very unhappy and there were difficult exchanges with the officer. They said that they'd never been told about giving evidence and if she'd known that, she wouldn't have agreed to the interview. The officer said the family had been told all along she would have to give evidence. I explained my role and assessed Upma in the presence of her father and Witness Service supporter. Upma cooperated but refused to give evidence. It emerged that she was scared about being seen by the defendant; when she was told he had already seen her police interview, this caused further outrage as the family said no one had told them this would happen. She was adamant that she would not give evidence if the defendant would be able to see her. Eventually it was agreed that the defendant would be screened in court so that he would hear but not see her over the live link. By this time, there was no trust left between officer and family so I just tried to maintain rapport with the family and informed them that I'd seen the screens in place myself.

While I was collating my thoughts about my assessment, prosecution counsel came in and handed me a list of written ground rules, saying: "The judge uses these in every case with children." I was then called to a meeting with judge and counsel and asked if I wanted to add anything to the "already agreed" ground rules – not the way it's supposed to happen.

Upma gave evidence in the live link room with me, the Witness Service volunteer and her father all squeezed in. She was fine and coped with the questions. I only intervened to raise concerns about sound and picture quality and repeat verbatim to the court what she had said. I was then released and have not asked about the verdict.

This case was talked about in Upma's community and I was concerned about the wider impact. Since this case, I have mentioned to officers that it's important to consider exactly what information is given to witnesses and their families about the court process. Although Upma's communication profile was roughly in line with her chronological age, the anxiety both for herself and her family had an adverse impact on her. (By the way, the dog survived.)

SEVEN

Negotiating professional space at the ground rules hearing

Courtrooms are traditional, deferential places in which everyone knows their place in the hierarchy and jealously guards their professional space. The intrusion of an outsider can be regarded with suspicion. We saw an example of this during our evaluation of real-time computer-aided transcription (Plotnikoff and Woolfson, 1993). As the judge, lawyers and witnesses spoke at trial, a highly trained stenographer (whose skills cost more than her equipment) created a transcript seen immediately on the computer screens of the judge and lawyers, allowing them to annotate text as it appeared. At the start of the evaluation, the stenographer was seated below the judge's bench, close to the witness box – the ideal position to hear what was being said. Nevertheless, a few days into the experiment, the stenographer was shifted to a seat further away where it was harder for her to hear accurately. She had been moved because she had taken the position normally occupied by the clerk when swearing witnesses and passing papers to the judge.

The ground rules hearing, a new type of case management hearing, is where intermediaries carve out their own space in professional, not merely physical, terms. For the first time, someone other than the judge or opposing counsel may interrupt questioning at trial (Henderson, 2015c, forthcoming). Those with a traditional view of the courtroom hierarchy may argue that intermediaries are unnecessary, that they are likely to interfere with witness cross-examination and possibly even compromise the judge's control of proceedings. Intermediaries try to allay such concerns at the ground rules hearing. It is designed to facilitate 'a more intense consideration of issues' by bringing together intermediaries, lawyers and judiciary to resolve how best to communicate with vulnerable witnesses at trial (Ministry of Justice, 2014a, p 4). This chapter explores how ground rules hearings came about and why, 10 years on, intermediaries sometimes still find themselves negotiating their professional space on a case by case basis.

The case management background

> Government objectives for 'active and effective case management' include the early identification of trial issues, 'achieving certainty as to what must be done, by whom, and when'; the early setting of a timetable for the progress of the case; monitoring compliance with judicial directions; discouraging delay; and encouraging the cooperation of participants in moving the case forward. (Ministry of Justice, 2014a, p 10)

Most intermediaries accept appointments across a wide geographical area. As outsiders to the criminal justice system, they are shocked to discover that the use of intermediaries and the extent to which their trials are managed ahead of time varies widely between court locations and even between different judges of the same court. Sometimes requests for a ground rules hearing are ignored and attempts by intermediaries to carry out their professional responsibilities are resisted. These problems are less surprising when considered in light of the long history of differences in local court practice and the chequered success of efforts to introduce national consistency in case management.

Policies to give priority to young witness trials

The gap between case management policy and vulnerable witness practice was evident 25 years ago. In 1988, a government minister announced that child abuse cases should be given 'greater priority' (Home Office press release, 18 February 1988); this policy was incorporated into the Criminal Justice Act 1991. In practice, the Act made no difference; these cases actually took longer than the national average to be completed (Plotnikoff and Woolfson, 1995). Despite frequent reiterations of the 'priority' policy, child witness cases still took longer than average to reach trial 20 years after the policy was first announced (Plotnikoff and Woolfson, 2009a). The latest commitment applies to children under 10 only (Association of Chief Police Officers et al, 2015).

Case management is a judicial responsibility but in England and Wales a single case is often dealt with by several judges; the trial judge is often not assigned until shortly before it starts (lawyers representing the prosecution and defence may also change as the case moves through the system and at the last minute). This gives our system flexibility in allocating judicial resources but contrasts with practice in federal courts in the United States where one judge handles a case from start to finish. Judicial continuity is favoured by American judges and lawyers (Gerety and Kauffman, 2014).

In 1995 the Lord Chief Justice introduced case management 'plea and directions' hearings (now called 'plea and case management' hearings) held before the trial in each Crown Court case. Judicial interviews revealed wide differences in their willingness to apply case management principles: while the majority welcomed a proactive role – 'If the judge is a neutral referee who only intervenes to apply the rules, then that is not case management' – others resisted the new approach, perceiving, for example, 'quite a widespread feeling that that plea and directions hearings are a waste of time' (Plotnikoff and Woolfson, 2002, pp 8–10). When the 2005 Criminal Procedure Rules emphasised the compulsory nature of case management hearings, the Lord Chief Justice and Lord Chancellor called for a complete culture change (Darbyshire, 2014). In recent years, significant cuts to justice system budgets have resulted in a loss of ground for active case management. 'Changing this culture ... is taking a long time' (Darbyshire, 2014, p 50).

Establishing the need for 'ground rules': the first pilot trials

'The ground rules hearing is an essential part of the trial process involving use of intermediaries. It is very important to get an idea

of the witness and it's of great assistance in trial management
– also to set the boundaries of intervention.' (Judge)

In light of wide variations in case management practice around the country, it is not surprising that in 2004 some courts in pilot areas gave no thought to how the new role would be integrated, assuming that intermediaries only needed to turn up for the witness's evidence (a belief that still seems to be current, given that some CPS requests for intermediaries are made on the eve of trial). There was little prior discussion about the circumstances or manner in which intermediaries would flag up communication problems to the court.

The first pilot trial to use an intermediary revealed just how badly things could go wrong. The teenage witnesses, R and G, had learning difficulties and aphasia, an impairment affecting the production and comprehension of speech. Interviews concerning alleged sexual assaults were conducted without an intermediary but one was appointed to assist them at trial. Following her assessment she concluded that questions should be short and taken slowly, giving them extra time to understand and form words in reply. She did not prepare a report and had no opportunity to discuss her recommendations with the judge.

The boys' police videos were shown to the court as their evidence-in-chief. They were then cross-examined, accompanied by the intermediary, over a live link to the courtroom. It was a textbook illustration that 'communicative competence' concerns not only the abilities of the witness but also those of the questioner (Saywitz, 2002a). From the outset, the defence advocate spoke quickly, using complex questions. The judge only intervened once to request that a question be simplified. Difficulties of the same sort arose during G's cross-examination. (The trial resulted in an acquittal.)

At the end, we spoke to all those involved. The judge saw no problem with the defence counsel's pace or questioning style but thought that the intermediary should have repeated all of the boys' answers. The intermediary had wondered whether she should do so but refrained because she had not had a judicial direction. She was frustrated that she had been unable to meet the judge beforehand; she had sent a message with the usher twice asking defence counsel to slow down and give the boys time to answer, but he did not do it. The prosecutor thought that they should all have spoken to the judge beforehand but the defence advocate disagreed: "We didn't need any guidance." R and G told us the intermediary had been "brilliant" but R would have liked to say to the defence lawyer: "Slow down, slow down, slow down."

The second trial was more carefully planned. This case was triggered when C, a young woman with mild learning difficulties, made an allegation of sexual assault. The police interviewed her but because her speech was difficult to understand, they concluded she could not give evidence. The case proceeded based on interviews with two other young complainants. The trial judge was aware that charges in relation to C had been discontinued and directed that an intermediary assess her communication and assist at a second police interview. At the start of the interview, the intermediary explained C's use of 'Makaton' signs and said that she would repeat and clarify C's answers where necessary. The intermediary also explained C's illustrated symbol book for everyday use to which she added a balanced range of pictures to support questions relevant to the case. When C used the book, the intermediary said aloud what C was pointing to and asked her to hold up the relevant illustration for the camera. Following this interview, charges in relation to C were added to the indictment.

The advocates, intermediary and judge met to discuss the intermediary's recommendations about how best to communicate with C. Her interview was shown to the court and she was cross-examined over the live link. The defence QC asked many complex questions. When C struggled to find words, the intermediary asked her to "show us in your book". The intermediary intervened quite frequently, speaking directly to the QC, for example: "C has difficulty with dates – can you use an event to help her?" The judge picked this up and made similar interventions. When C's answer was more than "yes" or "no", the intermediary would repeat her response and explain her 'Makaton' signs. Sometimes the intermediary said that she did not understand C's answer, and asked C to repeat it. At the close of C's testimony, the judge thanked C and the intermediary.

The defendant was convicted and imprisoned in relation to the charges concerning C, and was acquitted in respect of the two children. This was the first prosecution case that would not have entered the justice system without intermediary assistance.

Afterwards C told us that the intermediary was "very helpful" and made it easier for her to answer, although questions were "too fast". The lawyers praised the intermediary and the helpful pre-trial discussion; however, the judge was not given the intermediary's written memo of recommendations. The judge thought that, in future cases, the trial judge should convene a short directions hearing with the advocates and intermediary.

In most conventional justice system research, recommendations are considered only when the evaluation ends. In this project, we worked closely with those responsible for the pilot scheme and were able to pass on the judge's observations that a pre-trial planning meeting would be an important ingredient of effective intermediary use at trial. We identified two sources for a model procedure. The first was judicial guidance encouraging judges to issue directions on the questioning of young witnesses, including 'any areas on which the child might be led; and the tenor, tone, language and duration of questioning and cross-examination' (Judicial Studies Board, 2004, section 4). At the time, however, no use was made of this provision. The second source was a California judicial handbook recommending that judges set 'ground rules', specifying what would and would not be allowed in questioning children and stressing that if questions were developmentally inappropriate, the judge would intervene (Saywitz, 2002b, section 1.7).

Towards a ground rules hearing before every intermediary trial

'The ground rules hearing is essential in educating judges and lawyers who have not previously worked with intermediaries as to how the system can work well.' (QC)

'On occasion where the judge has not seen the need for a ground rules hearing, he has changed his mind when taken through it carefully by the intermediary.' (Barrister)

In 2010, the 'Application for a special measures direction' form was revised to indicate the need for a ground rules hearing in every intermediary trial. By 2011, rates of ground rules hearings had increased, but only to an estimated 76% of intermediary cases (Cooper, 2012). Guidance at the pilot stage had described the intermediary's presence at the ground rules hearing as 'desirable'. The 2010 provision made the intermediary's presence mandatory. Nevertheless, there are still instances where intermediaries say they have to "push in" and others where ground rules are discussed in their absence. In rare instances, judges decline to convene the hearing at all. Where judges turn down requests for a ground rules hearing, intermediaries report instances of questioning at trial so poorly managed that the witness breaks down – in one instance, smashing the live link screen – and the trial is discontinued.

The ground rules hearing requirement in all intermediary cases is now reflected in Criminal Procedure Rule 3.9(7) (2015) and Criminal Practice Direction 3E.2 (2015). Despite this, they are not yet systematically requested by the prosecution or scheduled by the court. While intermediaries report that the hearings are close to becoming the norm in their Crown Court cases, this often requires prompting on their part. Some consider that the position is improving and they "no longer have to jump up and down" while others feel that "It's categorically not getting easier," with one reporting that it took over 40 phone calls, emails and letters to ensure that the ground rules hearing was held. Magistrates' courts tend to be unfamiliar with the process; intermediaries may have to explain the purpose of the hearing and that it must be conducted by the Bench, not the legal adviser (Magistrates' court 'Preparation for effective trial' form, sections 5.2 and 10.2).

In the Northern Ireland pilot intermediary scheme, draft procedures initially made the holding of a ground rules hearing compulsory, drawing on experience in England and Wales. Before the pilot started, the judiciary in Northern Ireland decided that the ground rules hearing 'should not be a mandatory requirement but rather viewed as a helpful process' (Department of Justice, 2015, para 60). Its pilot cases have demonstrated the value of ground rules hearings; in due course, experience will surely result in policy confirmation that ground rules hearings are a prerequisite to effective intermediary use at trial.

Acceptance of the intermediary's role at the ground rules hearing

> [Intermediaries] are neutral and independent, offering assistance to the court and responsible to the court. Their presence is designed to assist the judge and the advocates and the witness to ensure that they all understand each other. (Lord Judge, 2013a)

The Code of Practice expects registered intermediaries to be impartial, neutral and to owe their paramount duty to the court (Ministry of Justice, 2012, para 1.23). Confidence in the scheme has grown, but intermediaries' independence is often tested at the ground rules hearing where they have to justify recommendations based on their assessment of the individual witness. They stress the importance of being "open", "collaborative", "not defensive" and "not on anyone's side". Even where the intermediary sits at the ground rules hearing must avoid any hint of bias. An intermediary who was invited to sit behind the prosecutor declined: "The prosecutor laughed and said: 'Oh yes, of course – why don't you move along the bench so you are in the middle, then you can be a plague on both our houses.'"

Policy requires intermediaries to be present if the application for their involvement at trial is contested, so that they can explain their recommendations (Ministry of Justice, 2012, para 2.46). In early cases they were sometimes excluded. In one such instance, Melissa was asked to attend the hearing but was left to wait outside the courtroom. Prosecution counsel came out and said that the judge had decided the child did not need an intermediary:

> 'He said he "rather agreed. We're all used to talking to young children, we've got children and grandchildren of our own." I heard later from the officer in the case that the child had collapsed sobbing in the live link room the next day and

was unable to give evidence. The trial had to be abandoned. Tragic, of course, but I couldn't help hoping the story would be different next time.'

The perception that an intermediary may not be needed for 'ordinary' children and some other witnesses has persisted. Intermediaries still encounter some ill-informed attitudes: "I don't need help with knowing how to talk to children;" "I've never had an issue questioning a child before"; "the witnesses were okay without you when the police interviewed them"; and once, appallingly, "I know how to talk to 'thick' children." Maria recalls a judge who queried the need for an intermediary with normally developing children aged six and seven. "The prosecutor agreed: 'Your Honour, we've read the intermediary report and it isn't rocket science.' I assured the prosecutor that it clearly was rocket science to some advocates and that I had several transcripts to illustrate the point."

Some judges may suggest that the intermediary can be dispensed with at trial, based on confidence (sometimes misplaced) in advocates' communication skills: "Intermediaries are seldom needed at trial – we follow the ground rules." The Judicial College's Equal Treatment Bench Book (chapter 5, para 47) dismisses the argument that an intermediary will not be needed because advocates say they will comply with guidance in the report:

> In practice, many advocates find it more difficult to adapt key questions than they anticipate. It can also be difficult to keep in mind all aspects of questioning that may be problematic for the individual witness. An intermediary who has already assessed the witness's communication is able to alert the court to any problems or loss of concentration.

It appears that most judges now concur. When Hazeley encountered an advocate who suggested she would follow the ground rules but did not need the intermediary at trial, "the judge was very firm, pointing out that she was opening 'a can of worms' and could not foretell the difficulties she would encounter".

Intermezzo

The need for realistic timetabling in a trial with multiple vulnerable witnesses

Hazeley and Paige (registered intermediaries)

This case involved an allegation of sexual abuse of a group of children from a Traveller community aged from pre-school to young teenagers. When we became involved, they were all in foster care. Initially the younger children were referred for an intermediary assessment and possible police interview. It was agreed that two intermediaries should deal with them. We subsequently learned that the older children had all been interviewed without an intermediary but the police agreed that we should also assess them for the trial. All were complex youngsters. We each dealt with some and agreed to provide each other with ongoing support and supervision.

Assessing the children was a challenge. Many standard assessment tools and intermediary approaches were inappropriate, either due to the children's unusual pattern of development or because the material and images used scenarios alien to their experience. We had to find appropriate visual material to help keep them focused. The children had little or no school attendance; they were unused to sitting still and their attention span was short. Their concept of time was impaired as a result of lack of structure in their lives; they were even uncertain of their birthdays. Two had a learning disability. Even the more able children had impoverished language skills affecting their ability to express themselves. Their use of tenses could be random and their personal pronouns were confused.

Interviews were more complex because the children found themselves conflicted about the allegations. They needed huge reassurance about their safety. In the end, only four could be called as witnesses. Setting up and arranging court familiarisation visits was a problem as they were fostered in different parts of the country. We divided them into two sets and each of us attended one court visit. Memory refreshing from their DVD interviews was also a challenge: they did not want to watch or be reminded of what they had said. We had to persuade them to view the DVDs beforehand; it would have been impossible for them to watch at the same time as the jury.

For several weeks prior to trial we made regular contact with the court. The prosecutor backed up our recommendations, organised for us to meet defence counsel and spoke in support of our request for individual ground rules hearings for each child. The judge was reluctant to allow enough time for this so, in anticipation, we prepared summaries highlighting how each child differed.

Hazeley spent an excellent session with defence counsel going over the questions to ensure they would be understood by the children. There were issues that we had not encountered before, including a message that the judge wanted all the children to promise to tell the truth at the beginning of cross-examination. We were concerned this would set them off on the wrong foot because of the apparent presumption that they would not tell the truth; the matter was never resolved.

The final timetable was overly optimistic and did not provide enough time for proper discussion of ground rules for each child. Once the trial started, adjustments to the schedule were made once or twice daily. (At one point one of the children said: "Are you coming to tell us you've changed your mind again?") On day three, after various problems had delayed the start of the children's evidence, the defendant pleaded guilty. Hearing the indictments read out was a chilling experience – we were aware we had only been told a fraction of what had happened to these children. On being told the outcome, their relief was immense. We heard later that the defendant received a lengthy prison sentence. One lesson from this trial was that, when the scheduling of multiple vulnerable witnesses is unrealistic, the potential for disruption is enormous. Too many changes can risk losing witnesses altogether if they become too distressed to give evidence.

EIGHT

Making the ground rules hearing effective

Ground rules hearings are now a requirement in intermediary cases. They must also be held where 'directions for appropriate treatment and questioning' are necessary, even if the case does not involve an intermediary (Criminal Procedure Rule 3.9(7), 2015; Criminal Practice Directions 3E.2, 3E.3, 2015; toolkit 1 and checklist, *Ground rules hearings and the treatment of vulnerable people in court,* www.theadvocatesgateway.org). The Court of Appeal expects ground rules to be discussed in every vulnerable witness case, except in 'very exceptional circumstances' (*R v Lubemba, R v JP* [2014] EWCA Crim 2064, para 42). The hearing gives intermediaries an opportunity to explain that their role is to assist everyone to communicate with the witness. Agreed ground rules minimise the risk of inappropriate questioning at trial and reduce the need for interventions by the intermediary or judge. There are benefits of making clear from the start 'where the boundaries of questioning lie' (Leveson, 2015, para 257). In practice, however, ground rules hearings are often squeezed into the court's timetable just before the witness's evidence begins, while the jury is waiting, leaving little time for meaningful discussion.

Criminal Procedure Rule 3.9(7), (2015) sets out an agenda for the hearing. This includes directions about the duration of questioning (discussed in this chapter); the use of communication aids (Chapter Five); what questions 'may or may not be asked' and the manner of questioning; (Chapters Ten and Eleven); and 'relieving a party of any duty to put that party's case to a witness or defendant in its entirety' (Chapter Twelve). The Court of Appeal suggests additional issues for discussion (*R v Lubemba, R v JP* [2014] EWCA Crim 2064, para 43) including the frequency of breaks (this chapter); general care of the witness, refreshing the witness's memory and introductions (addressed in Chapter Nine); and asking the lawyers to write out questions in advance (Chapter Twelve).

This chapter describes the characteristics of effective ground rules hearings and reasons for scheduling the hearing before the day of the witness's evidence. The Bench should give clear directions about the intermediary's ability to intervene orally, the rules to be followed at trial and its intention to take action if the rules are breached. If ground rules are not observed, or something else goes wrong during questioning, a further ground rules discussion mid-trial is likely to be helpful.

However, effectiveness of the ground rules hearing depends crucially on the advocates. As one judge told us:

> 'Experience of intermediary involvement has been highly informative. In my trials, they have been largely non-interventionist, which is testimony to the relevance of the proposed ground rules from the intermediary *and counsel's willingness to follow them.*' (Our emphasis)

Discussion before the ground rules hearing

> 'Speaking to the advocates before the hearing is the "bread and butter" conversation. I explain that I'm not there to interfere but to assist.' (Intermediary)

Professional barriers can be broken down where intermediaries speak informally to advocates before the ground rules hearing. Attempts to introduce themselves by phone or email are sometimes ignored. Persistence may be necessary – one intermediary "sits outside the courtroom keeping a 'beady eye' out". Even if a defence lawyer does not wish to speak beforehand, it is still worthwhile for intermediaries to discuss recommendations with the prosecutor. Well-briefed prosecutors can help persuade a sceptical judge of the importance of ground rules, ensure key issues are discussed and reinforce recommendations if they are queried. However, intermediaries describe some prosecutors as leaving them "to get on with it" in the ground rules hearing; they "appear to not want to rock the boat" or "risk upsetting the judge".

Opportunities for informal discussion between the intermediary and advocates are increasing with the introduction of review of questions (see Chapter Twelve). Sir Brian Leveson's *Review of Efficiency in Criminal Proceedings* anticipates that 'in due course, with the correct technological support' ground rules hearings 'may take place in a virtual environment' without the parties' physical presence, thus saving costs (2015, para 259). Virtual hearings would present a further challenge to intermediaries attempting to engage lawyers in informal discussion and ensuring that their own voice is heard.

Holding the ground rules hearing before the day of trial

> 'Ground rules need to be agreed and set before the trial so that counsel have no excuse for not complying and can have them in their mind when drafting questions.' (Judge)

The intermediary evaluation concluded that ground rules discussions left until the day of the witness's evidence were unhelpful for planning purposes and resulted in additional waiting time for the witness (Plotnikoff and Woolfson, 2007a). Criminal Practice Direction 3E.3 (2015) now recommends that ground rules hearings take place before the day of the witness's testimony. Where witnesses are due to give evidence from a remote location, the ground rules hearing must be held before the day of trial, to enable the intermediary to attend in person.

Discussing ground rules before the day of trial accords with advice from advocacy trainers who recommend writing out questions in advance not only to adapt questions to the witness's communication needs but also to plan the questions which the advocate wishes to ask. The risks of failing to do so are illustrated by the cross-examination of D, a witness on the autism spectrum who had complex communication needs. At the ground rules hearing, defence counsel rejected Melissa's advice about how to adapt his questions:

'He insisted: "I often don't know what my question is going to be until it's come out of my mouth." The Bench chairman paused then said: "In that case, we definitely need the intermediary's assistance to guide us." In cross-examination, defence counsel said to D: "I put it to you that you phoned the police just to cause more trouble for this man." I started to intervene but in fact D was able to respond: "Well, what you do if man knock your door down. He got a big hammer." End of cross-examination.'

Holding ground rules hearings in advance of trial also gives intermediaries time to create communication aids tailored to the advocates' questions and allows courts to make case management decisions in response to intermediary recommendations. Golightly contributes actively to such decisions at the hearing: "My role is to help produce 'best evidence' so this is what I should push for. Leaving the ground rules hearing to the last minute implies that it is a formality, rather than an opportunity to properly discuss or change practice."

Encouraging meaningful discussion

'I make ground rules hearings wholly informal. They have proved very useful.' (Judge)

Giving people a chance to say something at the start seemed to activate their sense of participation and responsibility and their willingness to speak up. (Gawande, 2011, p 108)

It is the judiciary's responsibility at the ground rules hearing to invite intermediaries to go through key points of their report and it is good practice to check at the end: "Is there anything else I should know?" Lucia observes: "It's hard if the prosecutor thinks they can talk for me and the judge addresses questions about my role to this person instead of me. It's confusing and harder for me to intervene in the discussion. It's best if the judge addresses questions to me directly."

Open, collegial discussion, demonstrating professional respect for the role, enables the intermediary to highlight subtle issues of communication that may otherwise be overlooked. Betsey feels strongly that objections to her recommendations should not emerge at trial but ought to be raised and resolved at the ground rules hearing, which she likens to the banns of marriage: "If anyone present is going to object to the intermediary's recommendations, they have to do it now." She tries to get across that "if we manage to get things right at trial, this child can be a very effective communicator". Her use of "we" emphasises the collective responsibility of good communication in the court context. Discussion is important because some things are "tricky" to explain adequately in the report:

> 'Bizarre behaviour is tough to handle: children who become giggly under stress, children who spit, bite, swear or masturbate in the live link room. I have an upfront approach to rude words: my reports say "Use the child's preferred words for private body parts and sexual acts," then I list them. I read them out at the ground rules hearing.'

Some judges inhibit discussion because of apparent disapproval of the recommendations. Equally problematic are judges who apparently endorse the intermediary's recommendations but dismiss the need for discussion. For example, one judge described ground rules hearings in his court as "short, since intermediary recommendations have previously been covered in the written report. Advocates almost invariably accept these recommendations." Many intermediaries are concerned that a token ground rules exercise does not flush out advocates' concerns about restrictions on their cross-examination which they resist or may have difficulty implementing, nor does it enable intermediaries to justify their reasoning. Alexa recalls a case where failure to permit discussion of the intermediary recommendations resulted in delays during the trial:

> 'The judge commented "We've all read this helpful report and will of course take note," but then did not

invite further input from me. He went on to indicate that visual aids should not be used "unless necessary. Let's see how the witness gets on without them." This ambiguous statement caused confusion later on. After some complex questioning in which I intervened, I thought it was appropriate to introduce a visual aid. The judge stopped the trial, expressed displeasure and requested that I send the proposed aid (which counsel had already seen) to the court via an usher. The judge then agreed its use and asked the defence to plan the remaining questions with me.'

Other intermediaries report similar experiences. When discussion of ground rules is curtailed, advocates may be left, as George says, "neither understanding the importance of the recommendations nor committed to applying them at trial".

Benefits of an informal approach

Informality is unusual in the context of criminal proceedings. Many ground rules hearings are held in court, on the record; the judge may wish the defendant to hear any restrictions imposed on his advocate's cross-examination. But the intermediary's active participation seems easier to achieve in the informal atmosphere promoted by some judges. Intermediaries and judges describe hearings in chambers as more productive, less pressured and more likely to stimulate discussion. When hearings take place in the courtroom, some intermediaries prefer to be in the witness box. Others find that "interaction is much more normal and polite" if they are outside the box and this in turn helps in establishing "proper working relationships".

However informal the discussion, it should always culminate in a clear statement by the judge of the ground rules that will apply at trial (discussed further below).

Alerting the court to a communication problem

'Intermediaries are very helpful. Counsel are assisted by the intermediary's interventions in posing questions.' (Judge)

'We are all very experienced here, so I wouldn't expect you to need to say anything. Please do not interrupt verbally, just raise your hand.' (Judge, quoted by intermediary)

One of the required decisions at a ground rules hearing is to 'establish how the intermediary will alert the court if the witness has not understood' (Application for a special measures direction, part F.1). Intermediaries must sit alongside the witness and are most effective when permitted to intervene verbally as necessary. Seated close to the witness, the intermediary can identify early signs of confusion, loss of concentration or distress; perhaps something as slight as a change in breathing. When witnesses are in the live link room, these indications are unlikely to be apparent to those watching in court. Interaction between witness and intermediary needs to be visible to those in court but despite this, intermediaries have sometimes been required to sit off-screen.

Intermediaries are trained to direct their interventions to the judge, for example:

Barrister: 'When you went to speak to the police ladies, do you know why you went to speak to them?'

Intermediary: 'Your Honour, L finds it difficult to understand "Why" questions.'

Judge: 'Mr T will re-phrase the question.'

Witnesses in the live link room can be confused by this because the intermediary is speaking to a disembodied voice belonging to someone the witness cannot see. As a result, judges sometimes permit intermediaries to speak directly to the advocate, for example:

Barrister: 'What do you call him?'

| Intermediary: | 'Can we clarify who you mean by "him"?' |
| Barrister: | 'Have you called Richard "dad"?' |

This less formal process is sometimes adopted by default during questioning where frequent intermediary interventions prove necessary and it becomes too cumbersome to keep making interventions via the judge.

Almost all judges agree that the intermediary should speak if a problem affecting communication arises but a few require the intermediary to intervene just by signalling to catch their attention. These judges may be unaware how difficult this is over the live link. Although those on the Bench have an overview of the live link room, the intermediary and witness see on screen only the person speaking – usually the questioner. (In contrast, the Australian state of Victoria provides the witness with two separate screens, one showing the questioner and the other always showing the judge.) The intermediary cannot tell whether the judge has seen the signal; the judge may be making a note or looking elsewhere (we have seen this happen where the judge later acknowledged not having seen the intermediary's hand go up). Sometimes intermediary signals may be seen but not acted upon. Paige was asked to wave a piece of white paper: "The police officer told me that to those in court it looked like some comic attempt at surrender, and yet I was still ignored."

Stifling intermediary intervention

The ground rules hearing should enable intermediaries to fulfil their role at trial, as described by the Court of Appeal, 'actively to intervene when miscommunication may or is likely to have occurred or to be occurring' (*R v Cox* [2012] EWCA Crim 549, para 28). Two practices, happily rare and perhaps now abandoned, have prevented intermediaries from doing so. A few judges have told intermediaries that if they intervened, they would have to come into court to discuss the reasons in the absence of the jury; a few have directed intermediaries not to intervene at all. In one such case, a judge restricted Bonnie to standing in the witness box next to M, a witness with schizophrenia and learning difficulties:

'The judge said he had years of experience of working with "these cases". I decided that ethically it was not correct to totally abandon M, who was very vulnerable, so I stood with her while the defence advocate asked questions such as "What do you think he thought you were thinking?" M became more and more distressed. Her voice became weaker and weaker and they kept telling her to speak up. She finally broke down.'

If judges ask intermediaries to keep interventions to an "absolute minimum", many now respond along the following lines: "Your Honour, if my recommendations and the ground rules are followed, I will probably not need to intervene at all."

Arguments to dispense with the hearing or the intermediary on grounds of cost

Intermediaries report instances in which the cost of their attendance (borne by the CPS at the trial stage when appointed for a prosecution witness) have been put forward as a reason not to hold a ground rules hearing in advance of trial or to dispense with the intermediary's presence, even in a complex case (Henderson, 2015c, forthcoming). Hector was appointed for B, whose communication relied on 'Blissymbols' (an ideographic writing system consisting of hundreds of basic symbols, each representing a concept), finger-spelling and gesture. After the trial, the judge commended the intermediary's work and "what can be achieved with careful planning, imagination and modern technology" but Hector felt that much more could have been achieved:

'There was a Monday meeting prior to the trial starting on the Wednesday. I wasn't invited to attend because of the costs involved. I was available on the phone if required, but no-one called me. At trial, the communication aids I'd prepared were useful but I could have provided additional symbols if there had been a discussion in advance. This would have avoided me having to "read" some finger-spelled words and would have saved court time.'

Alerting the court if the witness needs a break

'I sometimes feel that there is a battle between how best to use court time and what is best for the witness.' (Intermediary)

The judiciary and lawyers routinely invite witnesses to say if they want a break but many witnesses who lose focus or become upset elect to keep going and 'get it over with', with adverse effects on the quality of evidence. The 'Application for a special measures direction' form requires ground rules hearings to discuss how courts will be alerted to the need for breaks (part F1). Intermediary reports advise about the length of the witness's concentration span and suggest how frequently breaks may be required. Pre-arranged breaks encourage advocates to plan their questioning accordingly so as not to disadvantage either side.

Judges are responsible for managing the trial timetable; even when they have agreed to a schedule of breaks, some judges appear reluctant to take them (Henderson, 2016, forthcoming). When a ground rule stipulated that the witness would not be questioned for more than 40 minutes at a stretch, after 50 minutes Ramiro raised her hand to indicate that the witness needed a break: "The judge snapped 'no' at me before I could say anything."

Mini or 'in-room' breaks

Breaks in a Crown Court trial usually last 20 minutes or longer because jurors must return to the jury room. However, some witnesses need only a momentary rest to refocus and reduce tension. Intermediaries now often recommend 'in-room' breaks of up to three or four minutes, in which the intermediary and witness stay in the live link room and the judge, advocates and jury remain in court. An egg-timer may be used as a visual indicator for the witness. Court microphones are muted and the main camera is switched off but the judge continues to have an overview of the live link room. Jeeves observes that judges reluctant to take breaks without dismissing the jury may take "longer breaks than are ideal", to less effect:

> 'More explanations are needed to encourage greater flexibility. If judges think that breaks can never be shorter than 20 minutes, which I have sometimes heard said, they will resist taking them and respond: "Just a few more questions." Longer breaks disturb some witnesses' concentration so there are diminishing returns on their ability to give best evidence if a series of longer breaks are taken.'

Setting limits on the duration of questioning

> The judge, in our view, rightly recognised in hindsight that he had permitted cross-examination to go on too long. ... Cross-examination to challenge RB's account of maltreatment and to seek to establish the defence case could have been much simpler and did not need to turn over every stone. Much cross-examination was of a sort which was an oblique comment on the evidence, such as the attempts to demonstrate inconsistency, and could probably have been entirely disposed of or dealt with in much more summary form. (R v IA and Others [2013] EWCA 1308, para 72)

Some intermediary reports address the overall length of questioning that is developmentally appropriate for the witness. In all trials, lawyers are required to submit estimates beforehand of how long questioning will take. As part of general trial management judges may limit questioning and give directions about its duration (Criminal Procedure Rules 3.9(7)(iii); 3.10(d), 2015). The Court of Appeal confirms that the judge is 'fully entitled, and indeed we would say obliged' to impose reasonable time limits on cross-examination (*R v Butt* [2005] EWCA Crim 805). Duration should not exceed what the witness can reasonably cope with, taking account of his or her age and intellectual development. A 45-minute time limit on cross-examination of a 10-year-old gave counsel 'ample time to put what she needed in the time allowed' (*R v Lubemba, R v JP* [2014] EWCA Crim 2064, para 52).

Lawyers are expected to clarify matters in dispute before the trial; judges are expected to identify the issues between the parties 'as early and as clearly as possible' (Criminal Practice Direction 1A.1, 2015). Judges are therefore entitled to decide whether certain lines of questioning are relevant and 'may direct that some matters be dealt with briefly in just a few questions' (Judicial College, 2013, chapter 5, para 63).

Despite these exhortations, intermediaries observe that overall time limits are not set routinely and that cross-examination often ranges beyond the alleged offence, with a focus on peripheral detail – a characteristic of traditional cross-examination. Golightly describes a rape trial in which lawyers indicated that C, an 18-year-old with Asperger syndrome, would be questioned for two days. Questioning lasted for five days and the alleged offence was not addressed until the end of the week. Much time was taken up with questions about C, her diagnosis, anticipated exam grades and her job "with questions about the social skills and confidence it required". Golightly became uncomfortable with these topics and the length of time devoted to them:

> 'The questions were extremely complex and increased C's cognitive effort. My simplifying suggestions made the advocate flustered, so in the end I was almost acting as interpreter. He would ask a question, C would look at me, I would break it down or simplify the vocabulary, and then C would look at the screen and answer the advocate. The experience was distressing for C, as we were only told towards the end of each day that there would be another day of questions. We spent a hot week in a live link room where a noisy fan could only be put on during breaks. By the end of the week, C was completely exhausted and had a significant "meltdown" which meant taking a long break. It took a lot of work and encouragement to keep her going. I felt dissatisfied and alone in trying to put forward C's communication needs. In other trials, I felt that the judge took responsibility for this.'

In an early version of *The Advocate's Gateway* ground rules hearing toolkit, a Lord Justice of Appeal recommended a cross-examination total of two hours as the norm and half a court day at the outside. Intermediaries who recommend a limit to duration of questioning have had a mixed response. Some judges said that the idea of a half-day limit on cross-examination was "impossible" whereas others "stuck with this rigidly". Intermediaries report instances in which cross-examination has been restricted to 20 minutes, or to one or two hours taking account of breaks (see also section 28 pre-trial cross-examination pilots, discussed in Chapter Twelve; Henderson, 2015b, forthcoming).

Repetitive questioning

Criminal Practice Direction 3E.1 (2015) gives judges a clear responsibility to stop repetitive questioning of vulnerable witnesses. Intermediary assessments often address the witness's ability to respond reliably to questions that are repeated. As James says: "This makes witnesses think they have answered it wrongly the first time. They may change what they said to try to 'get the answer right' for the lawyer." If the judge fails to tackle repetition, a few intermediaries are prepared to highlight the difficulty but most feel the issue lies at the boundary of their role. However, if the intermediary report flags repetitive questioning as affecting the reliability of witness responses, the judge should address this in ground rules.

Setting ground rules for multi-defendant trials

Criminal Procedure Rule 3.9(7)(v) (2015) and Criminal Practice Direction 3E.5 (2015) recommend that in multi-defendant trials, allocation of questions among counsel should be addressed at the ground rules hearing, with the lead advocate asking most of the questions and other advocates asking only 'ancillary questions relevant to their client's case'. Practice is evolving rapidly in relation to management of these trials. A judge who describes himself as having "a firm, no-nonsense" approach timetabled the duration of cross-examination of a 12-year-old with a learning disability in a trial with five defendants. He told the lead advocate: "You can't have two-and-a-half hours, you can have one-and-a-half hours." In a recent trial with two defendants, Ramiro recommended limiting cross-examination to two or three hours: "In fact it took much less and was spread over two days with a break between, so the witness coped well."

Judicial efforts to control the length of cross-examination may nevertheless be thwarted. In a multi-defendant trial in 2013 which the judge described as "seared in the memory", he tried to curtail laborious questioning of a young teenage witness, whom a psychologist found to be 'deeply traumatised'. An intermediary was appointed but there was no ground rules hearing. The witness was asked at length about her statements to the police in order to try to draw out apparent inconsistencies. The following example from the trial transcript is typical:

Barrister: 'The next topic I'd like to ask you about is what happened with Tom. If you could turn to start with to page 136, if you count down from the top, the fourth entry of 322 we can see that the officer asks you: "Okay, so how many times have you had sex with Tom?" We see your answer is: "About two times." The officer says: "Okay. Can you tell me what date the first time you had sex with him was?" You say: "I can't remember." The officer says: "You don't know, okay, but what room were you in when it happened?" Your answer is: "He said, 'Let's go to Bill's room,' and I said no, so we went downstairs to that room." The officer there, a couple of lines down says: "What, Kevin and Pete's room?" And you're seen to nod your head. Were you telling the police officer there that the first time that you had sex with Tom was not in Bill's room it was downstairs in Kevin's room?'

Witness: 'No.'

The intermediary was entitled to intervene in respect of the length of such questions but failed to do so, perhaps in part because of the lack of a ground rules discussion. The judge's admonitions to the advocates became increasingly explicit. He delivered them at first in the presence of the jury and defendants and then in their absence:

> 'I think you may find economy helpful … You would not be criticised if you did not labour the point … I said once and once and for all, if you deal with it shortly no one will criticise you … It won't have escaped the jury's attention that as soon as you touch upon matters relating to sexual affairs the witness does not want to speak of them and I say for the record, so that no one is under any illusion, if you don't pursue matters of detail nobody is going to complain … I'm not preventing anyone putting proper matters but really, less is best.'

Despite these and other interventions, cross-examination lasted for four days, partly because of the length of questioning but also because of difficulties in managing the witness's behaviour. (This trial resulted in conviction of three of the four defendants.)

Later, the judge reflected that: "The jurisprudence has moved on." He identified as a learning point the need to "really get to grips with problems presented by a young witness, particularly a damaged one". In a forthcoming multi-defendant child sex exploitation case, he "certainly intends to do things differently": holding a ground rules hearing; requiring counsel to prepare a schedule of inconsistencies that can be explained to the jury but not put to the young witnesses; allocating topics for cross-examination according to the answers given by the defendants in their defence statements and relevance to the defendant in question; "and using a guillotine if necessary" (see also Henderson, 2015a).

Clear judicial decisions on ground rules

'The approach was thrashed out at the ground rules hearing, which meant that the intermediary was largely non-interventionist at trial.' (Prosecutor)

The ground rules hearing must be conducted by whoever will conduct the trial: the key output is a clear statement from the Bench about the rules to be applied. Criminal Practice Direction 3E.4 (2015) expects the judiciary to intervene to prevent further questioning that does not comply with ground rules 'and give relevant directions to the jury when that occurs'. However, intermediaries observe that some judges "seem to be okay with all recommendations at the hearing but then don't intervene when ground rules are not followed".

Criminal Practice Direction 3E.3 (2015) recommends that, after the hearing, a written trial practice note should be produced which the judge may use in ensuring that agreed ground rules are complied with. Sir Brian Leveson's *Review of Efficiency in Criminal Proceedings* describes such notes as essential, so that in the event of an appeal 'the entirety of the assistance provided by way of directions in relation to a challenged decision is then available to the court' (2015, para 283). Making a record of ground rules decisions is a feature of section 28 pilot hearings to pre-record cross-examination for trial (see chapter 12). While formal practice notes have not been routinely produced by the parties in other cases, judges occasionally make a list of what has been agreed or recap this orally. Some intermediaries bring their own checklist of recommendations and tick off those accepted at the hearing. Where no written note is produced, before the hearing ends advocates and intermediaries should push for clarity about which rules have been agreed.

Judicial College training introduced in 2014 emphasises the importance of firm control of ground rules hearings as part of case management. In 2013, we observed a ground rules hearing which discussed Jeeves' recommendations for R, an adult witness with severe learning disabilities and other complex problems. The intermediary report recommended asking simple, direct questions no more than six to eight words in length. It gave numerous examples of R's limited level of understanding. The defence QC, now a Crown Court judge, strongly challenged the role and independence of the intermediary and most of the recommendations, arguing that "It is essential to ask leading questions and the proposed restrictions would deny the defendant a fair trial" and that "The defence must be entitled to ask R if she is lying and why she is lying."

The QC's list of proposed questions for R were mostly long and complex, for example: 'Did you make up the story about J because you thought it would make your Mum change her mind about sending you away to live with strangers?' (a 27-word question centred on R's mother's feelings, an abstract concept). The intermediary provided detailed comments on the QC's proposed questions, explaining why they would be unlikely to result in reliable responses.

The 90-minute ground rules hearing was contentious. The QC signalled the intention to ask suggestive questions "for the jury to judge whether the witness can be influenced. To deny pressure on the witness is to deny the jury the opportunity to assess." The intermediary responded that such questions would be likely to confuse the witness. At the end of the hearing, the QC said: "I can't promise I'll abide by the intermediary's recommendations." The judge did not respond so that it was unclear which ground rules, if any, defence counsel was expected to apply. From the start of cross-examination, the QC ignored the recommendations and the intermediary had to intervene after almost every question. There were no interventions from the judge or prosecutor. (This trial resulted in an acquittal.)

The mid-trial ground rules hearing

'Stopping the trial to discuss ground rules further is a very effective way to quickly sort out and resolve a potential problem.' (Intermediary)

During a vulnerable witness's evidence, a further discussion of ground rules is sometimes requested by the intermediary or ordered by the judge. The intermediary may lay a foundation for this in the report – for example, suggesting reporting back to the judge periodically if the case involves more than one vulnerable witness or cross-examination is expected to last for more than one day. Prosecutors can request a further ground rules hearing but seem to do so only when prompted by the intermediary.

Many intermediaries, drawing on professional experience in a medical setting, describe what they call the 'paramedic moment' when urgent intervention is essential. These can also arise at court, where intermediaries encounter witnesses who run away, break down or threaten violence to themselves or their surroundings. It used to be almost inevitable that the trial would collapse in such circumstances, since it appeared impossible for questioning to continue. Judicial College guidance (2013, chapter 5, para 5) now suggests allowing a witness unable to give evidence because of distress or as a result of inappropriate questioning to come back the next day, if necessary, following a further ground rules hearing between the judge, advocates and intermediary outside the presence of the jury. The intermediary can explain the problem and suggest how it might be addressed. The judge can reiterate ground rules or issue new ones and may direct the intermediary to review remaining questions with the lawyer during the break.

Intermezzo

Kevin, aged six, and the 'paramedic' judge

Carroll (registered intermediary)

I worked with Kevin, a distressed six-year-old, the alleged victim of a sexual assault. The judge met Kevin to get to know him before proceedings. The judge and prosecution counsel were receptive to my advice but defence counsel was suspicious of my role. The judge warned defence counsel to keep questions simple. Nevertheless, his first few questions to Kevin were impossible – the judge and I between us had to intervene with each one – until Kevin refused to answer and ran out of the live link room. We broke for the day, hoping Kevin would feel better and for the defence barrister to prepare his questions.

The next morning we tried again, but as soon as Kevin saw defence counsel on the screen, he ran out shouting that he wouldn't answer any more questions. I spent 30 minutes trying to reassure and calm him. I tried asking him to answer from behind the door, or a chair, or curtains; using an iPad to indicate 'yes' or 'no'; nods and shakes of head only; or talking 'through' a teddy bear, but to no avail.

The judge adjourned the hearing and it looked as if the trial would collapse. However, the judge then suggested speaking to Kevin. We spent a while with him, sitting in his chair in the empty courtroom, visiting his chambers, looking at his family photos and talking about what he was going to have for lunch. Kevin then agreed to answer six questions if they were asked by the judge. Back in the live link room he was calm. The judge asked defence counsel's questions, much simplified, and Kevin answered confidently and assertively.

Afterwards, the judge wrote thanking me: "This was clearly a case where the services of an intermediary were necessary and, without your assistance and patience, I have no doubt that we could not have achieved completion of Kevin's evidence. Please accept my grateful thanks." Without such an understanding and patient judge, Kevin wouldn't have completed his evidence. It was teamwork. (The defendant was convicted.)

NINE

'Every reasonable step': preparation for giving evidence

In preparation for trial, courts are expected to take 'every reasonable step' to facilitate the participation of a witness or defendant, including giving directions for the appropriate treatment of the person, especially in intermediary cases (Criminal Procedure Rules 3.9(3)(b) and 3.9(6), 2015; Criminal Practice Direction 3D2, 2015). Intermediaries have become adept at turning this exhortation into practice in a variety of creative ways.

This chapter describes intermediaries' involvement in the witness's pre-trial familiarisation visit to the court; how they help ensure witnesses make an informed choice about how to give evidence and refresh their memories from their police statements; why intermediaries may recommend face-to-face questioning in the live link room; how they facilitate witness introductions to the judge and advocates; and how they collaborate with the Witness Service and Witness Care Units. The chapter concludes with examples of innovative intermediary recommendations which have helped maximise best evidence from vulnerable people.

Pre-trial familiarisation visits

> 'I was scared about it until I went to look round and then it made me feel more comfortable.' (14-year-old witness, in Plotnikoff and Woolfson, 2009a)

The Witness Charter entitles all witnesses to visit the court before trial (Ministry of Justice, 2013b, Standard 11). They and their families almost always find this helps to demystify the trial process and allay anxieties. Visits are usually conducted by the Witness Service, available to both prosecution and defence witnesses and staffed in every court by a paid manager and a team of trained volunteer supporters. (Citizens Advice took over management of the Witness Service from Victim Support in 2015.) Eight locations also benefit from a specialist Young Witness Service which continues to be managed by Victim Support.

Where staff schedules permit, witnesses can meet the supporter and the court usher whom they will see at trial. Sometimes pre-trial visits are not offered or witnesses fail to follow up. Intermediaries are usually proactive in arranging visits and are expected to accompany the witness. Their presence assists in facilitating communication between witnesses, supporters and court staff. Visits also give intermediaries the opportunity to see the court as the witness sees it, as Jeeves describes:

> 'The family of N, a young man on the autism spectrum, was anxious about him being a witness and delayed telling him that he'd be going to court. The court had an excellent Witness Service. We worked together to demonstrate our mutual roles. The family's relief at the end of the visit was palpable. Although I knew the court, I didn't see it through N's eyes until I visited it with him. For example, there's a long walk down dark corridors with flickering strip lighting. This was difficult for N because it highlighted his sensory difficulties. I recommended that he should hold his preferred stress toys to keep him calm as he walked down the halls and during cross-examination. There was a last-minute guilty plea but his family felt confident about the arrangements in place if he had been called to give evidence.'

James highlights the benefits of familiarisation visits for witnesses who are deaf:

> 'Deaf people have limited access to incidental information that most people take for granted.

Court visits enable them to visualise the physical environment. I show them the live link, describe the roles of the people who will be in court and explain about wigs and gowns. I also explain various signs: "jury" for example, which the deaf person would not necessarily know.'

If appropriate, intermediaries recommend more than one familiarisation visit to avoid 'information overload' through trying to cover too much on a single visit. While most visits take place just before trial, seeing the court at an early stage can help reassure witnesses about security arrangements. When C, aged 14, revealed that he was terrified of going to court, Alexa suggested that a familiarisation visit be scheduled quickly to alleviate some of his anxieties. The officer accompanied them. Just prior to the trial, they visited the court again but then the trial was postponed. They had a further visit before the actual trial: "These three visits had the beneficial effect of reducing C's anxieties. He attended the trial and gave evidence to the best of his abilities."

Expressing an informed view about how to give evidence

'I wanted to have more choice about how I gave my evidence.'
(14-year-old witness, in Plotnikoff and Woolfson, 2004)

Witnesses are often unaware that they are entitled to express a preference about how to give evidence (Ministry of Justice, Witness Charter, 2013, Standard 11; Ministry of Justice, Code of Practice for Victims of Crime, 2013, p 19). Their views should be reflected when requesting special measures (Application for a special measures direction, parts B5 and 6) but they need preparation to make an informed choice (Ministry of Justice, 2011a, section 4.84).

Options include giving evidence in court behind a screen or curtain, out of sight of the defendant and the public gallery, or doing so over a live link from outside the courtroom (Youth Justice and Criminal Justice Act 1999, sections 23 and 24). The live link allows witnesses to give evidence away from the potentially intimidating courtroom environment. The witness cannot see the defendant, but should be made aware that the defendant can see the witness on the live link screen in the courtroom. The screen can also be watched by anyone in the public gallery, unless the judge allows the witness's evidence to be given in private (Youth Justice and Criminal Evidence Act 1999, section 25).

If a witness wishes to use the live link but not be seen by the defendant, the screen and live link special measures can be "combined" (Criminal Practice Direction 29A.2, 2015), although some court staff are unaware of this provision. Intermediaries have obtained judicial permission for the defendant's live link screen to be switched off; for the defendant to be moved out of view of the screen (if necessary, out of the dock); and for the defendant's view to be screened with cardboard and masking tape.

A recent Criminal Justice Joint Inspection (2014a, para 9.16) notes that 'advocates and the judiciary prefer child witnesses to give evidence in person [in the courtroom]. The shared view is that it can impact directly on achieving a successful outcome'; in one area, counsel discuss special measures with witnesses in such a way that they opt to give evidence behind a screen. In our view, witnesses should not be pressed to give evidence in the courtroom, especially by implying that this may affect the outcome. Research shows no consistent difference to jury perceptions or conviction rates whichever special measure is used (Hoyano and Keenan, 2010; Ellison and Munro, 2013). On the contrary, choice gives witnesses some control over the process, which can help improve the quality of their evidence (Cashmore and De Haas, 1992).

Practising on the live link

Witnesses are entitled to practise speaking using the live link and to see screens in place on their familiarisation visit: 'simply being shown the live link room and equipment is inadequate for this purpose' (Criminal Practice Direction 29B.4, 2015). Familiarisation with the equipment is helpful because speaking to a screen can be disconcerting, particularly when there is a time lag in hearing the questioner's voice. Intermediaries will often arrange non-evidential question and answer sessions allowing the witness to practise 'rules' such as 'answer if you can', 'no guessing' and 'say if you don't understand'. The session gives the intermediary the opportunity to check camera angles and chair heights to ensure a clear view of the witness's face; additional adjustments may be needed for witnesses using communication aids. If the witness is distracted by the 'picture in picture' showing the witness on the live link screen, the intermediary may recommend that it is turned off or covered at trial.

There are two obstacles regarding this entitlement. Intermediaries are sometimes told that it is not local practice to hold such sessions and have had to refer to relevant policies or seek a direction from a judge. There is also a common fear, particularly among witness supporters, that non-evidential 'role play' constitutes 'rehearsing' the witness. This is unjustified (*R v Momodou* [2005] EWCA Crim 177; Plotnikoff and Woolfson, 2007b; Ellison and Wheatcroft, 2010). Intermediaries are usually successful in overcoming these objections.

Screens in the courtroom

Witnesses are not routinely shown screens in place in the courtroom, although screens are preferred by those who do not want to be seen while giving evidence. Roadrunner says witnesses are often simply told where the screen would be: "I have to ask for the screen to actually be put across the box if witnesses have a problem with abstract description or are very anxious and cannot decide which they would prefer."

Face-to-face questioning in the live link room

'The intermediary made the case to the judge as to how the child would be best able to give her evidence. Her recommendation was that both counsel went into the live link room and asked the child questions face-to-face rather than over the live link. This was agreed by the judge. Undoubtedly, the intermediary's assistance in this case was key to getting a conviction.' (Crown Prosecutor)

The live link practice session forms a key part of the intermediary's assessment and the findings may result in a supplementary report to the court. In 2012 Betsey observed P, aged four, practising on the live link and noticed that her communication was much less effective than when she was speaking face-to-face. Over the link P's face became less expressive, her use of gestures ceased, her concentration was impaired and her comprehension declined. At the ground rules hearing, the intermediary suggested that the lawyers move into the live link room with P to question her face-to-face.

The judge accepted this innovative proposal. The advocates and intermediary met to reorganise the furniture and camera angles and agree the use of communication aids. The intermediary provided a small chair for P. Both lawyers, the court usher and intermediary were in the room for P's cross-examination. P attended fully and responded to questions; the advocates shared the aids with her directly. Defence counsel saw it as an advantage that he could watch her reaction and adjust his tone of voice and pace, with the disadvantage that he could not see the jury's reaction (Wurtzel, 2012).

Subsequently, this arrangement has worked successfully with young children, teenagers and vulnerable adults. At Alexa's suggestion a switch to face-to-face cross-examination was even adopted during the trial when V, an adult witness, had difficulty answering questions over the live link but could not cope when the judge asked that V come into the witness box:

> 'At the judge's request, I went to the live link room during the lunch break and rearranged the furniture to accommodate everyone (both barristers, the supporter and myself). V was able to look directly at the questioner and in this way cross-examination was completed.'

Refreshing memory and watching the DVD

> 'The video was a great help. I don't think I could have done it without that. There was such a long gap that I wouldn't have been able to recall everything so clearly.' (10-year-old witness, in Plotnikoff and Woolfson, 2004)

Witnesses are entitled to refresh their memory before trial by reading their written statement or watching their police interview. Criminal Practice Direction 29C.1 (2015) requires that the DVD 'should not be seen for the first time immediately before giving evidence' and recommends that intermediary assistance be sought 'to establish exactly how memory refreshing should be managed'. The intermediary can help ensure that the witness is able to follow the written statement or focus on the DVD. However, ensuring that refreshing takes place is a police responsibility, and is sometimes overlooked.

The Criminal Justice Act 1991 allowed young witnesses' police interviews to be played to the court as their evidence-in-chief. The practice was adopted of having children – and, as the provision was extended, other vulnerable witnesses – watch their interviews at the same time as the jury rather than reviewing them at an earlier time as would occur with a written statement. Consequently, witnesses often waited for hours at court before the interview was shown. In 2009, children waited on average over five hours at the Crown Court and many were already tired by the time they started watching their DVDs (Plotnikoff and Woolfson, 2009a). More recently, a four-year-old who had spent almost two days at court was asleep when his turn finally came at 3 pm.

Many witnesses find watching their interview distressing or distracting. Maria recalls that S, aged nine, did not see her DVD until it was played to the jury: "As it started, S put her fingers in her ears and shut her eyes tight. I had to intervene and ask the judge to explain why it was important for her to listen and look. He spent time establishing rapport successfully and all went smoothly from then on." Roadrunner accompanied K, a woman with learning disability and "massive anxiety". The judge ruled that K must watch her interview at the same time as the jury, even though she had seen it beforehand:

> 'We sat side by side in the live link room. K kept shutting her eyes, trying to hug me and then, when I tried to stop her, she curled up on floor, shut her eyes and seemed to switch off. The judge could see the empty chair beside me on his overview. I knew K would not tolerate sitting up and watching the DVD so I asked the judge if she could curl up on a beanbag while the interview played. He agreed "as long as she listens to it". I checked from time to time that she had not fallen asleep and was listening. It stopped her freaking out and we got through it.'

There is no legal requirement that witnesses watch the interview at the same time as the jury. With an ingenious piece of lateral thinking, intermediaries negotiated with courts to allow witnesses to watch their DVDs before the trial and away from the court. This allows witnesses to take breaks as needed (it helps to let them control the 'pause' button) and makes it more feasible to begin cross-examination when they are fresh. This intermediary-led initiative is now enshrined in Criminal Practice Direction 29C.1–4 (2015).

A supporter of the witness's choice: an additional special measure

> Experimental and observational research confirms the common-sense view that potential benefits to recall and stress reduction flow from the presence of a known and trusted supporter and that reduction in stress can enhance the quality of testimony and decrease suggestibility. (Research summarised in Plotnikoff and Woolfson, 2009a, p 100)

A new statutory special measure allows a named supporter, known to and trusted by the witness, to provide emotional support while witnesses give evidence in the live link room. Their wishes regarding the choice of person must be taken into account (Coroners and Justice Act 2009, section 102; Criminal Practice Directions 29B.1, 29.B.2, 2015; Application for a special measures direction, part C3). Despite its status in legislation, use of a supporter of the witness's choice is influenced by local practice. In some courts the Witness Service appears to be uncomfortable about supporters other than its own trained volunteers; in others, judges prefer witnesses to be accompanied only by the usher. While the usher's presence serves other purposes, they should not be regarded as a source of emotional support (Judicial College, 2013, chapter 5, para 38).

Intermediaries can recommend that an application should be made for a named, neutral supporter to accompany the witness and intermediary in the live link room but describe this as a "very underused resource". However, some intermediaries contacted were unaware of this provision and suggested that police awareness is also poor, as officers do not raise it. Supporters chosen by witnesses to accompany them while giving evidence have included relatives, police officers, advocates from a charity and teachers. A staff member from a children's home accompanied a sexually exploited 15-year-old. Jeeves described this teenager as "a reluctant communicator, especially in stressful situations. At times she would either storm out or refuse to speak. In the presence of her worker, she was able to give evidence."

Judges may allow these supporters to sit within the witness's sight line or require them to be out of eye contact with the witness or out of sight of the jury. Some must be seated at a distance while others are permitted to be in physical contact; for example, the key worker of a young woman with learning difficulties and autism was allowed to hold her arm while she gave evidence. Golightly requested the presence of the carer who had supported Z, a woman with significant learning disability, at the police interview. The judge and defence counsel were concerned about physical contact between Z and her carer in the live link room. The intermediary explained that Z might reach out for the supporter of her own accord, so eventually this was accepted as unavoidable: "Z sometimes looked to the supporter for reassurance before answering, but the supporter's expression remained neutral. The supporter's presence made the difference in Z agreeing to go into the link room in the first place".

Emotional support and the intermediary role

Intermediary attitudes to supporters in the live link room differ. Some intermediaries describe emotional support as part of their own role, "with the understanding that witnesses can always ask to see their supporter waiting outside the live link room if they become distressed". Others feel more open to a supporter's presence because emotional support "is not something I can or should offer" and because "[having a separate source of emotional support] distinguishes my role more satisfactorily". These intermediaries agree that, to be effective, the supporter needs to be fully prepared on how to react to the witness while they give evidence.

'Therapy' dogs

There is scope for an additional special measure: the presence of a quiet dog to accompany the witness. A few judges bring their dogs to work and at least one introduces the dog to young witnesses. Many American courts allow vulnerable witnesses to be accompanied by a trained dog while giving evidence; the witness 'meets' the dog beforehand (National Center for the Prosecution of Child Abuse communication to the authors; 'Dogs are outstanding', *New York Daily News*, 15 July 2013, reports an unsuccessful appeal against use of such a dog). A dog's presence has been demonstrated to lower children's stress levels by reducing heart rates.

Permission has been granted for dogs to accompany witnesses in this country (however, a vulnerable witness who brought her caged canary to court, saying she wanted something to talk to while she was waiting, was sent home). A Witness Service volunteer saw that playing with the family dog helped calm a nine-year-old boy who was anxious about giving evidence about sexual assault. The judge agreed that a guide dog could accompany the child at court. The volunteer arranged for the child to meet the dog several times before trial. While the child gave evidence in the live link room, the dog lay by his feet. When the child was stressed, he stroked the dog and this enabled him to carry on giving evidence. Since then, intermediaries have obtained permission for quiet dogs owned by adult and child witnesses to accompany them in the live link room. One observed the calming effect for a young boy allowed to put his small dog in a wheeled chair and push it along the court corridor. (Dogs had already accompanied their owners at the police interview.)

Explanations and introductions

'I'd suggested that the Witness Service volunteer refer to the judge as "the boss of the court" but after she'd shown the seven-year-old round the court, she asked him: "What do you think about judges, then?" He replied: "Well, I don't like Simon Cowell."' (Intermediary)

Many intermediaries create materials that explain about the court, the trial and the people involved; they may include internet pictures of the trial judge and advocates. These illustrated booklets take the witness on a personalised step-by-step journey; the witness can tick off each step as it is completed at trial. Unfortunately, due to cutbacks, Young Witness Pack booklets are no longer reprinted. Online versions are available on the Ministry of Justice website but are seldom accessed.

Intermediaries who wanted to show witnesses pictures of actual courtrooms or live link rooms were baulked by a policy prohibiting the taking of photos inside court buildings. They have been successful in securing a change of approach. Criminal Practice Direction 3F.7 (2015) now encourages courts to permit photos to be taken 'to assist vulnerable or child witnesses to familiarise themselves with the setting ... having regard to the security requirements of the court'.

Meeting the judge and advocates

Where it would be of benefit, intermediaries encourage advocates and judges to meet witnesses before they give evidence. These introductions are increasingly common and often quite informal. Judicial guidance is gently encouraging:

> It is up to you whether to accompany the advocates but it can be a useful opportunity to 'tune in' to the witness's level of communication. Where justified by the circumstances, some trial judges have met the vulnerable witness with the advocates before the day of the witness's evidence. (Judicial College, 2013, chapter 5, para 27e)

It is preferable that judicial introductions take place in counsel's presence (*R v Lubemba, R v JP* [2014] EWCA Crim 2064, para 43). Usually this happens shortly before the witness's evidence starts. However, as the policy indicates, meetings may occur earlier by scheduling the witness's familiarisation visit to coincide with pre-trial hearings involving the trial judge and advocates. Introductions arranged this way can be less stressful for the witness than on the day of trial.

Waiting rooms and live link rooms are often small. Alexa tries to engineer "that we meet in another room where everyone can sit down: a shared eye-level is easier to cope with than 'being looked down on'". In multi-defendant cases, the intermediary may recommend introductions to defence advocates singly or no more than two at a time: for example, "Karen is asking questions for Tony and Mark is asking questions for Carl."

During introductions, judges sometimes use their first names – "I'm Anna, I'm in charge." Vulnerable witnesses often welcome a reassurance that the judge is in control. The choice of words requires some forethought. Roadrunner arranged for the complainant in a familial rape case to meet the judge: "He was friendly and informal. Just before seeing her, he said: 'I don't want her to be afraid of me. What shall I tell her to call me? "Uncle"?' Me, gulping: 'I think "Judge" would be better, Your Honour.'"

Intermediaries provide information about witness interests and help guide the conversation. They often explain court 'rules' to little children, including 'no pretending' when answering questions: similarly, they advise judges and lawyers against 'imagination' games to build rapport. "Within seconds of coming into the live link room to meet a stroppy four-year-old the judge was pretending to be a helicopter. I had to say 'In this place, we don't pretend.'"

Dispensing with wigs and gowns in the Crown Court is another special measure (Youth Justice and Criminal Evidence Act, 1999, section 26) about which witnesses can express a preference; the intermediary will pass this on. One judge when introduced to an anxious young witness made a point of taking off her wig, sash and gown so that the girl could see that she was "a real person underneath the uniform".

Judicial communication with the witness

Judges routinely give witnesses instructions over the live link just before the start of their evidence. However, intermediaries find it is easier to ensure language is developmentally appropriate if the judge explains the instructions when meeting the witness less formally: "Often the judge incorporates my suggestions when they repeat the instructions to the witness in court." As explained in Chapter Five, many intermediaries prepare visual aids to explain the rules for court. Copies are provided to the judge with, as Alexa says, "a gentle prompt that they can be used to help the witness understand what to do. On meeting the witness, judges have used them, saying: 'You have some rules that [the intermediary] has given you. We can look at them together.'"

Clear judicial communication is important not just for witnesses but because it models what is expected of the advocates. Recently, we saw a senior judge prohibiting the use of tag questions with a six-year-old. He then proceeded to tag each question he asked the child in front of the lawyers, for example: "You know about the rules, don't you?" When asked about this afterwards, he acknowledged: "It just goes to show how hard it is to change the way barristers speak."

Working with witness supporters and Witness Care Units

'When I was first told there would be an intermediary I wasn't really sure what that was. When they contacted me before the pre-trial visit I kept thinking – that's my role, that's what I do. I didn't realise how we would work together. However, at the visit I started to understand just how skilled the intermediary

was, helping the person feel in control and really giving them choices and helping them to communicate. I was able to help the intermediary understand the workings of the court we were in, who the key people were and how things usually run.'
(Witness Service volunteer)

Intermediary and supporter roles are distinct but complementary. The greatest benefits for vulnerable witnesses are obtained when intermediary and Witness Service or another supporter work together. Collaboration improves the understanding of both intermediary and supporter of their respective roles.

Best practice involves joint planning from before the familiarisation visit through to the witness's attendance at trial. The intermediary should alert the Witness Service to the witness's needs, either through a written summary (with the permission of the witness or parents), by phone or in discussion at the visit before the witness arrives. Intermediary advice covers communication but may also address, for example, the care needs of a witness who might become incontinent, or the fact that a witness with autism cannot use the court lift.

Finding out in advance who will conduct the visit allows for discussion about the information to be covered. Volunteers often have a 'script' when giving a court tour and intermediaries can help adapt this for the witness and show by demonstration what level of language is appropriate. They are, however, conscious of the need to intervene only when necessary for clarification. Many intermediaries report positive experiences in joint working with Witness Service personnel: "They are keen to work with you to do what is right for the witness." On occasion, supporters unfamiliar with the intermediary function have suggested that intermediaries cannot accompany witnesses into the live link room because "that's the supporter's job", and may disregard intermediary advice. This is a matter of training and gaining experience in working with intermediaries. It is encouraging that intermediaries are increasingly asked to contribute to supporter training. This benefits both groups.

Supporters' contact with witnesses post-trial gives an opportunity to assess the impact of the intermediary's contribution. A Young Witness Service manager observed:

"When we visit after the trial, we often see that children who had an intermediary, whatever the verdict, feel like they did their best job and understand what happened and why. That plays a big part in their being able to move on."

Witness Care Units, staffed jointly by the police and CPS, aim to provide a single point of phone contact for victims and prosecution witnesses, from the charging of the defendant through to the conclusion of a case. They are expected to identify witnesses who require special measures if this has been overlooked and to arrange assistance to help them get to court and give their best evidence. Intermediaries often liaise with them about vulnerable witness arrangements.

Alexa was appointed as intermediary for T, a woman with Asperger syndrome. She was due to stay at an unfamiliar hotel reached by a complex journey on public transport. This was likely to make T highly anxious, with an adverse effect on her ability to give evidence. Following Alexa's advice, the Witness Care Officer gave T written instructions for travel and arranged transport service escorts when boarding trains and moving between platforms and stations. On the day of trial, a police officer met T at her hotel and escorted her to and from court. T was able to give evidence.

Similarly, Heathcliff acted as intermediary for G, a man with Asperger syndrome who liked to mend fences, to the extent that if he was on a bus and saw a broken fence, he would get off the bus to fix it, losing all sense of time. Because of this, he was 90 minutes late for his first meeting with the intermediary. Heathcliff therefore arranged for the Witness Care Officer to phone G every 10 minutes when he was on the bus to court, to keep him focused. He attended on time and was able to give evidence.

Intermediary recommendations for greater flexibility at trial

'Some of the things the intermediary wanted I thought: the judge will never agree to that – but he did, after quite a bit of advocacy on the intermediary's part, and we were able to support them. Then, after the case was over, there were lasting effects at the

143

> court. Things have been adapted before so it makes it easier to
> ask the court to make changes for vulnerable witnesses again.'
> (Witness Service volunteer)

There are innumerable ways in which intermediaries have facilitated best evidence. This can involve considerable planning and negotiation. One example is recommending that witnesses – from children to the elderly – give evidence by a remote live link from non-court locations. Sometimes, as in the first intermezzo, confirmation that the witness will give evidence appears to trigger a guilty plea. In another such case, the CPS indicated that: "Information provided by the intermediary to the judge enabled us to obtain a video link from the victim's home address. The defendant finally changed his plea to guilty shortly after the judge made this direction."

Adaptations for children

Agreed adjustments for young witnesses have included allowing a four-year-old to give evidence while sitting on a relative's knee, and letting a child with urinary urgency go to the toilet without asking permission from the judge; arranging for a court usher to knit quietly during cross-examination because it was calming for the child and meant the usher was not obviously observing; agreeing to a child's request that a male usher would cover his face with a cushion when the child said 'naughty' words; and ordering defendants to be seated in the dock for 10 minutes at the start and end of the court day to ensure that young witnesses could enter and leave the building calmly. An intermediary obtained permission for a 15-year-old witness with psychological problems to pull up her 'hoodie' to create a sense of safety when she was stressed. With this reassurance, along with the presence of her supporter and the intermediary, the teenager gave evidence without covering her head. Sometimes just having the strategy in place increases witness confidence sufficiently that they do not need recourse to it.

Melissa acted as intermediary for G, a girl who had just turned four at the time of the trial, 21 months after the alleged offence. She describes it as "a textbook example of how it can work if the whole court pulls together". The judge convened a three-hour ground rules hearing in advance of the trial and required everyone involved to attend, including the usher, clerk and Witness Service. Every aspect of how G would be dealt with was discussed. Melissa then met both barristers to explain her use of communication aids to support their questions; these included miniature figures, furniture and cardboard shapes to represent the house where the offence was alleged to have taken place. The police obtained child-sized furniture for the live link room from a local nursery and camera angles were adjusted. Melissa accompanied G on three familiarisation visits to the court, on one of which she met the judge and barristers. During their meeting, the judge ended up with play stickers on his forehead. G also practised on the live link, answering non-evidential questions from the usher, who had already met G twice. G's cross-examination, conducted in 10-minute sessions, went smoothly and she was able to show and tell what happened to her. When G had finished, the judge came to the witness room to thank her. (The defendant was found guilty and received a long custodial sentence.)

Amelie assisted at an ABE interview with Y, a young teenager with normal communication but who felt unable to speak about the alleged offence. Y did not want the interviewing officer to look at or speak to her. The interviewer and intermediary planned that Y could type answers to questions typed by the interviewer. At trial, the judge agreed to adopt the same approach: a typist was brought in to type defence counsel's questions and a technology company supplied screens for the defendant and jury so that they could follow the typed interchanges (one screen per pair of jurors). If the intermediary needed to signal the judge on the witness's behalf, she used a prearranged code by typing on the computer: '1 = I don't understand a word', '2 = I don't understand the question' and '3 = I need a break'. In the live link room Y sat sideways to the TV screen; with the live link sound turned off, this arrangement enabled Y to focus on the written word on the laptop. The judge actively monitored the questions and many were deleted from Y's screen before the typing of the question was completed (counsel had declined to review his questions in advance with the intermediary). Cross-examination started around 11.30 am and finished around 3 pm, with lunch and three breaks in between. (This case resulted in a conviction.)

Betsey is adept at recommending 'extra-special' measures to accommodate the needs of small children:

> 'Many of these deal with the impact of trauma and hyper-arousal and how to keep the child calm enough to attend. This is another language to the court; it's hard for lawyers to understand. If young children are asked to recall violent or traumatic events, their hearts will be racing and they will feel sick and be desperate to run away.'

During assessment, this intermediary identifies rhythmic physical activities that help young children reduce heightened anxiety and 'settle'. P was a four-year-old whose favourite activity in foster care was vacuuming. At assessment, Betsey noticed that he became "much less anxious and oppositional while tidying up and sorting things". At the police interview, he was allowed to do this while answering questions. During breaks, he was offered both a hand-held and a full-size vacuum cleaner: "These activities lowered his arousal level and increased his ability to engage and attend." Use of the vacuum during breaks at trial was agreed with the judge. Other agreed break activities for four- and five-year-olds have included riding a tricycle, bouncing on a mini trampoline, crawling through a play tunnel and rocking in a small rocking chair: "The jury doesn't need to know about these recommendations."

Betsey broke new ground when helping the court plan how to take the evidence of two young children whom she described as "extremely traumatised". They needed high levels of support to watch what they described as the "rude" and "scary bits" of their DVD interviews, viewing them at a different time from the jury at a non-court location. J, the younger child, watched some of her DVD from inside a playroom tent, where she was much calmer. Consequently, Betsey recommended that J should answer questions from the chair in the live link room but be allowed, as necessary, to retreat to a "small, safe place" set up in the corner of the live link room so that she could calm herself quickly (see

Figure 9.1). The safe place would be out of the jury's sight but within that of the judge. He agreed that Betsey could create a makeshift den by placing two chairs back-to-back with a blanket over them and mats underneath. The blanket was pulled down to the floor while the child was 'inside'.

Figure 9.1

© Emily Henderson 2015

'Pause' and 'play' symbols with which these children were familiar were used to signal the start and end of breaks. Mini breaks were taken measured by an egg-timer, with sound to the live link turned off, while the jury waited in court. Betsey believed this would save time and the transition back to questioning would be briefer, which proved to be correct. The children were allowed to whisper swear words and 'rude' words to the intermediary, who repeated them to the court, and to manipulate 'Play-doh' while answering questions. The defendants could listen to but not watch the children's evidence on the court live link screen as the children were afraid of being seen. The judge required complete silence in the courtroom so that there was no chance of the children hearing the defendants' voices. Because these children were so fearful, Betsey asked the judge to confirm this rule periodically:

Witness, whispering to intermediary: 'He's gonna shout out.'
Intermediary: 'Your Honour, who is allowed speak in court?'

Judge: 'At the moment, only Mr P [the defence advocate] and me.'

Witness, whispering to intermediary: 'Everyone else has to be "shush"?'

Intermediary: 'Your Honour, has everyone else to be "shush"?'

Judge: 'Yes. Everyone else has to be completely silent.'

(The jury returned guilty verdicts on multiple counts.)

Recently, Betsey obtained permission for a boy aged nine to play his recorder for just a few moments (even shorter than an egg-timer mini break) during cross-examination when she felt this was necessary to regulate his breathing.

Adaptations for vulnerable adults

Modifications requested by intermediaries for vulnerable adults have included allowing a witness with autism and behavioural problems to give evidence with her back to the live link camera while the intermediary relayed her answers to the court. When a witness came to court without batteries for her hearing aids, the intermediary asked for a short delay and obtained replacements from a medical centre. Assessment revealed that movement helped another vulnerable woman reduce stress; the intermediary obtained permission for the witness to rock back and forward in the witness box.

  T was a woman in her 40s with Asperger syndrome. Her need for an intermediary was not identified until she had a panic attack during her pre-trial court familiarisation visit. Ashley was then appointed as intermediary and planned ways to manage T's anxiety by ensuring she knew what to expect at trial. She accompanied T on a further court visit with a 'walk through' of the trial day. Arrangements included coming in by the side entrance; identifying a 'time out' room for use during breaks; meeting a named Witness Service supporter; and practising answering questions over the live link. Just before the trial, the intermediary learned that it had been transferred to another court an hour away. She took this up urgently and it was agreed T could give evidence by remote link from the original court with which she was already familiar. Ground rules included the use of a 'stress scale' on which T could indicate her level of anxiety; scheduled breaks approximately every half hour; and use of the 'immediate break' card allowing T to go to the 'time out' room. At trial, the prosecutor took T through her evidence very slowly. When T was asked about the rape allegation, the intermediary described her as "really struggling" to speak:

> 'The prosecutor started to ask another question but I jumped in and said she needed more time. T said she had never been able to say the words out loud but then went on to give a detailed account. Cross-examination was difficult but we kept to the timetable and knowing we had scheduled breaks helped T to cope. We didn't need to use the "immediate break" card at all. With the right preparation and modifications to the environment and timetabling, T was able to give her evidence. The preparation meant that her ability to process verbal language was maximised and her anxiety was minimised. I only needed to intervene when it was unclear who or what was being talked about. The main intervention was achieved beforehand, by flagging up her needs to all who would come into contact with her. It was a real team effort from an excellent Witness Service, police officer and Witness Care Officer. The usher changed her shift so she could ensure her presence and continuity for the witness.' (The defendant was convicted and received a long sentence.)

Intermediaries have enabled many witnesses in extreme distress to complete their testimony. K, a woman with mental health concerns and learning disability, was highly anxious about attending court for the fourth time. The first trial was aborted due to technical difficulties; the second resulted in a hung jury; and during the third, K became so distressed that she took an overdose and was detained under the Mental Health Act. The original intermediary was unavailable for the fourth trial and Bonnie was asked to take over. She employed a wide range of strategies to enable K to complete her evidence:

'The atmosphere surrounding this fourth attempt was tense for all involved. Before questioning began, I assisted K with breathing techniques and the scent of aromatic oil that she found soothing; she also fidgeted with a soft stress toy. As soon as she started watching the DVD of her police interview, she sobbed and began to show signs of psychological disturbance. We had to take a break each time K became distressed but she was determined to carry on. Finally, I realised that there was nothing left but to put my arm around her shoulders and to rock her gently. I was anxious about how this would be perceived and during the next break I sent a message to the judge to explain that the physical contact should not be seen as a demonstration of affection but as a strategy to contain K's emotions and allow her to communicate. This was accepted, so I continued. During questioning, she coped with difficult questions, though I had to intervene in some to remind counsel of the ground rules. We were all very relieved when it came to an end.' (This trial resulted in a conviction.)

Tosca worked with R, a witness weighing over 20 stone who used a hoist at home and a heavy wheelchair. He wanted to give evidence in court behind a screen. All the courtrooms were on the first floor. The intermediary was advised that, in the event of a fire, the lifts would be out of action and R would be evacuated by an evacuation chair:

'There was a look of surprise when I said this wouldn't be possible. We decided that the only way for R to give evidence would be from a live link room on the ground floor. I was then told he wouldn't be able to get his wheelchair through the door. I asked for a tape measure, measured the door and rang his day centre, asking them to measure the width of his chair. It could just fit through. And yes, they could bring a ramp because the way in had a step up to it. In the end, the defendant changed his plea.'

Intermezzo

Danielle, the ticking clock and the 'deadpan' intermediary
Ashley (registered intermediary)

Danielle's case took over two years to come to trial. She was in her 30s, with learning difficulties, high anxiety and features indicating that she was on the autism spectrum. I assessed her at home following a visit from the officer to explain my role and a simple letter introducing myself. This officer went out of her way to establish rapport with the witness and support my role: her willingness to 'go that extra mile' made such a difference. Even so, when I met Danielle, she required frequent reassurance that she wasn't in trouble. I informally assessed her receptive and expressive language skills. We worked through a stress scale to identify what made her feel relaxed, from 1 (playing computer games and listening to music) right up to what stressed her at levels 4 and 5 (when people stare, new people and places and "when I have to remember many things at once").

I devised a timetable for her court familiarisation visit and sent another explanatory letter; however, on arrival Danielle 'froze' when trying to come through the security entrance. I obtained permission to take photos of Danielle sitting in the live link room. She was fascinated with the equipment – and the fire extinguisher – but did not like the lifts. I continued to assess her and to record the anxiety she 'communicated' through her behaviour: from low-level stress = sniffing her coat or putting the hood up, through to a very high level = 'freezing' or banging her head. Danielle was sensitive to my expression and continued to ask if she was in trouble. She interpreted things literally and said a 'witness box' didn't look like a box; she had difficulty when the Witness Service described the live link room chair as 'the hot seat'. Their usual approach to establishing rapport (chatting, sitting close and reassuring looks) doesn't work well with someone with autism, leading to greater confusion and an increased anxiety.

Following the visit, I made a booklet with photos and information about what we'd done and decided, such as using the stairs and coming in by the side entrance. I also explained that we'd have another court visit and watch the DVDs of her police interview. On the second visit she practised speaking over the live link again and then we watched her DVDs. She showed no obvious interest and commented more on the machine. She was adamant that she only wanted to attend the trial for one day.

Day 1 At the ground rules hearing, my suggested approaches to questioning were agreed. These included allowing Danielle extra time to process questions (wait five seconds before repeating); use of unambiguous language; and a timeline as a visual way of linking key undisputed facts (agreed with the prosecutor) to Danielle's age. We also agreed a visual schedule for her to follow, indicating what would happen next, and use of a chart to monitor her anxiety levels. (She and I had previously discussed strategies for what would happen at each level on the chart, such as use of the 'break' card and calming music on her MP3 player.) The hearing discussed what to do if she kept saying: "Do you believe me?" and "Am I in trouble?", which she'd done throughout the police interviews. We developed a script for counsel and I agreed to explain to Danielle again that "It's the lawyers who ask the questions." I took note of what the judge and counsel looked like, to prepare and familiarise her.

Day 2 The live link room was changed a number of times due to technology problems. This was very stressful for Danielle; she banged her head against the glass windows of the corridor. I had to ask everyone to be quiet and allow her to be still. This was another example of the different approach required when responding to a person with autism: attempted verbal reassurance or physical contact would have resulted in complete 'overload'. Despite Danielle having already watched her police interviews, I was told she had to see them again when they were played to the jury. At this point I was also informed that a jury member had reported in sick. I kept Danielle calm with agreed breaks and strategies and updated the schedule. She was allowed to go home as it would be impossible for her to be finished by the end of the day.

Day 3 A new jury was sworn and the prosecutor opened the case again. We were allocated a live link room with a ticking clock; I had to get it removed. Danielle and I sat down to watch the police interviews. As could have been predicted, she was uninterested. Again, I had a visual schedule for the day but was prepared with a 'write on/wipe off' whiteboard and pens in case of more last-minute changes. I knew that keeping Danielle focused was going to be difficult. I had prompt cards to remind her what to do for each 'activity': for example, 'watch and listen' when the DVDs were playing. She really tried, but at some points she was practically horizontal on the chair. If I made eye contact with her she'd ask me a question and if my facial expression showed anything she'd say: "You look worried. Are you cross with me?" I decided to look completely deadpan and to try to monitor what she was doing through sideways glances. During a break, the officer rushed in and said the judge had asked her to find out "what on earth is wrong with the intermediary – she is constantly rolling her eyes". I explained. By this time it was clear that Danielle's evidence would not be finished in one day. I suggested that cross-examination should at least start, as that was what she expected, but she was very stressed about coming back again.

Day 4 Cross-examination continued. The visual timeline was invaluable. It helped ensure that Danielle focused on the timeframe of each question (I would point to the relevant part). The defence barrister tried hard but it was obviously very difficult for her. The judge intervened as much as I did, which was great – I think the autism toolkit (at www.theadvocatesgateway.org) made a difference. We kept to the timetable and during breaks I reminded Danielle using visual prompt cards of 'rules' such as, 'If you don't know the answer, it's okay to say "I don't know"'.

Danielle was able to give detail which only those with autism can. We got into our routine and her anxiety was kept to a minimum. When I first intervened, she turned to me, smiled and said: "Thanks for your help." By lunchtime, her evidence was finished. The usher (who ensured that she'd be there to give Danielle continuity) commented that they'd never had such a complex witness at court before.

Despite all the delays, and against all the odds, Danielle had told her story. (This case resulted in a guilty verdict on all charges.)

TEN

Cross-examination: research, case law, training and regulation

This chapter summarises research on leading questions, showing that they undermine witness accuracy and pose a high risk for the quality of evidence of vulnerable witnesses. It then considers a series of Court of Appeal decisions which together signal the need for a changed approach from advocates and further empower judges to control cross-examination of vulnerable witnesses. These cases have greatly strengthened the ability of intermediaries to challenge conventional cross-examination strategies.

The chapter also reviews the provision of relevant training for the judiciary and advocates and regulation of the advocacy professions. The Judicial College has wholeheartedly incorporated the Court of Appeal's approach; the professions have yet to adopt an equivalent advocacy training requirement and regulation of advocacy standards has been strongly resisted. The response of those responsible for advocacy training has been slow at best, resistant at worst and, until recently, has lacked leadership. By default, intermediaries and judges (themselves still absorbing the new judicial training) find themselves playing a case by case educational role with advocates.

Cross-examination and research

> Cross-examination is 'the greatest legal engine ever invented for the discovery of truth'. (Wigmore, 1974, para 1367 at 32)

[E]mpirical evidence shows that [cross-examination] is a process that manufactures inaccurate evidence. (Cossins, 2012, p 111)

Perhaps the greatest skill comes from the ability to control the witness. Short answer questions, preferably 'yes' or 'no' answers allow the lawyer to dictate the examination ... An artful examiner will lead a witness ... down the primrose path and then, when they least expect it, slam the garden gate on them. (Meehan, 2011)

The objective of cross-examination in our adversarial system is to persuade the opposition's witnesses to change their version of events or to discredit their evidence (for a helpful discussion, see Hanna et al, 2010). Accordingly, questions that lead the witness by suggesting the answer and inviting the witness to agree are the preferred form. Advocacy training encourages cross-examiners to control responses and substitute their case for the witness's damaging testimony (for example, Hobbs, 2002, 2003; Hampel et al, 2008).

Several decades of research across common law jurisdictions shows that leading questions, along with other cross-examination techniques such as complex vocabulary and multi-part questions asked out of chronological order, mislead and confuse children and vulnerable adult witnesses (for example, Ellison, 2001; Hanna et al, 2010). Most children change previous accurate responses under cross-examination while some retract their account altogether (Zajac et al, 2012). The likelihood that vulnerable people will concur with suggestive questions increases when the questioner is an authority figure (Russell, 2006). Cross-examination techniques affect the reliability of even ordinary adult witnesses (Ellison and Wheatcroft, 2010; Henderson 2015d).

Research has informed guidance for police evidential interviewing (Ministry of Justice, 2011a) but made no impact on the closed world of criminal advocacy until the launch of research-based guidance on *The Advocate's Gateway* website in 2013, discussed later in this chapter.

Tag questions

The most powerful form of leading question is a statement followed by a short tag (with either the statement or tag usually in negative form) inviting the witness to corroborate its truth, for example: "He didn't touch you, *did he?*" or "You encouraged him, *didn't you?*" Such tagged questions allow the questioner to give the evidence and restrict the witness to 'yes' or 'no' answers, and consequently have become the cross-examiner's 'weapon of choice' (Graffam Walker, 2013, p 58). The extent to which leading questions is embedded in the legal psyche is demonstrated by Bar Council advice to litigants without a lawyer, issued in 2013. This guidance may baffle litigants in person:

> When cross-examining, it is best to ask closed questions. This usually means questions with a yes/no answer, which ensures that you have some control over what the witness says. For example: Don't ask: How did you get home? Do ask: You drove home, didn't you? (Bar Council, 2013)

Judicial College guidance (2013, chapter 5, para 64a) states that tag questions are 'unacceptable' for children and that these should also be avoided with adults whose intellectual development equates to that of a child or young person.

Assertions

Assertions treated as questions constitute another powerfully suggestive cross-examination strategy. Until recently, they have been regarded as 'good practice' for cross-examination of a vulnerable witness – for example, "You're not telling the truth, you just wanted Kevin out of your life" (Serious Sexual Offences Seminar DVD, Judicial Studies Board, 2009). Nevertheless, assertions are highly suggestive and therefore inappropriate for someone who may not even recognise that they are being asked a question to which they can respond. Lord Judge criticised the technique as "particularly damaging" for young witnesses (Judge, 2013b, p 9). However, Golightly describes a barrister as "genuinely confused" when asked to avoid assertions in the case of a young girl with Asperger syndrome:

> 'I explained that presenting a statement to this witness was going to confuse her. The barrister muttered "Of course it's a question … cross-examination is all about putting questions to a witness." I intervened constantly throughout cross-examination, feeling like a broken record asking "Could you rephrase that as a question?" I had to run through the court corridors to stop the girl leaving the building when she decided that she had had enough of (I quote) "that stupid woman".'

Intermediaries and leading questions

Intermediaries' challenges to leading questions began tentatively. During the pilot evaluation 'a few intermediary reports for trial flagged the possibility that such questions would produce unreliable evidence, but these types of questions were not the subject of a ground rules discussion before trial or of judicial intervention during the trial itself' (Plotnikoff and Woolfson, 2008, p 103). Around the same time, a leading law academic assured us that it was "entirely unrealistic to expect a cross-examiner to put his case to a witness without using leading questions".

However, as the number of intermediary appointments increased, so did their experience of vulnerable witnesses' inability to cope with leading questions. The statutory test for any special measure – the likely effect on the quality of the evidence in terms of its 'completeness, coherence and *accuracy*' (Youth Justice and Criminal Evidence Act 1999, section 16(5), our emphasis) – encouraged intermediaries to begin highlighting the risk that certain question types would elicit unreliable answers. As described in Chapter Four, intermediaries began to build into their assessments imaginative ways to test witnesses' abilities to understand and resist specific forms of leading question. As a result, the judiciary has been increasingly asked to rule on intermediary recommendations to restrict certain question types.

However, lawyers and intermediaries do not appear to share a common understanding of what constitutes a 'leading' question. In a study comparing intermediaries' and lawyers' analyses of mock transcripts of a child witness's evidence, tag questions were identified as leading by almost all intermediaries but by none of the lawyers (Krähenbühl, 2011). Intermediary recommendations must therefore be grounded in assessment of the individual witness and specify the type of question that the witness finds problematic.

Watershed decisions from the Court of Appeal

> The importance of the limitation on cross-examination in cases such as this is to protect the vulnerable witnesses and enable them to give the best evidence they can. (R v Wills [2011] EWCA Crim 1938, para 30)

> 'An unscrupulous counsel, playing within the rules, can play havoc in cross-examining a vulnerable witness and could render the case untriable.' (Judge)

The first four cases in the series concern the questioning of young witnesses, none of whom was assisted by an intermediary. (For a discussion of the theoretical approach of the Court of Appeal in these judgments, see Henderson, 2014.)

R v Barker

In May 2009 K, a child of four, gave evidence at the Central Criminal Court (the Old Bailey). She had been raped at the age of two and revealed what had happened to her when she was removed to foster care; she was three when the police filmed interviews with her. The trial generated enormous media coverage ('Tiny and scared: the Old Bailey's youngest witness', *The Independent*, 2 May 2009; 'She was four years old and scared. Justice has to find a better way,' *The Observer*, 3 May 2009). K's foster parents woke her at 6 am to bring her to court on Monday morning; they waited all day without her evidence being reached. On Tuesday, she had to be persuaded to return. Her police interviews were shown to the jury as her evidence-in-chief and she was 'exhausted and at the end of her tether' when cross-examination over a live link began in the late afternoon (Spencer, 2012, p 12). By the time K was asked about the alleged offence, she had been at court for around seven hours, and was yawning. She had to return to court for a third day for re-examination by the prosecution.

During cross-examination, K was asked many tag questions. Even journalists commented that when asked by 'a serious middle-aged man in strange circumstances, the [tag] construction must be particularly forbidding' – for example: 'He did not touch you with his willy, did he? Did he, K? I have to ask you one more time, please: he did not touch you with his willy, did he?' (*The Observer*, 3 May 2009).

The defendants were convicted and their lawyers appealed on the basis that K was not a competent witness. In what it later described as a 'specially constituted court' chaired by the Lord Chief Justice (*R v Lubemba, R v JP* [2014] EWCA Crim 2064, para 38), the Court of Appeal upheld the conviction (*R v Barker* [2010] EWCA 4). The court watched K's police interview, read the trial transcript and considered her to be a 'compelling as well as a competent witness' (para 52). The judgment emphasised that the purpose of the trial is to identify reliable evidence, whether from adults or children. Cross-examination must be adapted 'to enable the child to give the best evidence of which he or she is capable' while ensuring the defendant's right to a fair trial. When the issue is whether the child is lying or mistaken, the advocate should ask 'short, simple' questions putting the essential elements of the defendant's case. 'Aspects of evidence which undermine ... the child's credibility must, of course, be revealed to the jury, but it is not necessarily appropriate for them to form the subject matter of detailed cross-examination of the child' (para 42).

R v W and M

The judgment in *Barker* was followed in the same year (2010) by a case in which two boys aged ten and eleven were tried at the Old Bailey for sexual offences against R, aged eight (*R v W and M* [2010] EWCA Crim. 1926). So many reporters were in attendance that some sat in the dock; the child defendants sat in the body of the court (Wurtzel, 2011). The Court of Appeal thought this case should have been tried in the youth court, where reporting restrictions apply (paras 39–40).

R retracted much of her account during cross-examination, which consisted of a series of leading questions, for example (para 25):

Barrister:	'[The defendant] did not put his willy in your bum, did he?'
Witness:	'No.'
Barrister:	'[The defendant] did not put his willy in your minnie, did he?'
Witness:	'No.'

Contrary to practice at the time, despite R's retractions the judge let the case go to the jury. Both young defendants were convicted; these verdicts were upheld on appeal. The Court of Appeal took the view that R's answers to leading questions (and hence her retraction) were of limited evidential value:

> There is undoubtedly a danger of a child witness wishing simply to please. There is undoubtedly a danger of a child witness seeing that to assent to what is put may bring the questioning process to a speedier conclusion than to disagree ... It is generally recognised that, particularly with child witnesses, short and untagged questions are best at eliciting the evidence. By untagged we mean questions which do not contain a statement of the answer which is sought ... Most of the questions which produced the answers which were chiefly relied upon ... constituted the putting of direct suggestions with an indication of the answer: "This happened, didn't it?" or: "This didn't happen, did it?" The consequence of that is, as the judge remarked, that it can be very difficult to tell whether the child is truly changing her account or simply taking the line of least resistance. (paras 30–31)

Following the judgments in *Barker* and *W and M*, at the end of 2010 judicial guidance was issued recommending that tag questions not be asked of young witnesses (Judicial Studies Board, 2012, p 19).

R v Edwards

Cross-examination in *W and M*, as in *Barker*, was not adjusted to the child's developmental age. A more proactive approach was taken by the trial judge in a case involving C, aged six, who was taken to hospital suffering from injuries to her kidneys (*R v Edwards* [2011] EWCA Crim 3028). C told staff and, later, the police that the defendant had punched her. The judge ruled that defence counsel should not ask C about the alleged assault or put 'suggestion' questions to her. The judge explained this limitation to the jury as follows:

> The directions that I have given to [defence counsel] in this case are that he can and should ask any question to which he actually wants answers, but he should not involve himself in any cross-examination of [the witness] by challenging her in a difficult way. In this case the defendant has already set out in some detail what his defence is. It is not a question of putting it to a witness and challenging her about it, so you won't hear the traditional form of cross-examination. I thought you ought to know that from the outset. (para 7)

During cross-examination, defence counsel asked C some multi-part leading questions, combining tags and statements, such as 'And then you all went to bed? You went to your room? You slept in your bed, didn't you?' The judge sent out the jury and said to him:

> I am concerned you're making suggestions to the witness, and ordinarily that would be absolutely appropriate, but making suggestions to a six-year-old about matters so long ago [18 months earlier],

I wonder whether we're sure we're getting accurate information. Could you make the questions a little bit open so we can test whether she does remember? (para 25)

When cross-examination resumed, defence counsel again asked C some tag questions (eg 'Simon didn't stay in your room, did he?') and was again stopped by the judge. The defence appealed on the grounds that it had been 'deprived of the opportunity to confront' C in 'the traditional way' (para 28). The Court of Appeal disagreed:

> [W]e struggle to understand how the defendant's right to a fair trial was in any way compromised … The reality … of questioning children of tender years is that direct challenge that he or she is wrong or lying could lead to confusion and, worse, to capitulation. Capitulation is not a consequence of unreliability but a function of the youngster's age and the circumstances in which she finds herself. Experience … has shown that young children are scared of disagreeing with a mature adult whom they do not wish to confront. (para 28)

The Court of Appeal considered that the judge had clearly explained his reasons to limit cross-examination and the jury had been directed 'to make proper fair allowances for the difficulties faced by the defence in asking questions about this' (para 28). It concluded that conduct of the trial was 'astute, balanced, measured and fair' (para 30).

R v Wills

In *Edwards*, the Court of Appeal built on *Barker* to endorse limitations on defence counsel putting the case directly to the witness. This was taken further in a case in which eight young girls aged between 11 and 15 alleged sexual assault by two co-defendants (*R v Wills* [2011] EWCA Crim 1938). The trial judge directed that the defence advocates were not expected to challenge or put their case to the complainants. One barrister observed the judge's directions in this respect and his client was convicted. The other 'approached the cross-examination with only passing regard for the limitations imposed by the judge' (para 27); his client was acquitted. The convicted defendant appealed, on the basis that these differences in approach to cross-examination rendered the trial unfair.

The Court of Appeal disagreed, noting that the acquittal was in relation to the weakest count of the indictment. It went on to review how the complainants were cross-examined on behalf of both co-defendants. It confirmed there was 'every need for there to be clear limitations imposed on the cross-examination of the vulnerable young complainants along the lines of those set out by the judge' (para 23). The advocate who 'properly complied with the judge's directions' asked 'the necessary questions' and was therefore 'not unfairly hindered in asking questions which might progress' his client's case (para 26). The judge had intervened a number of times in the other barrister's cross-examination and at one point said: 'This is not the way to conduct cross-examination of a fifteen year-old. I have allowed you to go on longer than I should have done' (para 27). The Court of Appeal concurred:

> We have no doubt that the approach of counsel for the co-defendant did not comply with the proper limitations laid down by the judge ... The importance of the limitation on cross-examination in cases such as this is to protect the vulnerable witnesses and enable them to give the best evidence they can. We do not take the view that it follows that the type of cross-examination permitted means that the questions asked by counsel will be less effective in adducing the necessary evidence for the jury. Some of the most effective cross-examination is conducted without long and complicated questions being posed in a leading or 'tagged' manner. (para 30)

Although the trial judge had given the jury a direction in respect of the difference in styles adopted by the advocates, the Court of Appeal in *Wills* indicated its expectation that judges should manage such cases more robustly in future.

R v Farooqi

In 2013 the Lord Chief Justice, Lord Judge, used his final Court of Appeal judgment to emphasise that advocates have a duty to abide by judicial rulings (*R v Farooqi* [2013] EWCA Crim 1649). The judgment addressed 'flagrant misconduct and alleged professional incompetence' by one of the defence counsel in this case (para 1). Although the trial did not involve vulnerable witnesses, the principles are of universal application: 'In the course of any trial, like everyone else, the advocate is ultimately bound to abide by the rulings of the court … the trial process is not a game.' Advocates must ensure that their clients understand that they must abide by procedural requirements and practice directions and court orders (para 114).

Impact of the Court of Appeal decisions

Criminal Practice Direction 3E (2015) summarises the key points of these Court of Appeal decisions; in particular, case management guidance given in *Wills*:

> The judiciary is responsible for controlling questioning … All witnesses, including the defendant and defence witnesses, should be enabled to give the best evidence they can. In relation to young and/or vulnerable people, this may mean departing radically from traditional cross-examination … the court may dispense with the normal practice and impose restrictions on the advocate 'putting his case' where there is a risk of a young or otherwise vulnerable witness failing to understand, becoming distressed or acquiescing to leading questions. Where limitations on questioning are necessary and appropriate, they must be clearly defined. The judge has a duty to ensure that they are complied with.

Soon after stepping down as Lord Chief Justice, Lord Judge (2013a, p 8) warned that the impact of the five decisions from *Barker* to *Farooqi*

> has not yet been fully appreciated. Taken together, they have effected a major change in the way in which cross-examination should be undertaken. I strongly urge anyone involved in criminal trials whether as judge or advocate to understand the impact of these decisions … The advocate should go into the criminal trial anticipating that the judge will apply the legal principles to be derived from this group of authorities.

A recent Court of Appeal decision (*R v Lubemba, R v JP* [2014] EWCA Crim 2064) follows in the same vein. Key points of the judgment, written by Lady Justice Hallett, are described later in this chapter and also in Chapters Two, Eight, Nine and Twelve.

Other cases: influential for the wrong reasons

> 'You simply do not see unreasonable cross-examination of children. I cannot think of a single case.' (Barrister quoted in Plotnikoff and Woolfson, 2007a)

> 'The spectacle of multiple barristers with high IQs aggressively cross-examining the same vulnerable victim (who is likely to have a fairly low IQ), is a disgrace. We will look back on this in 100 years' time with the same disbelief that we have now at the notion of sending children up chimneys or down mines in Victorian days.' (Detective Inspector)

Cross-examination came back into public prominence as the result of adverse publicity surrounding vulnerable witness trials in 2013. None of these cases involved an intermediary, although some of the witnesses would have been eligible for intermediary assistance. We describe the cases here because the media attention helped influence a change in approach on the part of the judiciary and lawyers. This in turn has had an effect on the legal environment in which intermediaries work.

Guidance encourages judges to alert the jury to the adoption of stereotypes 'which could lead the jury to approach the complainant's evidence with unwarranted scepticism', for example, that someone who has been sexually assaulted 'reports it as soon as possible' or 'remembers events consistently' (Judicial Studies Board, 2010, chapter 17, para 12). In a widely reported 2013 case in which these rape stereotypes went unchallenged, the complainant was told by defence counsel that 'It beggars belief' that she would have stayed all night in the bed of someone who raped her and that if she was 'telling the truth about these matters, then I suggest that your answers would be consistent' ('Sex abuse victim's suicide sparks call for review of court procedures', *The Guardian*, 9 February 2013).

During cross-examination, the complainant was accused of lying or fantasising on at least 20 occasions; counsel described her evidence as 'ridiculous', 'nonsense' and 'utterly implausible'. The defendants were convicted but the complainant killed herself before the jury verdict. She had declined the offer of special measures before court and during the trial but was nonetheless a vulnerable witness with a history of suicide attempts and self-harm. The Serious Case Review following her death recommended that:

> Where a judge is of the considered opinion that a witness is vulnerable, even in circumstances where that witness has refused special measures, the judge should be proactive by introducing special measures that both protect the person deemed to be at risk of psychological or physical harm and the quality of evidence put before the court. (Brown, 2014, Recommendation 10)

Some of the high profile trials involved child sexual exploitation. The first report concerned the retrial of a case in the Midlands which had previously collapsed after four months of evidence ('Lawyers' treatment of gang grooming victims prompts call for reform', *The Observer*, 19 May 2013). In the first trial, a teenage complainant was 'aggressively cross-examined by seven barristers every day for three weeks'; she was repeatedly accused of lying and even asked if she 'repented her sins': she did not understand the question ('Humiliation in court: how the law treated abuse victims' and 'Abuse trial that shamed the British legal system', *The Times*, 23 May 2013). *The Times* reported that jurors seemed 'angry and dismayed' and the girl was reported to be 'so traumatised by her time in the witness box that she was said to be suffering flashbacks and panic attacks'; after the trial collapsed, the circuit's Presiding Judge was said to have described it as an 'unmitigated disaster'. The retrial was dealt with very differently. *The Times* reported the judge as saying: "The way things went the last time is just so wrong that we should all be ashamed that our justice system allowed it"; he intervened a number of times to control cross-examination. The defendants were convicted and received substantial custodial sentences.

Following a widely publicised trial in 2013 at the Old Bailey, seven men were convicted and given lengthy sentences after six teenagers gave evidence. Speaking afterwards, one of the girls described giving evidence as:

> 'probably scarier than the whole experience I went through previously. I can honestly say, even given the result, I wouldn't ever do it again. It was degrading. I felt completely torn apart ... I had to be told I was an unholy liar, everything I said had been made up ... It was absolutely horrendous. I can understand why people don't give evidence. If I'd known that was going to happen I would not have gone.' ('Woman's Hour' interview, BBC Radio 4, 18 February 2014)

In another sex exploitation trial, a 17-year-old took an overdose of pills after her first day in the witness box. She was taken to hospital and after being evaluated as fit to continue, she was cross-examined for six days by 10 defence barristers ('Why the witness box is such an ordeal in sex grooming trials', *The Times*, 6 August 2013).

The publicity generated by these trials added to a public perception that cross-examination of vulnerable witnesses is often abusive and that some professionals do not acknowledge any problem with the process. At the end of the trial described above as 'an unmitigated disaster', the advocate claimed that "If I hadn't cross-examined the girl in the way I did then I would have been negligent" ('Abuse trial that shamed the British legal system', *The Times*, 23 May 2013). At the close of the case in which the complainant committed suicide, the judge apparently described the way she was cross-examined as 'perfectly proper and correct' ('Victim killed herself after being "raped all over again" in court', *The Guardian*, 9 February 2013).

Training the judiciary

> 'I could have been a judge but I never had the Latin ... I didn't have sufficient to get through the rigorous judging exams.' (Peter Cook, Beyond the Fringe, 1961)

The Judicial Studies Board held its first child abuse seminars in 1996. The judge acting as course director said that it immediately became apparent how much practice varied, surprising those organising the seminars and those attending (Crane, 1999). The seminars ran for several years before being discontinued. 'Ticketing' (that is, compulsory training) of judges who conduct sex offence trials was introduced in 2002. In recent years this specialist training has been reinvigorated under the guidance of committed judicial trainers. High Court judges, Crown Court judges, Recorders (judges who sit part time in the Crown Court) and district judges who sit in the magistrates' court are required to attend two-day Serious Sex Offences Seminars in order to obtain their 'ticket'.

In June 2013 the House of Commons Home Affairs Committee *Inquiry into Child Sexual Exploitation and the Response to Localised Grooming* expressed deep concern about court language and recommended 'further specific guidance and training' for judges and advocates (para 94). In response, the Lord Chief Justice proposed new 'bespoke training' in child sexual exploitation and other vulnerable witness cases (letter from Lord Judge to Rt Hon Keith Vaz, Chairman, Home Affairs Committee, 26 July 2013). This additional training was extended to all judges holding a serious sex offence ticket. The first Vulnerable Witness Seminar was held in March 2013; by the end of 2014, 735 judges had attended the course. Although these seminars are not being repeated, induction and refresher Serious Sex Offences Seminars now 'prominently' address the treatment of vulnerable witnesses. Previously, ticketed judges were invited to attend refresher seminars every three years; this is now a monitored requirement (communication to the authors, March 2015).

No intermediary has been involved in delivering Judicial College training, at least in recent years, although their function is covered in presentations and delegates watch training films demonstrating how the role is performed at trial. Some judges attending Judicial College seminars as recently as 2013 and 2014 indicated that they had not yet worked with an intermediary either when they were advocates or since joining the Bench.

Magistrates

Induction and consolidation training for magistrates covers special measures; reference to intermediaries is made in the Adult Court Bench Book and the pre-reading for the consolidation course. More detailed training about vulnerability is given on courses for youth court magistrates and those who chair adult or youth court panels. Legal advisers who sit in court with (lay) Benches are also trained and should advise the Bench about the range of special measures.

The Judicial College is considering whether magistrates should receive more information about intermediaries (communication, November 2014). This would be a worthwhile exercise. When *The Advocate's Gateway* toolkits were launched, a Magistrates' Association representative advised us that there was no point in trying to train or encourage magistrates to read this material 'when the huge majority … will not be in a situation where it is relevant to them more than once every few years'. Yet vulnerable witnesses aside, over half of children and adults who offend have communication difficulties (Talbot, 2012; Criminal Justice Joint Inspection, 2014b).

Intermediaries report an increasing number of appointments in magistrates' and youth court cases but that magistrates remain unfamiliar with the scheme. A request on the Magistrates'

Association website for members' feedback about experience with intermediaries produced only one response. While this magistrate had dealt with two intermediary cases, she thought that "95 per cent of magistrates don't know what they do. Our Bench probably thought they were part of the Witness Care Unit or the Witness Service."

Advocacy training

> In practice, of course, a barrister could talk in baby language and still leave his listeners perplexed. (Grove, 2000, p 156)

> 'An element of torture [for the vulnerable witness] is inevitable.' (QC, 2013)

> 'We won't get this right until defence counsel are ticketed. Some shouldn't be doing it.' (Judge, quoted in Plotnikoff and Woolfson, 2011, p 13)

Current training provision is unsatisfactory. Mandatory e-learning training for all CPS prosecutors was introduced in the wake of adverse publicity surrounding child sexual exploitation cases; additional e-learning is required for CPS specialist lawyers who also have access to face-to-face refresher training ('CPS and ACPO call for national consensus on tackling child sexual abuse', CPS press release, 6 March 2013; communication from CPS, December 2014). External prosecution counsel for rape and child sexual abuse cases must fulfil requirements of 'experience, specialism and regular training' (Criminal Justice Joint Inspection, 2014a, paras 2.09, 2.11, 10.6). None of this training involves being tested or includes direct input from intermediaries. Apart from these limited provisions, advocates who defend or prosecute in cases involving a vulnerable person are not required to undergo specialist training.

Calls for advocates to receive training in questioning children date back at least to Judge Pigot's 1989 Home Office report. The approach at the time was exemplified by a defence barrister's letter to the Crown Court, arguing that his fee should be increased because the case 'required extensive preparation for a detailed and precise cross-examination of this young girl [aged 12], together with a full attack on her as to her previous sexual experience, her veracity and her character'; in another case, the CPS asked officers to warn a child witness that 'she can expect the defence will give her no quarter' (Plotnikoff and Woolfson, 1995, p 98).

In 2011 the Advocacy Training Council published *Raising the Bar: The Handling of Vulnerable Witnesses, Victims and Defendants at Court*, acknowledging 'a clear and pressing need' for specialist training (p 40). In October 2014 checks with the Advocacy Training Council (in respect of the Inns of Court and Bar Circuits), Law Society Advocacy Section and the Solicitors Higher Courts Advocates Association revealed that only a handful of ad hoc vulnerable witness training events were held in 2014; many organisations reported no training, showing that little has changed since we surveyed Inns of Court and Bar Circuits in 2010 (Plotnikoff and Woolfson, 2012, p 37).

The training that has taken place delivers inconsistent messages. We have seen some trainers disregard the Court of Appeal judgments: they continue to use tag questions in demonstrating cross-examination of vulnerable witnesses, criticise participants who carefully avoided tag questions and fail to challenge other aspects of poor questioning practice. At one 2013 event, a participant who queried the use of leading questions for a vulnerable witness was told by the trainer that cross-examination should always be leading: 'Evidence-in-chief is where the witness gives his evidence. Cross-examination is where I give the evidence and the witness says "Yes" or "No"' (Henderson et al, 2015 forthcoming). In her interviews with judges and barristers in 2013, Henderson (2015a, forthcoming) identified a sense among some QCs that case law restrictions on cross-examination apply to 'junior advocates only'. Trainers should be selected not just on experience but on their express commitment to best practice messages consistent with Court of Appeal decisions and Judicial College training. One barrister advised: "I have been an advocacy trainer in my Inn for 20 years and no one has ever asked us about our approach to vulnerable witnesses."

Raising the Bar recommended that training should no longer be the exclusive preserve of advocates but should draw on other disciplines (Advocacy Training Council, 2011, p 48). Intermediaries should be seen as an essential component of advocacy training regarding vulnerable witnesses. Commendably, the Criminal Bar Association has involved intermediaries in seminars and conferences and in development of its training film *A Question of Practice* in 2013. However, intermediary involvement in advocacy training is not routine. In 2013, 'hand-picked' trainers oversaw participants practising cross-examination without use of leading questions at an 'unprecedented and innovative event' (Ayling, 2014). Intermediaries were discussed – but not invited to assist.

In July 2013, shortly after the Lord Chief Justice's announcement of new judicial training, the Bar Council finally announced that it would 'support fully' the implementation of 'required' vulnerable witness training ('Bar Council encourages creation of a required training programme for cross-examination of vulnerable witnesses', Bar Council press release, 1 July 2013). The Advocacy Training Council asked His Honour Judge Peter Rook QC to chair an interdisciplinary group to devise courses for advocates across the professions and train the first cadre of trainers. The group aims 'to ensure high standards in the quality and consistency of advocacy' and 'to provide a focus for best practice'; while it cannot impose accreditation on the professions, the intention is for participation in its training to represent 'the appropriate standard' (communication, May 2014). The first pilot events began in 2015; they involved role play with feedback and input from registered intermediaries. (A similar working group has been set up to design training for advocates in the family courts: Judiciary of England and Wales, 2015, para 16.)

The European Directive on victims of crime, which Member States must implement by November 2015, requires them, 'with due respect for the independence of the legal profession', to make available both general and specialist training to increase awareness of victims' needs (European Union, 2012, Article 25.3). Judge Rook's committee is a vital move in this direction but there is a long way to go. The government made a commitment to 'devise a requirement' by March 2015 that, to be instructed in serious sexual offence cases, publicly funded defence advocates 'must have undertaken approved specialist training on working with vulnerable victims and witnesses' (Ministry of Justice, 2014b, p 6). No such training requirement had been announced when Parliament was dissolved for the April 2015 election. This delay is regrettable. Even after a government training requirement is in place, implementation will take several years, given the number of practitioners to be trained.

The current approach is piecemeal. Dealing with vulnerability should be part of foundation training for all criminal and family practitioners, with specialist training subject to 'pass/fail' accreditation before lawyers can participate in cases known to involve a vulnerable person. CPS lawyers, QCs and privately funded advocates (one of whom was responsible for the most egregious cross-examination of a vulnerable witness that we have seen) should not be exempt.

Quality assurance scheme for advocates

> The quality assurance scheme for advocates has 'one simple objective: to protect the public from the few criminal advocates who are not as good as they should be'. (Oliver Hanmer, Head of Quality at the Bar Standards Board, 2013)

> [Responding to proposals to introduce quality assurance] Outraged members of the Bar claimed never to have been so insulted in all their lives: 'been doing the job this way for 30 years, don't need someone to check how I am doing it now'. (Peter Lodder, Chairman of the Bar, 2011)

In 2009 and 2010, calls for specialist assessment of advocates dealing with children in criminal proceedings were rejected by lawyers' groups and the Council of HM Circuit Judges (Ministry of Justice, 2009; Joint Advocacy Group, 2010). However, in 2011, *Raising the Bar* acknowledged the desirability of accrediting or 'ticketing' advocates 'suitably trained, qualified and experienced' in this 'specialist skill' (p 3). Surprisingly, the report generated no formal response from the Bar Council (confirmed by the Council in June 2014). In recent years, concerns about declining advocacy standards have grown. A recent review of criminal advocacy reflected judicial disquiet which was 'remarkable for its consistency and the strength with which it was expressed' (Jeffrey, 2014, p 5; a survey for the Bar Standards Board in 2012 identified similar views).

The Joint Advocacy Group, representing the regulatory bodies of barristers, solicitors and legal executives, has developed a Quality Assurance Scheme for Advocates (QASA) which would require criminal advocates wishing to exercise rights of audience at a higher level to apply for accreditation at four levels of competence, including a rather vague standard in respect of the 'appropriate' handling of vulnerable witnesses (Criminal Advocacy Evaluation Form, QASA, 2013). If refused accreditation, an advocate would not be permitted to practice at a higher level. The scheme was scheduled to be introduced in stages, starting in 2011. Protests were vigorous from the outset. QASA has been the subject of four consultations and a Judicial Review. In October 2014 the Court of Appeal rejected challenges to the lawfulness of QASA:

> It is clear that this is a controversial scheme on which opinions are sharply divided. ... Those who oppose the scheme can at least take some comfort from the fact that the approved regulators intend to review it after two years. That is an important safeguard. (*Lumsdon v Legal Services Board* [2014] EWCA Civ 276, para 112)

The Supreme Court has granted campaigning barristers permission to appeal *Lumsdon*, while declining to hear any appeal on the basis that the scheme infringes advocates' independence. In the interim, the Bar Standards Board is seeking alternative ways of improving advocacy standards. This includes asking the body responsible for awarding Queen's Counsel status to develop a process for re-accrediting criminal silks as part of a continuous quality assurance scheme. The Board believes that QCs should not be exempt from quality assurance (Law Society Gazette, 'Bar regulator seeks QC re-accreditation scheme', 24 March 2015).

Advocacy in the youth court

Over 60% percent of young people in the youth justice system have speech, language and communication needs, compared with 10% per cent of children in the general population (Talbot, 2010). Their needs are often not picked up by professionals.

An enquiry into the effectiveness of the youth court chaired by Lord Carlile observed that it has been regarded 'as a safe place for inexperienced or inadequate advocacy'. The enquiry recommended that the regulatory bodies introduce 'without delay' accreditation to include training in communication difficulties, developmental needs and mental ill-health (Carlile, 2014, pp 31, 37) and that the Judicial College extend specialist youth training from district judges to all those dealing with young defendants.

The Bar Standards Board also regards advocacy in the youth court as a potentially high risk area: it has commissioned research to establish the extent to which regulatory intervention is required to ensure that youth court advocacy is delivered 'to a standard that protects the public interest' and to determine 'what training and accreditation might cover' (communication, September 2014).

Complaints against barristers

> In the few high profile cases regarding inappropriate cross-examination that received media attention, none of the parties (the witnesses, judges and prosecution or defence counsel) raised concerns with the Board. (Bar Standards Board communication, October 2014)

The Bar Standards Board provided the following information in respect of how complaints against the Bar are managed and, in particular, what procedures apply in relation to a complaint concerning cross-examination of a vulnerable witness (communication, October 2014).

> The Board will always consider, and take seriously, complaints about inappropriate cross-examination

of witnesses. Whether it is in a position to take the complaint forward depends on the circumstances of the individual case. When considering a complaint, the Board has to assess whether the barrister's behaviour amounts to a breach of the professional obligations as set out in the Bar Standards Board Handbook (January 2014; previously, the Code of Conduct 8th Edition). Neither the old Code nor the new Handbook contains specific provisions relating to cross-examination. However, this does not preclude the Board from taking action where allegations of inappropriate cross-examination are made.

The new Handbook moves away from prescriptive rules to emphasise core duties and outcomes, creating greater flexibility in addressing conduct issues. In relation to cross-examination, the following are relevant:

Core Duty 1 – barristers must observe their duty to the court in the administration of justice;
Core Duty 5 – barristers must not behave in a way which is likely to diminish the trust and confidence which the public places in them or in the profession;
Conduct Rule 3.2 – barristers must not abuse their role as an advocate;
Conduct Rule 7 – barristers must not make statements or ask questions merely to insult, humiliate or annoy a witness or any other persons.

The Handbook also creates new obligations on barristers to self-report serious misconduct and report serious misconduct by others. These obligations are designed to assist with creating a professional culture where serious inappropriate behaviour is not tolerated and may prove to be an avenue by which the Board becomes aware of conduct not previously brought to its attention.

The Board considers all complaints on their merits, taking into account the context, available evidence and the circumstances and individual facts of the case. The judge's attitude to counsel's behaviour is a central factor in determining whether regulatory action should be taken. If a judge condones or endorses the course of a cross-examination, this would inevitably make it difficult for the Board to establish that the barrister in question has acted inappropriately, but would not preclude the Board from taking action if the available evidence was sufficient to demonstrate that a barrister had breached his or her professional obligations. The Board's consideration of all the circumstances concerning a complaint about inappropriate cross-examination would include the attitude and reaction of a barrister to interventions by registered intermediaries, as well as the court's assessment, if any, of the barrister's behaviour. Where a barrister ignores agreements/rulings made in the course of a case this would provide a strong basis for regulatory action. If a barrister breached agreed ground rules issued by the judge, this would also provide strong evidence that the barrister had acted inappropriately and had potentially breached one or more of their professional obligations. (In 2014, in a different context, a barrister was suspended for four months for, amongst other things, ignoring the judge's rulings.)

It is always open to judges to refer a barrister's conduct to the Board if they have concerns about inappropriate behaviour in the face of their attempts to control the conduct. Indeed, even if a barrister complies with rulings/directions given by a judge, but the judge considers a barrister's approach to a case was inappropriate and/or unprofessional, the judge may still refer the conduct in question to the Board. A referral from a judge provides a strong basis for the Board to take complaints forward, but such referrals are rare.

Categorisations of complaints on the Board database do not currently allow the identification of specific cases about cross-examination. However, the Board identified one complaint in the past year about cross-examination of a potentially vulnerable witness in which there was insufficient evidence to progress to enforcement action. It has not identified any upheld complaints specifically about the cross-examination of vulnerable witnesses. The Board's categorisation of complaints is under review and this work will include considering how to identify more readily complaints about the treatment of witnesses, whether vulnerable or not. Nevertheless, in reality the Board receives few such complaints.

Henderson (2015a, forthcoming) found that even senior judges acknowledged being unable to control some counsel under current policies but none of the 25 judges in her sample had made a formal complaint about an advocate.

Consistent advocacy standards across the professions

The four branches of the legal profession (barristers, solicitors, solicitor advocates and legal executives) each has its own code of conduct, of which the Bar Standards Board Handbook is one. In *Farooqi* ([2013] EWCA Crim 1649, para 109), the Lord Chief Justice stressed that rules in the trial process 'apply whether the advocate in question is a barrister or solicitor, and to the extent that the rules of professional conduct of either profession are not consistent, they should be made so'.

The professions' provisions as a whole are neither consistent nor specific about what might constitute exploitative or unethical behaviour in respect of cross-examination. Only solicitor higher court advocates are required to be able to identify vulnerable witnesses, use appropriate questioning techniques and comply with relevant judicial directions (Solicitors Regulation Authority, 2010, Standards for Trial Advocacy 2(b), part 3).

The absence of clear expectations across the professions may be a contributing factor to the lack of complaints filed about advocates who ignore ground rules and who repeatedly breach judicial directions and interventions about how a vulnerable witness should be questioned. In March 2014, the government recommended that the rules of professional conduct be reviewed 'to identify inconsistencies and propose ways to align them for the purposes of trials of sexual violence cases' (Ministry of Justice, 2014a, p 4). Twelve months on, unfortunately there has been no progress in response to the government's recommendation. Action should be taken to make standards in respect of vulnerable witnesses and defendants consistent, irrespective of case category.

Advocacy Training Council guidance on *The Advocate's Gateway*

> 'Some advocates still fail to accept their limitations in questioning vulnerable witnesses due to ignorance, arrogance or misconceptions.' (Johanna Cutts QC, 2011, presentation at registered intermediary continuing professional development day)

> 'The judge can make such a difference about how effective an intermediary is. I worked with the same intermediary twice – the first time the judge and advocates stuck to the ground rules and the intermediary used brilliant aids and adaptations to help the witness give his evidence. The second trial with the same intermediary was very difficult – she constantly had to intervene and rightly so, as the witness was struggling to understand what was going on. Everyone was getting frustrated and it wasn't working. If that had been my first experience of intermediaries I'd have thought that they didn't help the process. As I knew how effective they'd been before, it made me realise that it's judges and advocates that need training.' (Young Witness Service supporter)

As advocacy training on vulnerability is not yet compulsory or consistent, guidance on best practice has a key role. For years, the only advice addressed to lawyers on questioning vulnerable witnesses was an admonition to avoid 'improper or inappropriate' cross-examination, set out in *Achieving Best Evidence*, government guidance aimed primarily at police officers (in its latest version, Ministry of Justice, 2011a, para 5.17).

The Advocacy Training Council report *Raising the Bar* (2011, p 49) recommended that:

> All advocates should be issued with 'toolkits' setting out common problems encountered when examining vulnerable witnesses and defendants, together with suggested solutions ... [these] should be considered amongst the essential elements of trial preparation.

We were inspired to respond to this recommendation via a rather unlikely route. Following his failed appeal in a Court of Appeal case, defence counsel complained in his chambers newsletter that the trial judge had not permitted him to ask 'even the simplest' question: 'It was not X that caused your injuries, was it?' If an intermediary had been involved in this case, he or she would have explained that this is not a simple question: it has a tag ending; the negative makes processing the question more complex; and the words 'cause' and 'injuries' are not within the average six-year-old's vocabulary. This barrister was experienced and his perception of 'simple' questions was no doubt typical of many of his colleagues at the time. How could awareness of these problems be raised across the professions?

We had previously written *Good Practice Guidance on Questioning Children* (Plotnikoff and Woolfson, 2009b) and had recommended that this be further developed through a code for questioning young and other vulnerable people at court, 'suitably endorsed and widely distributed for use in training and to inform ground rules discussions at court' (Plotnikoff and Woolfson, 2011, para 17). However, no action had been taken in response to this recommendation or that of *Raising the Bar*.

Inspiration struck during a lengthy dental appointment. *Raising the Bar*'s plea for toolkits would allow us to take forward our work relating to children and extend it to other vulnerable witnesses and defendants. We took the concept of a website hosting a range of toolkits to the intermediary trainers, Penny Cooper and David Wurtzel at City Law School, City University. (Penny is now a professor at Kingston University Law School and is chair of *The Advocate's Gateway* management committee, of which David is a member.) Penny kindly arranged for City University to design and host a demonstration website.

The Nuffield Foundation gave us a grant to develop three toolkits concerning young witnesses and defendants; our company, Lexicon, funded development of others covering case management, ground rules hearings, autism, learning disability and certain 'hidden' disabilities. The toolkits bring together research, legislation, case law and references to nearly 50 relevant policy documents. Intermediaries made a crucial contribution by providing anonymised good and poor practice examples; these include developmentally inappropriate questions and suggestions as to how they could be asked more effectively, something that judges reportedly find helpful. The toolkits provide a baseline of information which must be tailored to the communication and other needs of the individual witness or defendant. They are not a replacement for an intermediary assessment.

In June 2012, Nuffield hosted a seminar chaired by Lord Justice Hooper to demonstrate the prototype website. The Advocacy Training Council, under the leadership of Nicholas Green QC (now Mr Justice Green) generously offered to develop and host a permanent website; and *The Advocate's Gateway* www.theadvocatesgateway.org was launched by the Attorney General in April 2013. The *Gateway* continues to add toolkits by various authors on a wide range of subjects. It also lists relevant cases and other resources, including the Criminal Bar Association training film, *A Question of Practice*, demonstrating how to adapt questions for young and other vulnerable witnesses or defendants and exploring the circumstances in which advocates need not 'put their case' to the witness (Chapter Twelve).

The toolkits have caught on quickly. Criminal Practice Direction 3D.7 (2015) describes them as 'best practice' and advises judges and advocates to consult them. Lady Justice Hallett commends them as 'excellent practical guides' (*R v Lubemba, R v JP* [2014] EWCA Crim 2064, para 40); Sir Brian Leveson's *Review of Efficiency in Criminal Proceedings* recommends that judges promote the use of toolkits to raise and maintain standards of advocacy, and that their range be expanded 'to encompass as many areas of criminal practice as practicable' (2015, para 271). Frontline practitioners also report finding the toolkits helpful (Henderson, 2015c, forthcoming). Although judges increasingly refer advocates to the toolkits for planning their questions, many lawyers are apparently still unfamiliar with the *Gateway*. As non-lawyers, intermediaries are bemused to find themselves referring advocates to the toolkits, case law and policies, underlining the need for advocacy training. When an intermediary recently suggested to a prosecutor that he might find *Barker* useful, he responded: "Is it a text book?"

Intermezzo

Ken: four adjournments, three pre-trial hearings, three judges, two prosecutors – and an extra wig in court

Bradley (registered intermediary)

I was appointed as an intermediary for Ken, a man in his 60s with severe physical and communication difficulties resulting from a stroke. The allegations concerned theft and fraud by his carers. Over the following 22 months, the trial was adjourned four times. Before I was appointed, an officer took a written statement from Ken over a number of home visits. The CPS had been ready to throw the case out until an intermediary assessment was suggested.

I met Ken twice at his home along with the officer and Ken's social worker. His speech was difficult to understand at first; all conversation took a long time and tired him. It was to the officer's credit that he had taken the time to listen and try to understand Ken in order to obtain his statement. Ken was not receiving any ongoing support or therapy for his communication difficulties. He had significant physical limitations and was completely dependent on carers for all his physical needs.

My report concluded that Ken's language level was good enough to allow him to be cross-examined with my assistance to maximise the intelligibility of his speech. I recommended arrangements for wheelchair access, toileting and scheduling his evidence in the morning. While it was difficult for Ken to leave his flat, the physical barriers to getting him to court could be overcome: it was the communication obstacles that were harder to deal with.

I attended a court hearing in October and met the CPS lawyer and Prosecutor A. We discussed my report recommendations. Ken's police interviews had not been filmed. I was concerned that, if Ken had to tell the whole story from scratch, it would be tiring, time-consuming and difficult for the court and jury to understand. We discussed whether someone could read out his statement as his evidence-in-chief, with just a couple of clarifying questions from Prosecutor A. This was raised in court with Judge One and I thought it was agreed.

In November, I attended a court familiarisation visit with Ken and his social worker. This helped establish that Ken would communicate better in court rather than over a live link but that he might have trouble hearing speech across the courtroom. We practised where to position Ken's wheelchair so that I could sit next to him. Ken was able to get a feel for how it was to listen and speak in court. Just after the visit, we heard that the trial date had been postponed. The day before the rescheduled trial was due to start, I was told by the Witness Care Unit that it was adjourned again. I queried this with the CPS, which was unaware; on enquiry the trial seemed to have been cancelled in error. Ken's social worked visited him: "To say he's devastated would be an understatement. The upheaval of getting psyched up to the trial each time then to be told it's off is affecting him more than he's letting on. But he's a tough cookie and is determined to see it through."

I attended court again the following February. There was a change of prosecution counsel and, after waiting with Ken and his carer from 10 am, we met with the CPS lawyer and Prosecutor B. He was doubtful about Ken's ability to give evidence. He struggled to communicate with Ken, even with my advice, and concluded: "I can't understand a single word he said, I doubt this can go ahead even with your help." I tried to stay confident, asserted that my assessment and report findings were appropriate, and that I could support Ken to give his evidence, although I acknowledged that if he had to tell the court the whole story, it would be difficult. Eventually I was invited into court for the ground rules hearing, this time with Judge Two. It became apparent that any agreements made at the hearing with Judge One did not stand. After further legal argument, Judge Two conceded he could not guarantee the case could be completed in the time allotted for trial and adjourned it for another two months. Ken was therefore sent home again, after four hours in the waiting room.

In April, the day before the trial, it had to be relisted because of industrial action at court. I rang the CPS to discuss the possible impact of a further adjournment on Ken. They sought a change of trial judge so that the ground rules hearing could be dealt with the following week by Judge C, with the trial the week after. At the ground rules hearing, I was relieved to meet Prosecutor A again. We had a successful discussion before Judge C, who agreed that Ken's evidence should be presented in the way which best supported his communication.

Towards the end of April, I attended court once more and met the police officer, Ken and his carer. I invited Prosecutor A and the defence barristers to meet Ken and 'tune in' to his speech. Prosecutor A had a very different communication style from Prosecutor B. Legal discussions delayed the start of the trial; after two hours, we were told that the defendants had changed their plea to guilty. As Ken had made such an effort to attend, it was arranged for him to go into court to see his two ex-carers plead guilty to stealing thousands of pounds from his bank account. The judge praised Ken for his commitment and made positive statements about the intermediary scheme. I assisted the police officer help Ken make a victim personal statement as part of the sentencing process.

On a personal note, I fitted in these court dates around surgery and chemotherapy. All the professionals involved wished me well for my treatment and the judges were amenable to making sure any rescheduled court dates were suitable for me as well as the advocates. And, of course, I got to wear a wig in court, just like the judge and barristers.

ELEVEN

Cross-examination: intervention at trial

No guidance specifies precisely how intermediaries are expected to fulfil their responsibilities at trial. This is a matter to be worked out with the judiciary on a case-by-case basis. The intermediary's overarching obligation is to help improve the quality of the witness's evidence. Intermediaries monitor communication and must intervene only to seek clarification from the court or to draw its attention 'to any difficulty the witness may be experiencing in understanding what is being said or that may be distressing the witness'; they must not change the content of what is said or attempt to improve or elaborate on it (Ministry of Justice, 2012, Code of Practice for Registered Intermediaries, paras 1, 15–17).

The task is easier when vulnerable witnesses are able to indicate to their intermediary that they are confused by a question. However, many people with communication needs have difficulty recognising when they do not understand and even if they do, may be reluctant to say so in the intimidating court setting. In most instances it is therefore up to the intermediary to identify actual or potential communication problems and to tell the court.

The frequency of interventions depends largely on how well advocates comply with intermediary recommendations and the ground rules. At present, intermediaries describe lawyers' responses as ranging from "fully on board" through "trying hard to adapt" to those who are "stuck in the old ways". Until questioning is underway, it is impossible for intermediaries to gauge whether lawyers have adopted their recommendations, are resistant or are simply unable to comply. The judiciary is leading the transition to a new style of advocacy; the rate of intermediary interventions is therefore also related to the control of questioning exercised by the judge.

This chapter examines the respective responsibilities of the intermediary, judge and lawyers. Intermediaries are most likely to recognise communication difficulties in all their various forms but some questioning strategies that impede communication lie at, and sometimes beyond, the boundaries of their function. We follow them as they navigate a landscape of grey areas. Where judges and lawyers are reluctant to intervene and intermediaries feel constrained from doing so, vulnerable witnesses are left without a safety net.

Responsibilities for intervention

> Effective communication is the bedrock of the legal process ... Check that all parties understand ... the meaning of the questions asked and answers given during the course of the proceedings, otherwise the process of law is at best seriously impeded. At worst, justice may be denied. (Judicial Studies Board, 2012, Section 2)

> 'If I'd known that the defence barristers would treat me like that I'd never have agreed to do it. I could not go through that again. I would rather go to prison or kill myself.' (Witness who refused to give evidence at a second trial)

The presence of an intermediary throws into sharp relief the obligations of others in the courtroom. In order to understand intermediary interventions, it is necessary first to look at the corresponding responsibilities of the judiciary, CPS and advocates.

Criminal Procedure Rule 1 (2015) sets out the overriding objective 'that criminal cases be dealt with justly'. This imposes a duty on the judiciary to manage a trial with the aim of delivering a just result both for the Crown and the defence; 'a criminal trial is not a game under which a guilty defendant should be provided with a sporting chance' (Criminal Practice Direction

1A.1, 2015). The judiciary must take 'every reasonable step' to enable vulnerable people to give their best evidence, adapting the process 'as far as necessary'; this may mean 'departing radically from traditional cross-examination' (Criminal Practice Directions 3D.2, 3E.1 and 4, 2015). Some questions cannot be put to a witness without judicial permission. These include matters arising from information held by third parties, for example social work, education or medical records, or concerning previous sexual history.

A common strategy is for lawyers to make rhetorical comments directed to the jury, such as "You've told this jury a complete pack of lies" (a 'question' put to a vulnerable witness in 2013). Declarations like this can minimise the witness's responses yet be persuasive to juries (Klemfuss et al, 2014). Lord Judge, former Lord Chief Justice, says 'comment posing as cross-examination must stop' (2013a, p 7). While an intermediary can point out that a statement is not actually a question, only judges have the authority to halt comment as a routine practice, though it seems that not many do so. Interventions for other reasons also fall to the judiciary; for example, they are expected to stop repetitive cross-examination of a vulnerable witness and to prevent questioning that does not comply with ground rules (Criminal Practice Directions 3E.1, 3E.4, 2015).

Some judicial responsibilities for intervention overlap with those of advocates, although the respective policies are not always consistent. Judges and prosecutors are both expected to challenge defence use of stereotypes about the behaviour of a victim witness (Judicial Studies Board, 2010, chapter 17; Crown Prosecution Service, 2013, para 77). However, while the prosecution encourages the use of expert evidence (Crown Prosecution Service, 2013, para 77), this remains prohibited by judicial guidance (Judicial Studies Board, 2010, chapter 17, para 8). Notably in New Zealand, psychologists called by the prosecution are increasingly allowed to explain to juries about the behaviour of children who have been sexually abused. Unless jurors hear these 'counter-intuitive' research findings before children give evidence 'there is a danger the jury will have formed a view which is difficult if not impossible to reverse' (communication from Judge Duncan Harvey, March 2015).

Criminal Practice Direction 3E.1 (2015) requires judges to stop 'over-rigorous' cross-examination of a vulnerable witness. The statutory Code of Practice for Victims of Crime requires prosecutors to alert the court if cross-examination of a victim witness is '*too* aggressive' or 'inappropriate' (Ministry of Justice, 2013a, p 20, our emphasis); whereas the Witness Charter expects advocates to intervene if an opponent's questioning is simply 'aggressive' (Ministry of Justice, 2013b, Standard 16). The Charter also expects lawyers to flag up 'unreasonable' cross-examination if it is unfair, offensive or not relevant to the issues (Standard 16).

The CPS and independent advocates prosecuting on its behalf have responsibilities to intervene generally, in respect of prosecution witnesses under the Witness Charter, and specifically in respect of victim witnesses under the statutory Victims' Code. Intermediaries detect a significant 'duty gap' between practice and implementation of these policies. This is not confined to intermediary cases. In *Measuring Up?*, in which young witnesses were not assisted by intermediaries, only 13% of those who experienced comprehension or other difficulties (such as being interrupted during cross-examination) recalled the prosecutor drawing the Bench's attention to the problem. One 17-year-old said: 'I was told that if anyone said something wrong, your barrister would stop it. They made it out to be a fairyland. It did not turn out like that' (Plotnikoff and Woolfson, 2009a, p 120).

Intermediaries report that prosecutors seldom intervene when prosecution witnesses are confused by complex questions and fail to back up intermediary interventions when these are challenged by the defence. Some prosecutors acknowledge they do not initiate interventions. A QC advised that, even when a "sarcastic and patronising" barrister is cross-examining a vulnerable witness, "as prosecutor you have to be very careful. You can see the jury look sympathetic so you may not intervene. But it is potentially hard on the witness." Another barrister said:

'In my role as prosecutor it was arguably not appropriate for me to step in every time the defence tried to probe even with a badly phrased question ... the intermediary was in the perfect position, there to facilitate communication and acting independently and impartially.'

Poppy was appointed as intermediary for G, a witness with poor understanding of time concepts and difficulty in sequencing events. The judge ordered the intermediary to sit behind the prosecutor and tap him on the shoulder if she thought G was struggling to understand. The prosecutor failed to support Poppy's protestations that she would have difficulty performing her role if not beside the witness or able to communicate her concerns directly to the court:

> 'Despite me pointing out to the prosecutor when questions were inappropriate and when a break was required, he did nothing. The judge saw me but appeared to ignore me. G's cross-examination went on for two-and-a-half hours before the judge asked how much longer the advocate was going to need, because they could all do with a break. By this time, G's answers were all over the place as the rapid-fire questions were confusing him. The case was eventually thrown out and I felt absolutely useless.'

A High Court judge has criticised prosecutors who 'failed to stand up for [vulnerable] complainants and to object, and object again, and to continue to object until such time as their objections were paid heed to' (Green, 2014, para 21). Despite the various policy obligations of the judiciary and lawyers described here, intermediaries find that when communication problems arise, most interventions fall to them.

Principles of intermediary intervention

> 'The key is thinking on your feet but not shooting from the hip.' (Intermediary)

> 'Intervention is an art, not a science.' (Intermediary)

Intermediaries' decisions on whether or not to intervene require concentration and split-second timing. They stress: "Don't underestimate how hard it is to jump in." They must weigh up the risk of putting off the witness by interrupting against the harm caused by questions that may produce unreliable answers. Many describe themselves as intervening "too little" or "less than colleagues" but accurate comparisons are difficult as they rarely observe one another's practice at court. Nevertheless, differences in their approach are apparent: some intervene in questioning from the outset if they see the need. Others tend to hold back.

For 'early interveners', "jumping in promptly is justified because you cannot wind back the clock". They are concerned about the consequences of failing to flag up the first inappropriate question, even if it is relatively innocuous. They wish to be consistent from the start: "It can be hard to justify your later interventions if, early on, you fail to show concern and then suddenly start to intervene when the questions become more evidentially significant"; "If you wait to intervene the witness can be bamboozled." If an agreed ground rule is breached, some may interrupt even before the advocate reaches the end of the question:

> 'It's a matter of me getting in before the witness answers. If I let something go because it seems okay, the second time it may not be okay for the witness, but a precedent has been set so the defence could object if I intervene for the same reason later.'

Those intermediaries who tend to 'wait and see' apply different principles. Even if initial questions are problematic, they prefer to let lawyers get into their stride and allow witnesses to settle into listening to and answering questions because the witness "may be self-conscious and doesn't want to look foolish in front of the jury". This gives the court an opportunity to observe how the witness responds and sometimes reveals witnesses who cope better with questions at court than they did during the intermediary's assessment. But even the 'wait and see' group are aware of possible drawbacks: "The trouble is, it's a gut feeling and the decision has to be so quick." Sometimes alternative communication strategies fail to work because the intermediary waited too long to suggest their use. Even for experienced intermediaries, deciding when to intervene can be "a constant source of angst".

Most interventions are made without explicit reference to the intermediary's report or ground rules. Nevertheless, some intermediaries, including several in the 'wait and see' group, find it harder to intervene if they have no explicit foundation for the objection. In contrast, 'early interveners' do not feel so constrained. They stress that it is simply not feasible to anticipate every type of problem that may affect communication at trial; some include a statement to this effect in their reports. Golightly, for example, intervenes irrespective of whether a concern has previously been discussed: "Cross-examination can place a high cognitive demand on the witness, with context, emotion and fatigue all having the potential to make communication variable with a marked impact on how language is processed and understood."

Intermediary interventions: advocates' language

> [V]ery often the forensic techniques used to challenge the account being given by RB or to seek to demonstrate inconsistency are in reality examples of questioning where the questioners failed sufficiently to adapt their questions in order to take account of RB's difficulties in communication. (*R v IA and Others* [2013] EWCA 1308, para 64)

Intermediaries aim to ensure that questions posed to a vulnerable witness are short and simple, contain one idea and are expressed in familiar vocabulary. Chapter Ten explains why intermediary reports may conclude that leading questions with tag endings or in the form of statements are likely to affect the reliability of a vulnerable person's responses; Chapter Twelve explores judicial restrictions on 'putting the case' to a witness through use of such questions.

If advocates adapt their questions according to the intermediary's recommendations, there is little need for the intermediary to intervene. However, the accuracy and completeness of responses can be subverted in many ways, either inadvertently or by design. All of the following are common recommendations in intermediary reports and, if ignored at trial, are likely to be the subject of intermediary interventions. They also fall within the scope of interventions by the judiciary and prosecutor, in policy if not in practice. (The examples are from real cases, though not all involved an intermediary.)

Multi-part questions are confusing, especially when they invite a simple 'yes' or 'no' answer: for example, "At Carl's house you didn't have any food, you didn't have any tea and you didn't have any sex. Is that right?" Moreover, to give an accurate response, the witness would have to confirm or deny all three negative assertions. In a similar vein, the following question was posed to a young teenager:

Barrister:	'Kev did not have sexual intercourse with you in your vagina or in your bottom or anywhere else, did he, no sex at all? Do you agree or disagree?'
Witness:	'No.'
Barrister:	'When you first went to Kev's house ...'
Intermediary:	'Your Honour, could we please clarify what the "no" was? Is it, "No, you're wrong" or "No, he didn't"?'

Questions are also more complex if padded with redundancies, for example "To your knowledge ..." and "I put it to you ..." or, if asked in the passive voice, "Were you to have been taken to Jim's house that day?" Negatives also make a question harder to process. While judges are alert to confusion caused by double negatives ("Isn't it the case that you weren't touched ..."), even single negatives are harder to process ("I suggest that he didn't touch you") than their affirmative counterparts ("Did he touch you?"), as are negative forms ('inappropriate', 'unhappy') and concealed negatives ('unless').

Failure to specify names and places frequently results in misinterpretation: "How often did *he* ask you to go *there*?" (This question is even more complex for a witness who has difficulty with frequency and timing.) Questions that jump around in time are confusing, as when a lawyer asked: "When was the last time you say he did this to you before the one we have been speaking of? We have been speaking of just one in February, obviously, when was the last time you say he interfered with you before that?" An intermediary would ask for this to be broken up, with questions asked in chronological order.

Figurative language is problematic for those who interpret literally. "Are you close to Jane?" was asked of a child with autism, who answered "No, she's not here." An adult with autism was asked: "Did you get cold feet in the middle?" After looking at her feet and stomach, she answered: "I haven't got cold anything." A four-year-old who was asked: "Have you ever seen a blue movie?" thought the question was about the children's channel 'CBeebies' (children of this age cannot reliably process questions about 'ever' and 'any').

Intermediaries are alert to apparently simple words with the potential for misinterpretation. For example 'touch', a crucial word in the context of sexual offences, can be understood in different ways. A four-year-old who was asked "Did he touch you?" answered "No. He washed me on my private, everywhere." A six-year-old asked the same question also replied "no" but in response to a later question said: "He licked me." Interpretation of 'active' touching may differ, for example the question "Did you touch John?" was answered "No" but the same child later said: "He put his willy in my hand and in my mouth."

Any of these formulations make processing questions more difficult. A single question may offend on several counts, as in this extract of cross-examination of a seven-year-old who was giving evidence in respect of an alleged sexual assault against another child:

Barrister:	'I put it to you that because of the absence of light in the room, it was not possible for you to have seen what you say you saw, was it?'
Intermediary:	'Your Honour, that's a long and complex question.'
Judge:	'Counsel, please rephrase.'

Barrister:	'I put it to you that you did not see John doing any of those things, did you?'
Intermediary:	'Your Honour, that's a negative and tagged question.'
Judge:	'Counsel, please rephrase.'
Barrister:	'Did you see John doing those things?'
Witness:	'John was doing those things. I did know.'
Barrister:	'But if as you say it was dark outside, and if as you say there was no light on in the room, it would not have been possible for you to see what was happening on the bottom bunk, would it?'
Judge:	'Counsel, you must ask one question at a time.'
Barrister:	'If it was dark, you could not see what John was doing, could you?'
Intermediary:	'Your Honour, that's a negative tagged question.'
Judge:	'Counsel, you must make your questions simple and untagged.'
Barrister:	'How did you know what John was doing?'
Witness:	'Well, John was doing the willy in the private thing to her, so the bunk beds were going like this' [shows with hands, up and down and side to side]. 'Jigging.'

Intermediary interventions are not restricted to defence cross-examination; they may also be necessary during questioning by prosecutors. Lawyers are not permitted to ask leading questions of their own witnesses so, at least in theory, the prosecutor's questions should be more straightforward. This is not invariably the case. Like defence lawyers, those who prosecute may experience difficulties in simplifying their style (bearing in mind that independent advocates may prosecute one day and defend the next, in contrast to CPS in-house lawyers who only prosecute). Roadrunner describes one prosecuting barrister as "extraordinary. Her questions were highly complex, muddling the witness better than the defence could have done." An intermediary has also had to intervene when a prosecuting barrister contravened policy prohibiting advocates from asking witnesses to demonstrate intimate touching on their own body (Criminal Practice Direction 3E.6, 2015). Alternative methods for addressing this type of question are described in Chapter Five.

Rephrasing the advocate's questions

Following an intermediary intervention, judges often give the advocate one opportunity to reword a question and, if the advocate still cannot remedy the problem, the intermediary is invited to rephrase. It is relatively straightforward for the intermediary to suggest a word more familiar to the witness but rephrasing a question in the heat of the moment, without changing the content, requires a quick response under pressure: a few lawyers observe that intermediaries are sometimes unable to offer alternatives. Rephrasing can be particularly stressful when combined with other intermediary tasks. Hermione worked with D, whose speech was almost unintelligible, in a live link room where the sound quality was poor. Hermione needed to repeat everything that D said "and, in addition, many questions needed to be reworded. This was very intense and involved immense concentration on my part." While some intermediaries are comfortable with rephrasing, others actively avoid it: "I'm fearful of losing my concentration for a moment and not being fast enough;" "It can be hard as the moment is often particularly stressed, and because of the need to suggest something which will be legally acceptable."

Frequency of intervention and the need for the intermediary to rephrase comes down, in the end, to the abilities of the lawyer. We observed a youth court trial in which the intermediary intervened in almost every question asked by a prosecuting barrister who was taking a hearing-impaired teenager through her evidence-in-chief over the live link. Difficulties were apparent from the outset. The witness, who relied heavily on lip-reading, could not see the mouth of the prosecution barrister, who looked down to read from his papers. Despite frequent requests from the intermediary and the magistrates, he did not raise his head to face the camera. (This problem aside, the live link is unsuitable for someone reliant on lip-reading, which requires face-to-face proximity.) The intermediary therefore had to relay the prosecutor's questions to the witness. The prosecutor ignored her recommendations for questions to be short and simple so the intermediary also had to rephrase them:

Barrister: 'It was about 1 pm. What was the weather
               condition? Was it sunny, rainy, foggy, what
               was the situation, what was it like?'
Intermediary: 'What was the weather like?'

In our observation, the intermediary was forced into such a proactive role because of the prosecutor's inability to ask simple questions as recommended by the intermediary and to look at the camera while speaking.

Intermediary interventions: witness answers

'The witness had a bad speech defect. The jury would not have understood him. We could not have got the evidence out without the intermediary.' (Prosecutor)

The intermediary role as a facilitator of communication covers answers as well as questions (Youth Justice and Criminal Evidence Act 1999, section 29(2)). They routinely relay responses that are very quiet or unintelligible; read out written or typed replies from nonverbal witnesses; or speak the answers given by witnesses who use visual aids or gestures.

Intervention is appropriate if a pattern of responses suggests that the witness is beginning to acquiesce or to lose attention. During the evidence of S, Alexa intervened when S began to look inattentive and confused, repeating "I'm not sure" and "I don't remember":

'The judge sent out the jury and firmly reminded me that I wasn't there to interpret S's answers. I confirmed that I understood this and explained my reason for intervening, which the judge accepted. Following this, he decided that S was tired and that cross-examination should stop and resume the following day.'

Intervention by the intermediary is necessary where the witness's answer indicates the question was misunderstood. This example comes from cross-examination of a six-year-old witness who had just been asked where her grandparents lived:

Barrister: 'Does your mother have a different address?'
Witness: 'I don't think she does.'
Intermediary: 'It may help to use the word "house".'
Barrister: 'Thank you very much. Does mummy have a different house?'
Witness: 'Yes, she has a flat.'

Some witnesses blurt out their replies, not giving the intermediary time to raise a query about the question until after the answer has been given. Roadrunner worked with E, who tended to give automatic responses, without thought:

'E quickly answered the first part of a multi-part question but I knew she wasn't dealing with the whole of it. I intervened because I didn't want a precedent to be set. The judge said E's response had to be noted, but asked the defence to rephrase question in simple, single questions. E then answered each question, giving a different answer to the first one, consistent with her previous evidence.'

The position is most contentious where the answer queried by the intermediary is a departure from the witness's previous testimony and is therefore favourable to the cross-examiner. The defence may challenge the intervention as partisan. Hazeley worked with H, aged seven, when the advocate switched topics without signposting the change of subject. H replied: "Nothing happened." Hazeley intervened because it appeared to her that he was still talking about the previous subject, but she was told cross-examination was finished:

'It looked as if I was only intervening because of H's "admission". I don't think the court realised that he was still talking about something else. This was incredibly frustrating. I didn't expect the turn the very last question would take and I was not quick enough.'

One of the few concerns about intermediary interventions voiced to us by an advocate related to a question that the advocate felt the witness had "clearly understood and answered" and that the intermediary had objected "on the basis that it was a tag rather than whether it was understood. The intermediary was therefore undermined." Such comments explain why intermediaries find it difficult to intervene after an answer has been given. In our view, however, intermediaries cannot be silent and rely on the prosecutor to correct a possible misunderstanding at the end of cross-examination. The prosecutor may be unaware that the question has possibly been misunderstood.

Intermediary interventions: judicial language

'It's because of gremlins in the live link equipment.' (Judge, apologising to an eight-year-old witness for a delayed start to his evidence)

When judges interrupt cross-examination to ask evidential questions of the witness, it is generally because an advocate is struggling to be understood or an issue needs to be clarified. Judicial questions tend to be more direct and developmentally appropriate than those asked by advocates but they are necessarily asked without preparation, which can result in a lack of clarity. Interrupting a judge is more daunting than intervening during an advocate's questions but may nevertheless be necessary if there is a possibility of miscommunication. For instance, wording a question for those on the autism spectrum can be challenging because of their literal interpretation. We observed a case in which the intermediary intervened in questions to J, a 10-year-old with autism. The judge then asked a sequence of questions but his language was replete with figures of speech, such as: "Do you follow?" He also said: "I am trying to help jog your memory. I am trying to paint you a picture." J laughed at the word 'jog', and his face lit up at the mention of 'paint', the first thing he seemed to have grasped clearly in several minutes. He then reverted to looking puzzled when the promised picture did not materialise. The intermediary intervened in several of the judge's questions.

All judges speak to witnesses at the start of questioning to give them instructions and help put them at ease. If the language is complex, the witness may be confused even before questioning begins. Delays have been explained to a vulnerable witness because of "an interminable wait for a transcript". Another was told by the judge "If you have a problem, don't hesitate to ask Y, the intermediary," which was understood by the witness as "Don't ask Y" (another example of why a negative makes a sentence harder to process). Golightly recalls a judge speaking over the live link to W, a woman with a significant learning disability and poor level of comprehension:

> 'He said "You don't need to be too concerned about what I am doing right now … I'm just adjusting the camera angle and positioning the camera so that only the appropriate people are within view." (Not even a "Hello.") The witness looked towards me; and I said "That's the judge … he's making sure his picture on his telly is okay."'

Most intermediaries opt not to interrupt the judge while instructions are given: "If the language is not about the evidence, it is a careful balance between being regarded as disruptive and irritating and assisting the court and the witness." Instead, when the judge has finished speaking, the intermediary may ask to check the witness's understanding and explain if necessary. It is easier if there is an opportunity for the judge to give explanations to the witness before formalities begin (see Chapter Nine).

Judicial interventions

> I was 'powerless to stop a barrage of hostile questioning during the trial'. (Mr Justice Kay, at the end of an eight-month trial of a paedophile ring, *Daily Telegraph*, 10 August 1994)

> We have to get the message across: old habits die hard, but die they must ... The old-style methods of cross-examination have to be outlawed. (Judge Peter Rook QC, 'Lawyers must stop court humiliation of sex victims', *The Times*, 14 June 2014)

It was a long-standing practice that judges did not interfere with cross-examination, even when there was cause to do so. Writing 20 years ago, we reported comments from judges who 'feel they cannot curtail cross-examination where the child clearly does not understand the questions' (Plotnikoff and Woolfson, 1995, p 98). Studies of transcripts from that period compared cross-examination and judicial interventions in cases involving witnesses with learning disabilities and 'ordinary' witnesses; the comparison found no significant differences in the way the two groups were questioned and no increase in judicial intervention where witnesses had learning disabilities (O'Kelly et al, 2003; Kebbell et al, 2004). Even where specialist education was provided to judges and prosecutors in Australia, children were still subjected to complex questioning and judicial intervention varied (Cashmore and Trimboli, 2005).

One illustration of judicial non-intervention concerns the treatment of 'previous sexual history' evidence. Legislation was introduced to restrict the questioning of rape complainants about their sexual experience and relationships with someone other than the defendant; this is now prohibited unless a judge rules that exceptions apply (Youth Justice and Criminal Evidence Act 1999, sections 41–43). Written applications to admit such evidence must be made before the trial, specifying which exception applies and the questions the defence wishes to ask. The intention is to provide both judge and prosecution with the opportunity to assess and, if appropriate, challenge the application.

A Home Office study found that most previous sexual history applications did not fulfil statutory requirements as they were delayed until trial and made orally (Kelly et al, 2006). Training in the management of previous sexual history matters is now a central plank of Judicial College serious sex offences training. While observing in court in recent years, we have seen some instances of judges allowing oral applications just before cross-examination. It is not known whether this practice is still common.

Leadership and the shift in judicial practice

Following the introduction of new vulnerable witness training in 2014, intermediaries report that judges are increasingly exercising their powers to manage inappropriate cross-examination and referring in court to messages from the Judicial College. However, active control of cross-examination is not yet the norm (one senior judge said: "It's too late to send me on the 'super sex' course" – the colloquial name for the new seminar).

A common concern about persistent judicial intervention in the face of poor cross-examination practice is a fear of perceived bias if the case goes to the Court of Appeal. However, members of the Court of Appeal often speak on Judicial College courses to offer support for robust case management. Lady Justice Hallett, Vice President of the Court of Appeal Criminal Division, emphasises that:

> The trial judge is responsible for controlling questioning and ensuring that vulnerable witnesses and defendants are enabled to give the best evidence they can. The judge has a duty to intervene, therefore, if an advocate's questioning is confusing or inappropriate ... Advocates must adapt to the witness, not the other way round. (*R v Lubemba, R v JP* [2014] EWCA Crim 2064, paras 44–45)

In *Lubemba*, the trial judge had 'interrupted 11 times at most' (para 37).

Feedback from judges, intermediaries and lawyers suggests there are significant variations between individual judicial styles and readiness to intervene. Intermediaries observe that even intervention-minded judges are most likely to act in relation to relatively straightforward problems such as double negatives, questions with a tag ending and multi-part questions. Other strategies which undermine the witness's credibility, such as a disbelieving tone of voice, usually go unchallenged. Judges often perceive a limit to the number of times they can intervene. A senior judge described the fine line between appropriate control and interference as follows:

> 'You can only interrupt or send the jury out so many times. If I interrupt four out of seven questions, I can't do it again ... [and even if poor practice is brought to the attention of the head of chambers] they come back and do it in exactly the same way. Their role is to get the client off and they will.' (Plotnikoff and Woolfson, 2011)

This perception was still current during Emily Henderson's interviews in 2013. Her respondents acknowledged that advocates took advantage of weak judges; one advocate commented in despair: 'Again and again I hear [judges] say "I intervened five times and I can't do it again." But if you have reason to intervene then how is that?' (Henderson, 2015a, forthcoming). Almost all of Henderson's 25 judicial interviewees acknowledged the existence in their courts of a small group of advocates who were recalcitrant 'through ignorance, incompetence or intention'; the judges felt that intervening in cross-examination was possibly the most difficult aspect of their role and many acknowledged that, in practice, they rarely did so (Henderson, 2015a, forthcoming). Many of her barrister interviewees complained that 'judges are still not interventionist enough' (Henderson, 2015b, forthcoming).

In his *Review of Efficiency in Criminal Proceedings*, Sir Brian Leveson observed that despite 'ample scope' to do so, judges 'rarely exercised' their powers to timetable or control questioning (2015, para 280). He recommended that court power be 'specifically and unambiguously' extended 'to prevent repetitious or otherwise unnecessary evidence and to control prolix, irrelevant or oppressive questioning of witnesses' (para 264).

Judges working with intermediaries

One manifestation of a changing judicial style is the way some judges work in tandem with the intermediary. This example is from cross-examination of a six-year-old:

Barrister:	'Just one thing that I need to mention, to say to you before moving on. If I say that M was not in the bathroom with you, would that be telling a lie?'
Intermediary:	'That is a difficult question. It has several parts to it.'
Judge:	'Do you mean while she was washing her hands?'
Barrister:	'Yes.'
Judge:	'Just ask her "Are you sure M was in the bathroom when you washed your hands?"'
Barrister:	'Are you sure if M was in the bathroom when you washed your hands?'
Witness:	'Yes, I am sure.'

When a communication problem arises, more judges are seizing the initiative to remind advocates of ground rules and intervening even before the intermediary begins to speak. Jeeves recalls a judge who refused the defence advocate's request at trial to ask "just a few 'time' questions". The judge responded: "These are exactly the type of questions the intermediary said you shouldn't ask, so no, I am not going to let you ask them."

Golightly acted as intermediary for C, an 18-year-old whose Asperger syndrome had only been recently diagnosed. C had little understanding of what her condition meant; the intermediary had therefore recommended that C not be asked about it. The advocate's opening question was: "So, C, you have a diagnosis of high functioning Asperger's. Can you explain to us how this impacts upon your ability to form social relationships?" The judge and intermediary intervened simultaneously to clarify that the nature of C's needs made it impossible for her to answer.

Where the judiciary agrees with intermediary interventions, this should be made clear to the advocates. In a case described by Hazeley, the judge spoke to her privately:

> 'The advocate was persistently breaking the rules, becoming very irate with my interventions and sounding angry. The judge told me to continue intervening as much as possible, that he was determined the questioning would be done correctly. Although this was good, I was disappointed that it was not done in front of the advocate and the rest of the court.'

Some judges withhold criticism from advocates even when problems flagged by the intermediary exploit the vulnerable witness's developmental limitations. We observed a ground rules hearing where the intermediary had recommended that N, an adult witness with an IQ in the mid-50s, should not take the oath ("… that the evidence I shall give …") because she would not understand all the words. The QC argued against this and demanded in addition the right to put questions to demonstrate to the jury that N was easily confused: "Even if you don't get a productive answer, that's not a reason not to ask a question." The judge made no comment.

At trial, N was required to take the oath. The QC's first question to her was "What does the word 'evidence' mean?" The intermediary intervened to say that N did not understand the word but the judge ignored the intervention and allowed this and many other developmentally inappropriate questions to go unchallenged. (The defendant was acquitted.) Such a passive judicial style leaves intermediaries having to decide whether to persist in their interventions or give up if the lawyer does not respond.

Overlapping responsibilities to intervene

'A system is an assembly of interacting parts: the biggest problems arise at the interfaces.' (Anonymous)

We have seen that judges and advocates have specific responsibilities to intervene where questioning is unfair, unreasonable, aggressive or offensive or otherwise 'inappropriate'. If advocates and the judiciary fail to exercise their responsibilities, intermediaries are put in an invidious position. They recognise the problem but the duty to address it is not theirs.

The first suite of toolkits on *The Advocate's Gateway* website included the following statement approved by the senior judiciary: 'Questioning that contravenes principles for obtaining accurate information from a witness by exploiting his or her developmental limitations is not conducive to a fair trial and would contravene the [professions'] Codes of Conduct.' Intermediaries provided numerous examples of questioning that could be classified as exploitative.

Questioning that is 'unreasonable' or 'unfair'

Cross-examination that is 'unreasonable' or 'unfair' should be prevented (Ministry of Justice, 2013b, Standard 16). Questions have been permitted that are, on the face of it, unreasonable. Maria was recently appointed for two young children. The alleged offences had taken place 18 months to two years previously.

> 'It was not possible for either child to remember details about when the offences had taken place. Questions were asked about whether one waved to her friend passing the window and if the other visited her nanny in the pub where she worked on the day in August 18 months ago when she was at "grandad's house". In both cases, the questioning was frankly ridiculous. It is not my role to point out that these little children could not possibly remember these details but inside I am shouting.'

Questions have been permitted even after an intermediary pointed out that they were beyond the witness's abilities and were therefore, by definition, unfair. An intermediary who tried to alert the judge to the witness's lack of understanding of questions about 'time' was told: "You are not allowed to give evidence." Hazeley worked with T, a woman with a moderate learning disability:

'In his cross-examination, the defence barrister was allowed to highlight T's confusion with dates and times, although I had stated in my report that this was an unreliable area for her. Part of the cross-examination went back many years and her answers showed some confusion. The defendant was found not guilty, and the police officer told me afterwards that the confusion with dates led to T being viewed as not credible.'

Alexa felt that information she supplied about D was used by the defence barrister to mislead the jury about the witness's abilities:

'The advocate read my report and asked me to write a short synopsis describing the witness's educational needs. I did so. She began cross-examination by asking D if he went to the local school, if he was doing exams and if he planned to go to college. He proudly answered that he was doing all of these things. Actually, D was in the lowest ability set and had been supported in a group of eight pupils and two teachers for most of his time at school. He was taking the lowest level exams with limited expectations and was going to college to do a life skills programme. I felt that the barrister manipulated the information I gave her to reinterpret the witness's abilities for the jury. I didn't feel able to challenge any of this as all the questions had been posed entirely appropriately.'

'Offensive' or 'aggressive' questions

'Aggressive' or 'offensive' cross-examination should be stopped (Ministry of Justice, 2013a, p 20; Ministry of Justice, 2013b, Standard 16). Questioning has been permitted that was experienced by the witness as offensive. Barristers have a duty not to abuse their role and this includes an obligation not to 'make statements or ask questions merely to insult, humiliate or annoy a witness' (Bar Standards Board Handbook, 2014, rule C7.1). Tosca's assessment of N, a woman in her late 50s with Asperger syndrome, found that although N needed strategies to control her anxiety, she could respond reliably to tagged questions. The defence barrister asked N a series of questions such as: "You aren't stupid … [long pause], are you?", to which N replied "Well, I must be." N said to the intermediary: "This is sick" and "I feel dirty, I want a wash." The judge and prosecution did not intervene but although the intermediary thought the questioning was 'bullying" she felt she could do nothing "as defence counsel was not breaking any recommendations".

Intermediaries find it hard to challenge some strategies that impede communication but are not apparent in a trial transcript. Tone of voice of an authority figure at court can have a powerful impact. In *Measuring Up?*, half of the young witnesses described cross-examiners as "aggressive", "sarcastic", "rude" or "cross"; they also complained about the fast pace of questions (Plotnikoff and Woolfson, 2009a, p 107). In South Africa the intermediary acts as interlocutor and relays all questions to the young witness who neither sees nor hears the cross-examiner. This distances children from a potential cause of stress.

In interviews following intermediary pilot trials, judges invariably failed to identify difficulties caused to witnesses by the pace and tone of cross-examination (Plotnikoff and Woolfson, 2007a). According to intermediaries, this is still a common difficulty, as is a soft, persuasive tone when it encourages acquiescence. (Valuable insights can be obtained by listening to the voice recordings of questioning at trial from which transcripts are prepared: the Court of Appeal occasionally does this, for example in *R v Wills* [2011] EWCA Crim 1938.)

A barrister with over 30 years' experience in child protection found that working with intermediaries made her appreciate the effect of an advocate's manner:

'It never occurred to me that some witnesses may be affected by the loudness of the questioner's voice, which may upset them and make them feel they are being harangued. It's helpful to be told that this may need to be "toned down" for particular witnesses.'

Facial expression or body language (for example, a nodding advocate who seeks an answer in the affirmative) can also have a detrimental effect on communication. Inappropriate mannerisms include where "the lawyer adopted a world-weary manner and addressed all his questions to the ceiling" and one simply described as: "Tut, blow, roll eyes, sigh." Shelley requested a meeting with the judge and advocates where, although defence counsel's questions were asked "in a fairly calm way", his facial expression "conveyed irritation, frustration and impatience":

> 'The witness (mis)interpreted this as him being angry with her, which had a profound effect on her ability to think and respond. Defence counsel explained to me that his irritation was directly solely at the judge who was not letting him question as he had planned. The witness "crumbled" and was only persuaded to continue giving evidence once she was reassured that no-one was angry with her, helped by a significant change in the body language of counsel.'

Intermediaries should alert the court to any factor that may affect the quality of communication. Sylvia was concerned about the potential adverse impact of questions revealing a witness's transgender status; this was likely to be perceived as offensive by the witness, resulting in closing down answers. The intermediary's report did not disclose this sensitive information, referring only to how the witness might respond if asked about emotive topics and to consider this in the schedule of questioning, but the intermediary raised it in discussion before the trial.

Accusing the witness of lying

Accusing the witness of lying may be considered 'inappropriate' (Ministry of Justice, 2013a, p 20), 'unfair' or 'unreasonable' (Ministry of Justice, 2013b, Standard 16) depending on the witness and the circumstances. Telling the truth but not being believed is particularly stressful for vulnerable witnesses; children regard it as one of life's most stressful occurrences (Yamamoto et al, 1987). Emotional arousal can cause the witness to give inaccurate answers or to agree with the suggestion that they are lying simply to bring questioning to an end (Schuman et al, 1999). Guidance states that:

> Allegations of misconduct by a witness may not be made unless the legal representative has reasonable grounds for making them. Some legal representatives routinely ask child witnesses 'Do you tell lies?' but this is a practice that ought to be avoided unless the legal representative has grounds for thinking that the witness is an habitual liar (other than the fact that the witness's evidence contradicts that of the defendant). (Ministry of Justice, 2011a, para 5.17)

In response to highly publicised cases in which vulnerable witnesses were accused of lying throughout cross-examination, Judicial College guidance states that an assertion that the witness is lying or confused:

> should be addressed separately, in simple language, at the end of cross-examination. Repeated assertions to a young or vulnerable witness that (s)he is lying are likely to cause the witness serious distress. They do not serve any proper evidential purpose and should not be permitted. (Judicial College, 2013, chapter 5, para 64i)

Intermediaries cite many examples of vulnerable witnesses who have become distraught through even a single accusation of lying. Melissa worked with D, a 10-year-old with significant developmental and language delay:

> 'D provided detailed evidence in cross-examination in a calm and clear way. It ended with:"Just one more question. You're lying aren't you? You're just making

this up. You didn't want to get into trouble for being late home" [a developmentally inappropriate tag question, followed by two assertions]. D answered in a very little voice, pointing at the screen, "If he says I'm lying, he must be right." There were no further questions. D then became hysterical, collapsed on the floor and sobbed for a long time. I was left wondering how I could have intervened to get the question changed.'

Intermediaries are entitled to advise the court about anything that may distress a vulnerable witness, including how the witness may react to an accusation of lying. This should be routinely addressed in intermediary reports; for example, one intermediary advised the court that the witness so accused was likely to wet herself. It should also be a routine consideration at the ground rules hearing (as is the case when section 28 pre-trial cross-examination procedures are invoked – see Chapter Twelve). In respect of multi-defendant trials, one judge told us that he will allow only one advocate to suggest that the vulnerable witness is not telling the truth. In some circumstances, however, the judge will not permit the assertion to be put to the witness even once (*R v Edwards* [2011] EWCA Crim 3028). We have seen a judge at a ground rules hearing emphasise this to counsel: "It is never appropriate to call a child a liar. 'Did he really do it?' is as far as you need to go."

The 'stinger' question

Exploitation of a vulnerable witness's developmental limitations becomes acute in what is sometimes known as the 'stinger' question. The advocate obtains the desired answer and sits down: cross-examination is over. Many vulnerable witnesses are especially susceptible to a string of relatively innocuous questions inviting a series of 'yes' or 'no' answers, followed by the crucial question asked last. A compliant witness may be able to respond accurately to a single tag question yet acquiesce and agree with the questioner after being cued to answer a sequence. In a case involving a six-year-old witness, the defence counsel told Maria that although he would mostly avoid tag questions, he could always "throw in the stinger at the end". We have seen a senior trainer suggest this as an appropriate response to an intermediary's recommendation advising against tag questions: "The odd tag question here or there doesn't matter. Put your case and finish with: 'It didn't happen, did it?' Even if the child doesn't answer, silence is what you want the jury to hear."

'Stinger' questions are particularly hard for the intermediary to deal with and they report that judges also seem deterred from intervening once an answer has been given, especially if cross-examination is then ended. Only one of 25 judges interviewed recently was prepared to reopen questioning once defence counsel had concluded:

> [T]here are those situations where the defence counsel gets a very favourable answer to a question which I don't believe the witness fully understood, because the question was too complicated, but it's at odds with their other evidence. Often counsel will sit down, [but] I've got no compunction in reopening the question. (Henderson, 2015b, forthcoming)

The judge did not intervene in any of the following three examples where intermediaries were unhappy about the lack of a clear answer to the final question asked of the witness. Melissa was appointed for P, a pre-school child, who had given "very clear" answers about what had happened and who had done it. Counsel's final question was ambiguous: "Was mummy there?" P answered "yes" before Melissa could ask the barrister to clarify the location. The defence case was that P's mother was in the room where the offence occurred, but P's reply could equally have meant that she was in the house. The intermediary felt that she should have intervened, "but I didn't. Unfortunately, no amount of training can prepare you for these split-second decisions." In the second example, Golightly was the intermediary for G, aged five, who was asked only one cross-examination question: "Did your cousin tell you to say this?" G agreed and questioning was over: "I should have intervened to ask that we explore her understanding, whether her cousin said 'tell' what happened or that her cousin 'told her what to say'."

The final question put to M, a teenager with learning difficulties, was "Did you tell the boy in the white T-shirt that you did not want sex?" M responded "No," an answer which could have meant either that she had no such conversation or that she told the boy 'no'. The advocate said "No further questions," before Poppy could ask him to simplify the question: "The judge ignored my hand and let the question go."

Intermezzo

Pre-recorded cross-examination of Faye, aged four, and the tight squeeze

Golightly (registered intermediary)

I was appointed as the intermediary for Faye, a four-year-old witness whose cross-examination was filmed before trial as part of a pilot scheme [see Chapter Twelve]. The judge and both counsel were fully on board and there was a very constructive discussion at the ground rules hearing. Defence counsel had prepared a small number of questions using my report and recommendations from *The Advocate's Gateway*; the questions were openly shared. There was a discussion as to whether Faye would have the ability to distinguish between 'inside' and 'outside' in relation to sexual offences alleging penetration. This had not been clarified or explored fully during the police interview, which was conducted without an intermediary. Use of various communication aids to explore her understanding were considered but it was decided that this element of the alleged offence should not be pursued, resulting in a change of counts in the indictment.

I recommended in my report that Faye be questioned face-to-face by counsel in the live link room. Recording equipment for the pilot scheme had been set up in the smallest link room in the court and there was concern that it might not be possible to fit everyone in. In the event, face-to-face cross-examination was agreed by the judge, but it was a very tight squeeze and unlikely to suit larger witnesses or those needing more space.

It was worthwhile having the judge view the facilities. He was appalled by the dingy, bare rooms assigned for the hearing and requested that court staff consider how they could be made more child friendly. When Faye arrived the area was filled with posters, toys and child-sized furniture.

Both advocates met Faye twice, during her familiarisation visit to the court and again before the pilot hearing. The judge met her on the morning of the hearing. These meetings were very useful and child friendly. The lawyers and judge picked up on Faye's interests, which we had discussed during the ground rules hearing. This helped to build her confidence. It was agreed that her aunt could accompany her during questioning. I had made a booklet for Faye so she was aware of what would happen and what toys she would play with while being questioned. A small room opposite the live link room was made available for her parents to sit in. The door in the live link room was left open; Faye knew that she could leave to find her parents if she wished. Faye appeared comfortable during cross-examination and did not need to leave the room.

Both counsel, Faye, myself and her aunt sat at small-sized furniture arranged in a horseshoe shape. The judge watched from the courtroom. Defence counsel had asked that I introduce the topic of cross-examination, for example, "Thomas wants to ask you about ...", at a point where I felt Faye was adequately settled and attending well. Questioning was completely based around play into which a small number of questions were interspersed. Defence counsel tended to ask two to three questions at a time, allowing the witness to return to play as her attention reduced. This worked well for Faye, who liked to take an active role in play and conversation, rather than follow questions posed by others. The approach felt very natural rather than 'interrogatory'.

During the ground rules hearing it had been agreed that I should intervene at any point if I felt a question needed to be rephrased, repeated or supported with the use of a doll or other aid. Everyone was keen that I intervene in a conversational, play-based manner, rather than by making a suggestion via the judge or counsel. I intervened on a number of occasions to repeat or slightly rephrase a question. For example, I regained Faye's attention and asked a question again using a framework such as "Thomas wants to know …" or "Can you show Thomas on the doll …?" Faye sometimes spontaneously pointed to her own body or used a phrase, such as "my bits", but on other occasions used a rag doll with removable clothing to show 'on top of' or 'under' clothing. Defence counsel did not depart from the questions agreed at the ground rules hearing and the prosecutor did not ask any follow-up questions after cross-examination. Towards the end of the cross-examination, I did not intervene to repeat one of Faye's answers that had been very quiet as it was clear that the answer had been heard by those in the live link room. However, it turned out that her answer was not heard in the courtroom and may not have been evident on the recording.

Faye's parents were anxious about their daughter giving evidence. Explaining the measures that could be put in place to support Faye helped, in part, to alleviate their anxieties. I felt that Faye had a positive experience of being at court. Having a child-friendly judge and barristers, and face-to-face questioning made a big contribution to ensuring that the process did not feel so alien for her. I had proposed quite drastic adaptations to cross-examination; the judge gave them careful thought and asserted that the court would make it work. (Following the section 28 recording, it was decided that there was insufficient evidence for this case to proceed to trial.)

TWELVE

Cross-examination:
challenges at the cutting edge

Since special measures were introduced by the Youth Justice and
Criminal Evidence Act 1999, courts have implemented a raft of
changes to help vulnerable witnesses give their best evidence.
The process has acquired new momentum and scope through
the input of intermediaries. The most recent of the changes
are also the most profound; they involve reshaping the core of
conventional cross-examination.

Three of the ways cross-examination is changing are dealt
with in this chapter. All have emerged or developed significantly
during the period of writing this book: none has yet reached
a 'steady state'. The first involves the defence disclosing cross-
examination questions to the court, and sometimes even the
prosecutor (until recently, unthinkable), and subjecting them
to possible revision by the judge and the intermediary (until
recently, unimaginable).

The second issue relates to the development of practice, in
light of Court of Appeal decisions, around restrictions on defence
lawyers 'putting their case' to the witness. There is a sharp divide
between the objective of cross-examination as defined by the
justice system and that perceived by many defence practitioners.
This chapter explores the resulting tension, its impact on cross-
examination and some unanticipated effects on 'best evidence'
that remain to be addressed.

The final issue concerns a pilot project to pre-record cross-
examination before trial. Section 28 of the Youth Justice and
Criminal Evidence Act 1999 is the last special measure of the
Act to be implemented. It was first proposed by Judge Pigot

over 25 years ago (Home Office, 1989). Used in combination with provisions to admit the film of the police interview as evidence-in-chief (Criminal Justice Act 1988, section 32A, as amended), this allows the whole of the witness's evidence to be captured before the trial and played again at a retrial if that proves necessary. Implementation was delayed due to strong resistance, in part because of anticipated difficulties in expediting the prosecution's pre-trial disclosure to the defence of material that might assist the defence case.

Western Australia introduced pre-recording of cross-examination for young witnesses in 1992 (Jackson, 2012). This is done routinely for those under 10 and is often granted for older children on prosecution applications supported by recommendations from the Child Witness Service. Significant benefits include completing evidence more quickly than at trial (advantageous not just for younger children but for self-harming older adolescents); enabling parents to focus on the child's needs at the pre-recording while themselves giving evidence at trial; judges are better able to take witness needs into consideration; and time spent on pre-recording often saves trial time and may remove the need for a trial altogether (communication from the Child Witness Service, March 2015). The State of Victoria introduced pre-recording of cross-examination in 2006 in respect of children and cognitively impaired witnesses (communication from the judge in charge of the sexual offences list, March 2015). While concerns remain in both jurisdictions about delays before pre-recording can proceed, the process in both has been largely unproblematic.

Judge Hal Jackson's enthusiastic description of Western Australia's experience of pre-recording at a 2011 Cambridge conference triggered a resurgence of interest in section 28. However, the pilot scheme did not receive a government 'green light' until the storm of adverse publicity surrounding child sex exploitation cases in 2013.

Reviewing the advocate's questions in advance of cross-examination

'I was very impressed by the intermediary's practical and helpful suggestions at the ground rules hearing. She made clear the types of questioning that were likely to be problematic and "vetted" a draft of cross-examination at the request of the defence advocate.' (Judge)

'As defence counsel, I always type out all cross-examination. I then ask the judge for leave to sit with the intermediary and look through questions to see if they are appropriately phrased. If not, I take their recommendations on board and rephrase or reorder questions.' (Barrister)

A recent development is helping to fuel cultural change in respect of cross-examination of vulnerable witnesses. Advocacy trainers often advise lawyers to write out their questions for a vulnerable witness in advance (required when asking questions about the witness's previous sexual history: see chapter 10). In 2014, Judicial College seminars began encouraging judges to invite lawyers to submit these questions to the court for advance scrutiny. Lady Justice Hallett confirms that: 'So as to avoid any unfortunate misunderstanding at trial, it would be an entirely reasonable step for a judge at the ground rules hearing to invite defence advocates to reduce their questions to writing in advance' (*R v Lubemba, R v JP* [2014] EWCA Crim 2064, para 43).

Review of questions is an increasingly common intermediary recommendation – "I pester for time to be made available" – or judicial direction. The exercise does not mean the intermediary has 'pre-approved' questions; interventions will still be made if necessary during cross-examination. However, if the agreed format is observed, interventions are minimised. Intermediaries report many "very positive" experiences. Paige describes the opportunity to review questions as "a brilliant strategy. Rewording questions to ensure the witness understands them works very well in terms of reducing cross-examination interruptions. It also allows jurors to see that the advocate is not trying to trip up the witness."

The exercise can have other benefits. Hermione worked closely with the judge and advocates to review questions before each of two child witnesses gave evidence:

> 'Meetings with the judge and counsel facilitated the development of a working relationship between us. This allowed me to feel confident that I could intervene in certain ways that would be helpful to the court and also that counsel and judge had fully understood and agreed with the recommendations. At the first meeting, the judge made it clear that I should ask permission to intervene but could not do so until he allowed me to speak. After the second meeting, I felt able to raise this again with the judge who said it would be fine for me to intervene whenever it was necessary. This was a big shift in his initial response.'

Most judges who review questions do so working closely with the intermediary. For example, in section 28 pilot cases discussed in the final section of this chapter, some judges not only scrutinise the questions but also discuss with the intermediary what would be appropriate as alternative follow-up questions, depending on the witness's answers. However, a few judges may not yet appreciate the value of the intermediary's expertise. Melissa recently encountered a judge who asked to see the lawyer's questions for a five-year-old witness but excluded Melissa from the review process. While the children were already at court, waiting to give evidence, the judge revised defence counsel's questions and reduced the number significantly but did not simplify the content. The first question was: "If I said that K told you that if you said S did something to you, she would get some money. Do you agree?" Other questions passed by the judge were equally confusing. Melissa made a number of interventions but in the end she said she felt "completely defeated. This was a child who was perfectly capable of giving clear evidence with the help of suitable strategies."

Response of advocates

With the exception of the section 28 pilot scheme, discussed below, submitting questions to the court is not a requirement. In interviews conducted in 2013, Henderson (2015c, forthcoming) identified strong resistance from around half of the barristers she interviewed, particularly QCs. While this seems to have diminished, an intermediary's offer of advice is not always taken up. Marsha acted as intermediary for B, an eight year-old with language disorder:

> 'At two ground rules hearings, defence counsel could not suggest any questions for me for me to review. His cross-examination consisted of three questions, including: "Do you know what truth means?" and a question with a tag ending. In response to the final question, B started to say "My daddy did …" but the defence cut him off with "No further questions." The judge did not intervene. B was distressed and asked "Is that it? Why doesn't he [defence counsel] want to talk to me about what happened?" This experience was more "disabling" than "enabling".'

Where responses differ, this can result in an anomalous position in multi-defendant trials where some advocates provide their questions to the intermediary for review and others do not, or reveal only a list of topics. These differences in approach have an impact on the witness and on the need for intermediary intervention. Nevertheless, the offer of advice is often gratefully accepted, particularly where advocates have little relevant experience. Tosca acted as intermediary for N, a seven-year-old witness, where defence counsel "was happy for me to see her questions because she was not experienced at talking to young children":

> 'She proposed introducing herself to N by saying "I'm here on behalf of [the defendant]." I explained that N wouldn't understand "on behalf of" and he'd never used the defendant's name in the police interview. I

suggested that she adopted the phrase N used. I then suggested changes to questions, for example from "Where would you have been?" to "Where were you?"; and "Would you have been upstairs?" to "Were you upstairs?" Her cross-examination was short, about 10 minutes, and to the point, getting relevant information from N. The defendant was acquitted but this was of no consequence. I felt I'd done a good job and enabled the defence to ask questions in a way that N could understand.'

Golightly worked closely with defence counsel when she was appointed for three adult witnesses with varying levels of learning disability. She went through the advocate's proposed questions before each witness gave evidence. Although the advocate "was keen to get this right", at first he said that "it was still too difficult for him to completely rethink how to ask questions":

'I provided a structure and theme to the questions and showed how to introduce a new topic and then pause. I split up complex questions, changed vocabulary, simplified concepts and identified some questions that would not be understood at all, for instance, around what other people might think and feel. I changed leading questions to direct questions and showed where symbols or gesture could support communication. For example, where counsel wanted to put his client's case to the witness, we agreed a framework of how to do this and how the witnesses could use symbols to indicate if they agreed, disagreed or didn't know. With one witness, he worked with me to devise a visual schedule to show her which areas she would be questioned on, because she needed time to accept that she wouldn't be asked questions about some topics of most importance to her. I could refer her back to the visual schedule if her responses went "off topic". By the third witness, I had to change very little as counsel had learned how to adapt his language.'

As an officer of the court, the intermediary aims to assist all parties in communicating with the vulnerable person, and vice versa. The intermediary can speak to the defence or prosecution lawyer alone, though it is good practice to let the other side know. The defence representative may wish to discuss questions in the absence of the prosecutor. A defence QC explained the sensitivity:

> 'I may not be able to ask some of the questions on my list but in terms of strategy, there may be questions here that are relevant to other witnesses. The prosecutor could damage my case beyond repair if she was armed with it.'

A judge encouraged lawyers to send the intermediary their questions and was at pains to point out to the defence that she would not tell the prosecution what he was going to ask, declaring "the intermediary is a tool of the court – so use her". Some intermediaries decline to see the defence alone for fear that something they say may be taken out of context. This can, on occasion, be a realistic concern. In Elliot's first trial as an intermediary, P, the 12-year-old witness who had a significant learning disability, ran out during cross-examination and refused to start again. The judge came to the live link room to speak to P and reassure her. The judge also asked Elliot to work with the advocate on his questions but he was hostile to the advice given:

> 'I gave him examples of how to change his questions but he said he couldn't change them "as a matter of law". I said she wouldn't understand them. In court he told the judge: "The intermediary concedes the questions can't be changed." I spoke up and the judge said to him: "You have to try to change your questions." When P's cross-examination started again, I had to intervene. There was quite a lot of huffing and puffing. The judge backed me up. At the end the barrister said "I'm going to ask one more question." The judge said "No, you're not." I think it backfired

on the barrister but it was difficult for me to stand up to him.' (The defendant was convicted.)

In *R v FA* [2015] EWCA Crim 209, for the first time the Court of Appeal heard live evidence from a witness with intermediary assistance. Counsel for the appellant submitted her proposed cross-examination questions to the intermediary in advance. They were commended for working as a team 'better to promote the interests of justice in the conduct of this case' (para 13).

Departure from 'agreed' questions

Intermediaries sometimes find that the approach to questioning 'agreed' beforehand is not observed at trial. The judge asked the defence to indicate the subjects for cross-examination of Y, who had Down syndrome, so that Bonnie could prepare appropriate symbols and communication aids relating to allegations of historic sexual abuse. The judge requested that anatomically detailed dolls be made available:

> 'This was helpful in formulating a way forward and it felt like a team approach, reflecting on the needs of the vulnerable person. But my carefully prepared aids were not used. Once cross-examination started, the defence advocate switched to a completely different angle of questioning and suggested that Y had made this allegation in order to obtain money via compensation. This was beyond Y's cognitive ability. After a few questions and a very confused look on Y's face, I asked if the defence could define "compensation" and suggested she asked the witness what it meant. Y said she didn't know. The judge suggested it was not appropriate to continue.' (The defendant was convicted.)

A more rigorous approach to the review of questions prior to cross-examination is described in the final section of this chapter about the section 28 pilot scheme.

Time and timeliness

The timing of the provision of draft questions to the intermediary should be set by the judge, preferably to take place before the ground rules hearing. It is unreasonable to expect the intermediary to help reformulate questions during the course of the ground rules hearing. As Melissa points out, this seldom allows time to explain the rationale for suggested changes:

> 'It was very hard thinking on my feet like that, with the court waiting. I wouldn't ever do it again. The defence barrister had framed all her questions as statements. I suggested changing them to "Did you …?" When cross-examination started, she followed this advice, but added "– or not" to each question. She got very upset when I kept intervening, saying, "But I'm doing it just how you said."'

The review process can be complex and intermediaries need time to perform it properly. Intermediaries always try to respond but they report often receiving questions over the weekend or late at night for a trial next day. In a case in which Strider acted as intermediary for T, aged five, the judge directed that the defence advocate share her questions with the intermediary, but these were provided only 15 minutes before cross-examination started:

> 'Her questions included a number of adult terms and leading questions. She got very irritated and said "We just don't have time for this." Cross-examination involved my intervening a lot and T looking quite confused. I had to ask for permission to repeat questions in a different format, which the judge granted, but it was messy.'

Leading questions and 'not putting the case' to the witness

> [Advocates] cannot insist upon any supposed right 'to put one's case' or previous inconsistent statements to a vulnerable witness. If there is a right to 'put one's case' (about which we have our doubts) it must be modified for young or vulnerable

witnesses. It is perfectly possible to ensure the jury are made aware of the defence case and of significant inconsistencies without intimidation or distressing a witness ... (Lady Justice Hallett, *R v Lubemba, R v JP* [2014] EWCA Crim 2064, para 45)

The victims of offences of this kind are frequently damaged young people ... They can be difficult, emotional, contradictory, aggressive and on some occasions wholly uncommunicative ... The courts now have a far greater understanding than hitherto as to the difficulties that exist for vulnerable witnesses and the need for care in assessing whether inconsistent or varying accounts given on different occasions necessarily mean that the underlying allegation is untruthful or unreliable. (Lord Justice Fulford, *R v Uddin and Ali* [2014] EWCA 2269, para 54)

In conventional cross-examination, lawyers 'put their case' to the other side's witness by asking leading questions – typically suggesting that the witness is mistaken or lying. Barristers are obliged not to 'make a serious allegation against a witness whom you have had an opportunity to cross-examine unless you have given that witness a chance to answer the allegation in cross-examination' (Bar Standards Board Handbook, 2014, rC7.2). As we saw in Chapter Ten, suggestive questions are often problematic. The persuasive tag ending, for example "He didn't do it, *did he?*", may lead a vulnerable witness to give the answer the questioner wants and assertions such as "You didn't want your mum to think you were out getting drunk" may not even be recognised as a refutable suggestion. Intermediaries should not simply recommend 'no leading questions' but should explain, based on their assessment, the types of question likely to produce an unreliable response from this witness. A firm ruling in response to the recommendation should then be given at the ground rules hearing.

In what Criminal Practice Direction 3E.4 (2015) describes as a radical departure from conventional cross-examination, courts are now authorised to:

dispense with the normal practice and impose restrictions on the advocate 'putting his case' where there is a risk of a young or otherwise vulnerable witness failing to understand, becoming distressed or acquiescing to leading questions. Where limitations on questioning are necessary and appropriate, they must be clearly defined. The judge has a duty to ensure that they are complied with and should explain them to the jury and the reasons for them. If the advocate fails to comply with the limitations, the judge should give relevant directions to the jury when that occurs and prevent further questioning that does not comply with the ground rules settled upon in advance. (see also Criminal Procedure Rule 3.9(7)(b)(i), 2015; *R v Lubemba, R v JP* [2014] EWCA Crim 2064)

A senior judge told us that, as a result of working with intermediaries: "I do not now require any defence advocate to assert positively their case. In fact, in most cases I insist that they do not." An illustration of the shift in practice was provided by Golightly's experience at a recent ground rules hearing concerning a seven-year-old witness:

> 'Defence counsel made a half-hearted attempt to suggest to the judge that he had to use leading questions to put his client's case. The judge smiled and said: "We've come a long way in recent years, and can no longer expect to use this in our practice with children. Anything you can't put to the child through open questions will have to be put to the other adult witnesses, or presented as issues to the jury at a later point." This is so different from my early experiences as an intermediary, when I had to battle hard to get these points across.'

The defence response

Intermediaries see an increasing number of advocates who try hard to adopt new approaches to cross-examination, although some have yet to grasp the basic principles. Barney recently encountered a defence barrister who said he had prepared his questions "with a tag at the end of each one, just as suggested by the intermediary's report":

> 'The prosecuting barrister and I both replied in alarm and in unison "The report says *not* to use tag questions." The defence said he'd go and have another look at the report, which he did, and then said "Yes, it does say not to use them. I must have misread it." I didn't know whether to laugh or cry. I suggested how he could rewrite the questions, which he did straight away. It was all right in the end but I felt a bit sad for him because he was clearly trying to do the right thing and adhere to my recommendations – he just got it all the wrong way round.'

Restrictions on leading questions are not necessarily accepted. Lawyers sometimes continue to argue that they *have* to put their case in this way, even to pre-school children. It is, of course, to their advantage to do so because powerfully persuasive leading questions are likely to result in a vulnerable witness acceding to the advocate's proposition, even if the suggestion is incorrect. A ground rules hearing concerned L, a witness in her 40s, whom Roadrunner assessed as having the level of understanding of a six-year-old. The advocate said: "I'm sure L will tell us if she doesn't understand what we are asking her" (a task well beyond L's cognitive ability) and also insisted that he would need to ask tag questions:

> 'He said: "I have to be able to suggest L is wrong by saying 'You didn't ... did you?' I can't put my case another way." After the judge directed the advocate to rephrase his questions, he had to accept that he could not give the exact nuance he wanted. He did self-correct but made comments like, "Oh, this is very difficult" and "If I can't say that, can I say this?"'

Paul Mendelle QC, former chair of the Criminal Bar Association, argues that this lawyer's view is a misunderstanding of the professional obligation to put his case to the witness. The duty to put the defendant's case is owed to the witness and the court, not to the defendant. If the judge says that the lawyer does not have to or is not allowed to put the case to the witness, then there is no duty: 'and if a vulnerable witness cannot understand what the advocate is putting, then it's not fair to the witness and the advocate should neither do it nor be required to do it' (Mendelle, 2014, paras 70, 74). In those circumstances, the jury will be told that the defence disputes the witness's evidence and on what grounds.

The restriction on 'putting your case' does not actively prevent lawyers from asking the witness key questions in a simple, non-leading way. As the Lord Chief Justice said, 'it should not be over-problematic for the advocate to formulate short, simple questions which put the essential elements of the defendant's case to the witness, and fully ventilate before the jury the areas of evidence which bear on the child's credibility' (*R v Barker* [2010] EWCA Crim 4, para 42). However, lawyers do not invariably wish to ask 'short, simple questions' about 'essential elements of the defence case'. They may prefer to avoid asking the question at all rather than use a straightforward non-leading alternative proposed by the intermediary or by the judge.

Judicial input to the form of the question

Judicial involvement in the content of cross-examination has evolved considerably since leading questions such as: "X did not put his willy in your bum, did he?" were asked of an eight-year-old witness who then retracted much of her evidence (*R v W and M* [2010] EWCA Crim 1926, para 25, discussed in Chapter Ten). In a recent case Betsey acted as intermediary for F, who had just turned six. The defence case was that the sexual offences alleged by F did not happen. Counsel proposed to ask F three tag questions: "M didn't put his willy in your mouth, did he?"; "M didn't put his willy in your bottom, did he?"; and "M didn't put his willy in your moomoo, did he?" Betsey recommended that the questions be rephrased simply, without tags. The judge agreed that each question be reframed as two short statements followed by a question, for example: "You said M put his willy in your mouth. M says he didn't put his willy in your mouth. Did M really put his willy in your mouth?" Cross-examination of F proceeded as follows:

Barrister:	'You said M put his willy in your mouth. M says he didn't put his willy in your mouth. …'
Witness:	[before the barrister could ask 'Did M really put his willy in your mouth?'] 'Well, he is joking with you, because he did put his willy in my mouth.'
Barrister:	'You said M put his willy in your bottom. M says he didn't put his willy in your bottom. …'
Witness:	[again, before the barrister could ask 'Did M really put his willy in your bottom?'] 'Well, M is just joking about with you guys down there. Because he really, really did put his willy in my bottom, loads of times.'

Defence counsel did not go on to ask the 'moomoo' question. (The defendant was convicted and received a lengthy sentence.)

We observed a ground rules discussion about whether the defence case could be put to the witness. The judge asked defence counsel: "Isn't it easier to ask: 'Do you like going to stay with X?'" The advocate responded that he was reluctant to ask that question, "because if what she says is true, she will say she didn't like sleeping at X's house". The judge then warned: "You cannot ask generalities [of the witness] and then go into specifics with the jury later." The advocate said he would need to take instructions before discussing questions with the intermediary. When the ground rules hearing reconvened, the advocate told the judge he wanted to ask: "Didn't X sleep on the couch?" The judge said: "Ask 'Did he sleep on the couch?' … That's you putting your case."

While it is preferable for the form of questions to be resolved before cross-examination starts, sometimes the judge addresses this in the course of cross-examination. Tosca was the intermediary for G, a 12-year-old with a learning disability, who was asked by defence counsel: "He didn't put his hand down your pants, did he?" She intervened to indicate that G looked confused. "The defence said: 'Well that's as may be' and before I could say anything further, the judge said: 'Just ask a simple question ... Did X put his hand down your pants?'"

Similarly, a judge recalled intervening in respect of a 13-year-old with a severe learning disability:

> '[D]efence counsel wanted to say "you've lied about
> that, haven't you?" and I intervened ... I just smiled
> and said "You're asking a tag question. Why don't you
> ask an open question: 'Are you telling the truth?' ...
> that is the only way you can ask this." And he did ask
> and got the answer "yes". He sat down.' (Henderson
> 2016, forthcoming)

The judiciary can ask questions to clarify the evidence and need not adopt the questioning style of the cross-examiner. In a case in which cross-examination broke down after 15 minutes, the Court of Appeal saw 'no grounds for criticism' of a judge who asked a 14-year-old some of the defence advocate's questions but declined to ask questions that were 'mere comment or would unproductively inflame the witness' (*R v Cameron* [2001] EWCA Crim 562, para 10).

The judge may also ask a key question that has not been posed by the advocate. This was addressed by the Court of Appeal in a case where the defence alleged that the judge's questioning amounted to 'oath helping' and the trial was unfair in part because the judge 'devalued a number of [counsel's] questions by indicating that they were either irrelevant or of little value' (*H v R* [2014] EWCA Crim 1555, para 68). Following cross-examination of the 16-year-old witness about a note she had written saying she wished she could be 'amoral', the judge questioned her further about what she meant:

> Remembering her age, the judge asked her what her
> understanding of morality and amorality was and,

having obtained her explanation for the terms, asked the question [about the intention of the note]. In our judgment, that did not constitute a question designed to bolster X's credibility; *rather, it gave her the chance to deal with the implication in the cross-examination.* (para 63, our emphasis)

The judgment rejected the defence submission that the judge had gone:

outside the bounds of that which was appropriate ... a trial judge is not only entitled but under a duty to ensure that no improper advantage is taken of a complainant's vulnerability and, in this case, the judge did no more than was necessary pursuant to his duty of fairness. (paras 69–70)

The tension of differing objectives

While chairman of the Bar Council, Maura McGowan QC described the trial process as "not necessarily a search for the truth" but as "a test of the case against the defendant" (BBC 'Today' programme, 21 December 2013). This tension is implicit in the description in Criminal Practice Direction 1A.1 (2015) of a criminal trial as '*a search for truth* in accordance with the twin principles that the prosecution must prove its case *and that a defendant is not obliged to inculpate himself*, the object being to convict the guilty and acquit the innocent' (our emphasis).

Speaking shortly after leaving the office of Lord Chief Justice, Lord Judge called for traditional cross-examination strategies to be discarded when questioning vulnerable witnesses. He stressed that '[T]he objective of cross-examination is to investigate the truth by questions which must be clearly understood by the witness' (2013a, p 8). This is not a vision shared by all defence practitioners:

'It's a fallacy to say our system is about truth ... If it's just to get to the truth you'd put [the questions] in a very stark way but it's not: it's to create doubt.

The aim of defending is to try and undermine the prosecution case.' (Henderson, 2015b, forthcoming)

'[I]f I want to say "he didn't touch you, did he?" I can't ask "Did he touch you?" because that just leads to more information ...' (Henderson, 2015a, forthcoming)

'More information' here means an answer that the defence lawyer does not want the Bench or the jury to hear. A barrister who is an advocacy trainer explained:

'If a witness can answer tag questions and the defence case can properly be put and answered, then I think it should be, [but] there is no obligation upon the defence to ask a question which they know will produce an answer adverse to their case and I do not believe a judge can compel counsel to ask one. The prosecution can re-examine and the judge can always ask it themselves.'

A judge who is also an advocacy trainer agreed that an advocate cannot be forced to ask a question:

'However, experienced judges will step in and say what the case is and put it to a witness (any witness) if the defence advocate fails to do so. I have done it frequently. However I do not weigh in without warning. I usually say to the advocate (if something central to the case hasn't been put and there has been a discussion about the point, because it is usually in the defence statement): "If you don't put it, I'm sure the prosecution will ask the witness about it in re-examination. And if they don't, I will." In those circumstances, the defence advocate realises they have lost "control" of the situation and they ask the question. But of course, you need resilient judges.'

There is an equal need for resilient magistrates. In this example, a lawyer in the magistrates' court did not want to use the communication aids Hermione had developed for use by L, a witness with severe expressive difficulties:

> 'The advocate was keen to avoid introducing any vocabulary that went near the evidence. He was highly inappropriate, shouting at L and asking her "How …" questions. I explained to the magistrates that L, who had become very frustrated, could only respond to questions requiring a "yes" or "no" answer. The Bench chairman asked her "Was it a hammer?" No further questions were asked when she answered in the affirmative.' (The defendant was found guilty.)

'I only want an answer if it's the answer I want'

As we have seen, some advocates decline to put a question at all if prevented from doing so in a leading way. Betsey and some other intermediaries have identified instances where experienced but disingenuous defence advocates actively embrace the restrictions:

> 'They announce at ground rules hearings that they expect to be told to ask no leading questions during cross-examination, often framed as "I imagine the intermediary will advise against me putting my case and therefore, Your Honour, I will have to present my case directly to the jury after cross-examination." They seem absolutely delighted about being told not to ask leading questions, and quite perturbed when I suggest otherwise. I have had several bizarre ground rules hearings where I have had to argue strongly that the witness could be asked appropriately framed questions that put the defence case.'

It is clearly in the interest of best evidence that a vulnerable witness is not asked a question in a way likely to produce an unreliable answer. However, where witnesses are denied the opportunity to answer simple questions that appear to be within their capability, intermediaries complain that, 'the baby is being thrown out with the bathwater'. When restrictions on putting the case are imposed, jurors are advised, as in the case of *Edwards* ([2011] EWCA Crim 3028, p 7), that they will not hear the witness confronted with the defendant's version of events in 'the traditional form of cross-examination'. We wonder what jurors make of this admonition. One juror observed about such a discussion: 'What on earth was going on? We had no more idea of "the rules" than of quantum mechanics' (Grove, 2000, p 150). Jurors may be justifiably mystified as to why the witness has not been asked a simple question about the essence of the case.

Practice around the avoidance of leading questions, 'not putting the case' and the substitution of simple, direct questions is developing rapidly. There should surely be a presumption or expectation that the defence case will be put to vulnerable witnesses provided this can be done in a form they can understand and cope with, without coercive syntax. If the defence declines to ask a key question that the witness is capable of answering, then it should be asked by the prosecutor (overcoming the reluctance illustrated in the previous chapter) or the judge.

In our view, alternative steps to further explain the defence case to the jury should only be triggered where the intermediary confirms that the witness is unlikely to understand or be too distressed to cope with questions on the topic asked in a straightforward way. This seems to accord with the position of the judge who warned the defence advocate that he could not ask 'generalities' of the witness 'then go into specifics with the jury later'. More reflection is needed about 'putting the case' to the vulnerable witness, without suggestion, in ways that are fair to both the witness and the defendant.

A unique approach was adopted in a recent young witness case with two defendants. As a result of the intermediary's early observations, trial counsel collaborated to avoid the need for the child (who had significant learning disabilities) to be cross-examined. This was achieved by having the intermediary assist at a further police interview at which the advocates agreed in advance what should be asked, with intermediary advice. The original police interviews, edited by agreement, were shown to the jury, as was the supplemental interview. The defence teams then made short statements to the jury informing them of what was agreed, what was challenged and the position of each defendant. The limitations of putting detailed challenges to children were explained. One of the barristers said: "It was an example of how proper collaboration between all parties can achieve the desired goals and also, I believe, command the respect of the jury for having the sensitivities that were clearly demonstrated." (This case was the subject of Attorney General's References Nos 113/2014, 114/2014 [2015] All ER (D) 115: the sentences were increased as having been unduly lenient.)

Section 28 pre-trial cross-examination

'This case was the first to use section 28 and as such there was a high degree of interest. I have received positive feedback from a number of parties, in particular the judge who was extremely grateful for the intermediary's assistance. He indicated that he felt that the cross-examination of the witness would have been impossible without her.' (CPS lawyer)

'I prosecuted a case where the victim was an adult female with a mental age of around four. She was child-like in her responses and behaviour and had a short attention span. The intermediary was extremely helpful and provided cards for the witness to point to instead of answering questions directly. She also provided guidance on questioning the witness and advised the court about how the witness would appear. The witness got upset during cross-examination and burst into floods of tears on many occasions, causing the court to have to take frequent breaks. Pre-recorded cross-examination would have been preferable.' (Barrister)

Section 28 of the Youth Justice and Criminal Evidence Act 1999 provides for cross-examination of eligible witnesses to be filmed at a pre-trial hearing and played to the jury at trial. The witness need not attend the trial. If a request to question the witness further satisfies legislative criteria, the court can authorise this but the questioning must also be pre-recorded via live link. Ground-breaking pilot projects to pre-record cross-examination were introduced at the Crown Court in Liverpool, Leeds and Kingston-upon-Thames in April 2014. Their aim is 'to improve the court experience' of young people, victims of sexual abuse and vulnerable witnesses (HM Courts and Tribunals Service, March 2014). The formal evaluation period ended in October 2014, having involved around 200 cases (HM Courts and Tribunals Service, November 2014). However, the section 28 procedure continues to be used at the pilot courts, at least for the time being. The government has committed to complete national roll-out of section 28 by March 2017, subject to the findings of the evaluation (Ministry of Justice, 2014b).

Pilot procedures

The judiciary has issued a protocol governing section 28 cases (Judiciary of England and Wales, 2014a). Whether or not cases involve an intermediary, they must all have a ground rules hearing conducted by the same judge who presides at the pre-trial recording; 'it is highly desirable' that the same judge also conducts the trial (para 60). Some pilot cases have had more than one ground rules hearing, with exchanges of emailed questions and amendments by lawyers and the intermediary in between.

In order to control pilot scheme numbers, eligibility for inclusion was restricted in the case of young people to those under 16, as opposed to those under the age of 18 covered by the 1999 Act. Although vulnerable adults were eligible, most pilot cases involved children. Intermediaries were appointed for only a small proportion of witnesses involved in the pilot although all were, by definition, eligible for the intermediary special measure. This was due primarily to the continuing lack of awareness on the part of police and CPS of the types of witness who would benefit from intermediary assistance; where an intermediary was appointed, it was often post-interview. Intermediaries were appointed in almost all pilot cases where they were requested; only one request failed to be 'matched' (communication from the National Crime Agency, December 2014). The limited observations in this section are drawn only from pilot cases in which intermediaries were involved.

The section 28 protocol details some of the issues to be discussed at the hearing, including any restrictions on the advocate's usual duty to 'put the defence case' (Judiciary of England and Wales, 2014a, para 33). The pilot courts' Guidance Note expects lawyers to indicate the need for judicial directions as to whether it is appropriate to 'put the case' in full (for example, whether the witness is lying) or whether, due to the vulnerability of the witness, the advocate should not do so; to confirm they have read relevant *Advocate's Gateway* toolkits (see Chapter Ten); and to prepare their cross-examination for the judge's consideration, particularly 'where the witness is of tender years or suffers from a disability or disorder' (Liverpool Crown Court, 2014). Intermediaries describe ground rules hearings for section 28 hearings as longer (often lasting several hours) and more thorough than is the norm, allowing more time for discussion and review of proposed questions.

Observations on some pilot cases involving an intermediary

The section 28 protocol requires the ground rules hearing to discuss the possibility of cross-examination by a single advocate if the case involves more than one defendant (Judiciary of England and Wales, 2014a, para 62). Maria was appointed for a five-year-old in a case with four defence advocates. The ground rules hearing lasted several hours, with clear directions from the judge about the process to be followed and what was expected regarding language and communication. It was agreed that the first defence advocate would cover most questions: 20 minutes were allowed per advocate, with questioning in total to take no more than an hour. The intermediary looked at proposed questions and changed all those listed by the first advocate; questions from the others were more appropriate. In the end, only two defence advocates asked questions. The prosecutor then asked a couple of questions, the first of which was a statement with a tag ending: "Both the judge and I asked her to rephrase together."

The ground rules hearing should take place at least a week before the section 28 recording to allow enough time for preparation (Judiciary of England and Wales, 2014a, para 20). We observed a ground rules hearing which was held the day before the recording; it took half a day to finalise cross-examination questions for the following morning. The judge's active involvement was striking. She asked the two defence lawyers about the purpose of their questions and screened them not just for clarity but for relevance, something obviously beyond the scope of the intermediary role.

A break was taken to give the advocates and Alice, the intermediary, time for discussion. Alice said this took a long time because she had recommended "no tag questions" with the witness and defence counsel "insisted on being allowed to ask 'just one tag'". Counsel raised this when the ground rules hearing reconvened. The judge directed the advocate to put his case by asking the question without a tag ending. The judge went on to query the form and language of other questions. At the end of the ground rules hearing, the judge asked for questions to be written out again in their final form and provided before the end of the court day, typed up overnight and provided again in the morning, when the intermediary would be invited to review them once more. The judge made clear that no deviation was expected from these questions in cross-examination. The judge referred to a previous section 28 hearing in which "the prosecutor nearly had the girl in tears" so if the prosecutor wished to ask questions in re-examination, there would be a break in which these questions could be discussed with the intermediary: "It shouldn't be necessary, but sometimes it is."

The protocol suggests that for child witnesses, the section 28 recording should 'conclude before lunch time' (Judiciary of England and Wales, 2014a, para 23). Many of the cross-examination recordings were scheduled early in the morning to fit them in before the start of normal court business; intermediaries expressed concern that in some instances where witnesses lived at a distance from the court, this schedule meant "dragging the child out of bed too early."

In the case we observed, cross-examination by the two defence counsel lasted less than 10 minutes; there were no questions from the prosecutor and the child was free to leave the court by 10.15 am. One of the defence advocates commented that because half a day had been devoted to discussing the questions, "that's why we were able to be so brief this morning". His colleague observed: "These ground rules hearings are time-consuming and can't just be 'slotted in'." The judge, who dealt with other cases while the lawyers were in discussion with the intermediary the day before, thought that fewer other matters should be put into the judge's court list on days when they are dealing with section 28 hearings, but that the listing office had not yet appreciated "these cases take a lot of planning". However, when circumstances require, a section 28 recording can be arranged at very short notice. Bradley was the intermediary for an woman of 88 whose case was adjourned on the day of trial at a pilot court. The intermediary suggested that, as the parties were all available, the witness's evidence be recorded. This took place at a section 28 hearing the following day.

A judge whom we interviewed in 2012 after the first use of face-to-face cross-examination with the lawyer in the live link room favoured the concept but was uneasy in case any subtle interaction in the room, for example anything that might seem intimidating to the witness, was not evident to the judge watching from the courtroom. This can be a realistic concern: Annie describes an advocate turning his head away from a child aged six who leant forward trying hard to make eye contact. Pilot cases broke new ground when not only the advocates but also the judge moved to the live link room, an option recognised in the section 28 protocol (Judiciary of England and Wales, 2014a, para 38). In one such case with two defence advocates, Bradley was appointed to facilitate communication with G, who had severe communication problems as a result of a stroke but no learning disabilities:

> 'I sat next to G, with the advocate asking questions sitting in front of him slightly to his left and the judge in front of him slightly to his right. The two defence barristers swapped seats when their time came to question, leaping over a small table and the judge's knees. The prosecution counsel and usher sat behind us. The judge and I had about 12 inches of space between us. It was cosy but it worked for this witness. Rather than G having to speak via live link,

communication for him was much better face-to-face. It was especially beneficial here as this judge wanted to be able to intervene at a moment's notice.'

The jury's view of the witness and the live link room

As with any pilot, teething problems need to be resolved. For example, the initial intention for section 28 filming was to show the jury a split screen, with the advocate in court on one side and the witness and intermediary, if there was one, in the live link room on the other. This provided insufficient detail of the witness's face or use of communication aids (irrespective of camera focus, it is good practice for the judge to direct the intermediary to describe what happens as aids are used). In any future rollout, the screen will show a larger image of the witness and a smaller image of counsel or judge. In the section 28 recording we observed, and in several others, the intermediary was off-screen and therefore not filmed, contrary to the protocol requirement that the intermediary be visible (Judiciary of England and Wales, 2014a, para 37).

Court facilities and the use of remote live links

Pilot procedures did not allow for pre-trial recording of cross-examination to be conducted away from trial courts because it was considered necessary to work out basic principles first. This was a disappointment to those working with vulnerable witnesses because facilities in many courts are uncomfortable and not 'witness-friendly'. At one pilot court the live link room equipped for section 28 was "a dusty box room in the basement". At another the room was not air-conditioned. Betsey took part in a section 28 recording "on the hottest day of the year so far. The room was like an oven, which gave the six-year-old witness – who had learning difficulties, autism and attention deficit hyperactivity disorder – an added reason to escape, which he did, several times."

Intermediaries mentioned several instances where witnesses actually or nearly encountered the defendant at court on the day of the section 28 hearing (despite everyone's best efforts, this is also a common problem at trial). This risk would be avoided if evidence was given from another location. If section 28 is rolled out as the government intends, pre-trial recording using remote links should be tested as the next step. By March 2015, the government is committed to increasing the opportunity for vulnerable witnesses to give evidence away from the court building, 'with at least one such location available in each court region' (Ministry of Justice, 2014b). Some regions will have remote links in at least three locations: while no official announcement was made prior to the April 2015 election, work was ongoing to 'get the sites ready'; they will be section 28 compatible (Ministry of Justice communication, March 2015). Court regions are large and inevitably some courts will not be close to a remote link site. This has implications for ease of access for judges and lawyers in face-to-face cross-examination cases.

Early impressions are promising

In proposing pre-trial cross-examination, Judge Pigot was concerned about delay in child abuse trials and wanted cross-examination to be expedited (Home Office, 1989, para 7.9). Section 28 has, at least in theory, the potential to allow a witness's cross-examination to be reached more quickly. Target timescales for each case stage have been established for the section 28 pilots and for cases involving any child witness under the age of 10 (Association of Chief Police Officers et al, 2015, para 3.3). In practice, some cases had been in the court process for a considerable time before being included in the pilot scheme, so it is unclear whether the evaluation will demonstrate much reduction in the time vulnerable witnesses wait to go to court.

However, time saving would be of little benefit if inappropriate cross-examination is simply brought forward (Plotnikoff and Woolfson, 2012). In experimental research, children were cross-examined either a few days or eight months after they watched a target event (Righarts et al, 2014). Despite highly accurate initial reports, children's performance during cross-examination was very poor, even when cross-examination took place shortly after the target event. In Western Australia, even after decades of pre-recording experience, Cossins (2012) concludes that it failed to tackle endemic problems of cross-examination. In the State of Victoria, judges

> 'have been lulled into thinking that counsel know how to ask questions after years of programs designed to train them (and judges) in dealing with these vulnerable witnesses. However, I have been brought up suddenly in recent trials, as have others, so I plan to circulate the judges with a memo suggesting they revert to the original practice [of setting ground rules]. These will still be general in nature, unlike the tremendous assistance that an intermediary would provide.' (Communication from the judge in charge of the sexual offences list, March 2015)

Early impressions of the pilot scheme in England and Wales indicate that it has given a small, determined group of case management minded judges an opportunity to demonstrate what can be done to improve the cross-examination of vulnerable witnesses through tight control of the content and length of questioning. Sir Brian Leveson's *Review of Efficiency in Criminal Proceedings* concludes that 'Technological problems aside, [the pilot] is proving to be a huge success, due in no small part to the very substantial effort of all those involved' (2015, para 259). The Family Justice Council sees 'no reason why similar techniques could not be employed for use in family proceedings' (Judiciary of England and Wales, 2015, para 26).

Advocates describe the section 28 procedures as a 'sea-change when it comes to both the speed and methodology of trial preparation' (Stevenson and Valley, 2014). Intermediaries consistently praise the effort of all involved, stressing the "goodwill and exceptionally strong willingness to get it right" and the "serious commitment to make it work". One intermediary said: "The best thing is the feeling of calm and having enough *time*."

It remains to be seen what juries will make of pre-recorded cross-examination. However, benefits for witnesses are already evident. Witness waiting times at court have been short; judges visit live link rooms with the intermediary to discuss the most appropriate setup for the needs of the witness; and ground rules hearings are more exacting and more effective because lawyers are better prepared – one ground rules hearing was adjourned because counsel had not read the intermediary's report. Questions are reviewed carefully and, as a result, duration of questioning is much shorter than the norm. One judge said: "Whatever the difficulties, when the witness arrives at 9.15 am, is cross-examined immediately and is on the way home by 10.30 because everything has been arranged properly beforehand, it has to be positive for everyone involved – and this is now happening regularly in this court."

Intermezzo

Use of acupressure and a quiet room at court for Simon, a defendant with symptoms of mental illness

Poppy (registered intermediary)

I was contacted by solicitors representing Simon, a man in his 30s with a diagnosis of schizoaffective disorder (a combination of psychotic symptoms, similar to schizophrenia, and mood symptoms of bipolar disorder). He was accused of an offence of violence to be tried in the magistrates' court. Once confirmation of my funding was secured, I assessed Simon in the presence of his solicitor. Simon never raised his head and could not make eye contact. He was experiencing auditory hallucinations and delusions, had difficulty concentrating, poor listening skills and low self-esteem, all of which affected his ability to communicate. As the trial date approached, he became more stressed and anxious. Before the trial, I asked the solicitor to book a quiet room at court for Simon to wait in and use during breaks; at trial we had to change rooms because the first was too close to a noisy lift. At the ground rules hearing I explained about the voices Simon heard and visual hallucinations that he may need to filter out during questioning, and the potential effect of these on his ability to communicate.

During the case we had breaks every hour or more frequently if necessary, with 10 to 15 minutes for rest and quiet. This enabled him to participate more fully while in the courtroom. I explained proceedings as we went along but we took five minutes during each break for anything additional that needed to be covered. In court, we used 'pressure-pointing' and 'tapping' to distract Simon from his delusions (tapping on acupressure points can help relieve stress and anxiety). He was quite distracted by the time each break occurred but he was adamant that he wished to continue. Over lunch he had a sandwich with his psychiatric support worker and then rested for 45 minutes in the quiet room.

After lunch he was cross-examined. At the ground rules hearing, I had requested long pauses so that he could process and answer the questions and I had to ask for longer pauses as the trial went on. I also intervened a number of times to ask the prosecutor to simplify and reduce the length of questions. Simon's mannerisms became quite unusual while he was in the witness box and the magistrates asked if we needed to adjourn to another day. This would have increased his stress so the solicitor asked that we continue. At one point I requested a short five-minute break in the darkened quiet room as Simon was really struggling to filter information. He said that he was so stressed that he was beginning to see alien lights approaching him from all angles and was trying to avoid them. This was making it difficult for him to listen. The break served to 'stop the lights' and we returned to court.

The strategies for managing his mental health symptoms enabled Simon to give his evidence clearly and comprehensively, even though towards the end of the trial he heard nothing as his stress levels had become so high. However, as planned, during the next break the solicitor explained everything to him. After the magistrates deliberated, he was acquitted. Simon said he would not have managed to complete the day and follow the proceedings without the communication support provided.

THIRTEEN

The uneasy position
of vulnerable defendants

An intermediary sometimes assists a vulnerable person called
to court as a prosecution witness; that person can appear in a
different case as a defendant, without intermediary help. As
intermediaries observe, only the side of the fence has changed,
not the person's communication needs. The overriding objective
in Criminal Procedure Rule 1 (2015), 'that criminal cases be
dealt with justly', includes dealing with the prosecution and
defence fairly and recognising the defendant's rights to a fair
trial under Article 6 of the European Convention on Human
Rights. Courts are obliged to take 'every reasonable step'
to facilitate the defendant's participation, including setting
directions and ground rules, especially in intermediary cases.
The aim is to enable defendants to give their best evidence,
understand the proceedings and 'engage fully' with their
defence; the pre-trial and trial process should be adapted as
necessary (Criminal Procedure Rules 3.9(3)(b), 3.9(6) and 3.9(7),
2015; toolkit 8, *Effective participation of young defendants*, www.
theadvocatesgateway.org). This requires the judiciary to ensure
'by any appropriate means' that defendants understand what is
happening and what has been said by those on the Bench, the
advocates and witnesses (Criminal Practice Directions 3D.2 and
3G.9, 2015).

Many defendants would meet the criteria governing the
provision of special measures, including intermediary assistance,
as set out in the Youth Justice and Criminal Evidence Act 1999;
however, the Act specifically excludes defendants (section 17(1)).
Over half of children and adults who offend have communication

247

difficulties: many have learning difficulties and mental health problems, often combined with alcohol or drug misuse (Talbot, 2012; Criminal Justice Joint Inspection, 2014b). However, for reasons of political expediency and cost, the Act excluded vulnerable defendants from eligibility.

Pressure as a result of court decisions has led to a grudging legislative response. Some defendants under the age of 18 may now give evidence by live link (Police and Justice Act 2006, section 47, creating new section 33A-C, Youth Justice and Criminal Evidence Act 1999). A provision permitting appointment of an intermediary, on narrower grounds of eligibility than for vulnerable witnesses and restricted to the giving of evidence, has not been put into effect (Coroners and Justice Act 2009, section 104, creating new section 33BA(4), Youth Justice and Criminal Evidence Act 1999). The government continues to delay implementation on the grounds of resource implications.

In an effort to redress the imbalance between witnesses and defendants, courts have exercised their inherent powers to appoint an intermediary to assist the defendant's communication, either when giving evidence or throughout the trial and, where necessary, in preparation for trial (Criminal Practice Direction 3F.3, 2015, which cites the relevant case law). The term 'registered intermediary' is restricted to those recruited by the Ministry of Justice to assist witnesses under the 1999 Act. Those appointed as intermediaries for defendants are classed as 'non-registered' and as 'private and unregulated' (HM Courts and Tribunals Service, undated; Cooper and Wurtzel, 2013). Courts can appoint anyone to act as an intermediary, whether or not professionally qualified. In practice, those who take on defendant work are either already registered in respect of witness work but also willing to accept defence appointments, or are professionals working exclusively with defendants. This latter group tends to work for two private sector providers of defendant intermediaries, Communicourt and Triangle.

The rest of this book tells the story of witness intermediaries. In this chapter, we hear from registered intermediaries who also undertake defendant work and from defendant intermediaries whose appointments come through private companies. These intermediaries take us to the other side of the courtroom, sitting alongside the defendant in the dock. Like their counterparts for witnesses, they operate as neutral officers of the court but they are creatures of case law, operating without a legislative foundation, official guidance, approved training or regulation. The chapter explores what these intermediaries do and why their assistance is often needed for the duration of the trial. As with witness intermediaries, their work with defendants behind the scenes may not be recognised by others in the courtroom.

Profile of intermediary appointments and private sector providers

'The intermediary was of great assistance in helping the client understand what was going on and facilitating communication between him, his legal team and the court. Her work was of a high standard.' (Defence solicitor)

'The intermediary was invaluable to me in taking instructions from my client. She was able to break down significant legal processes into simple terms that he understood.' (Defence solicitor)

We have put together information for 417 defendant appointments by combining limited Ministry of Justice figures and unpublished data from the two private sector providers. Details of 97 Ministry of Justice defendant appointments for the two years ending in August 2009 were quoted in *R (OP) v Secretary of State for Justice* [2014] EWHC 1944 (Admin). In addition, Communicourt and Triangle provided details of 250 and 70 appointments respectively.

Information from all three sources is remarkably consistent: most defendant intermediary appointments are for the duration of the trial, with under 10% restricted to assisting defendants while giving evidence (overall, between a quarter and a half of these defendants did not give evidence). Ministry of Justice figures were not broken down by trial length but most private sector intermediary appointments are for more than one day. Triangle acts exclusively for defendants under 25; half of Communicourt's clients are also in this age group. Both have teams of around 20 intermediaries and are led by registered intermediaries. For both organisations, the majority of appointments are for Crown Court trials. Common presenting problems are learning disability, autism spectrum disorders and attention deficit hyperactivity disorder.

The backgrounds of the Triangle team (a mix of employed and self-employed) include psychology, teaching and speech and language therapy; all have significant experience working with vulnerable children and young people. Communicourt's team (all of whom are employed) are qualified speech and language therapists; many are recent graduates but some have forensic experience or have worked in prisons. Both teams include some intermediaries on the Ministry of Justice register and both provide training and monitoring; their members follow a report template. There is continuity of intermediary between assessment and trial in the majority of appointments; if there is scheduling difficulty, another team member attends the trial.

Registered intermediaries working in a non-registered capacity with defendants receive no training from the Ministry of Justice for this aspect of their work and are not required to follow a specific report format but will try to provide continuity of service from assessment to trial if court scheduling permits.

Finding and funding a defendant intermediary

'The defendant is only 13 (and, it is fair to say, not the brightest 13-year-old). He, of course, is not entitled under the statute to the benefit of any special measures. There is a danger of the playing field not simply being uneven but being on a considerable slope.' (Defence barrister, objecting to an application for a witness intermediary: Plotnikoff and Woolfson, 2007a, p 68)

'The intermediary was helpful in explaining the difficulties that people with learning difficulties and mental health problems face in criminal proceedings, and how even apparently simple questions have to be "deconstructed" before they are understood.' (Defence barrister)

Initially, the Ministry of Justice's Witness Intermediary Scheme matching service responded to requests to find a registered intermediary on behalf of defendants. It had made around 100 such appointments when this service was withdrawn in August 2011, because of the pressure of requests for witnesses. Since then, the matching service has provided registered intermediaries for defendants only when obliged to do so as a consequence of litigation. Shauneen Lambe of the charity Just for Kids Law, who has brought such cases, argues that defendants are disadvantaged when their lawyers cannot access the range of registered intermediary skills provided by the matching service. In a 2014 case brought on behalf of a defendant with learning disabilities and autism, the Divisional Court agreed that a registered intermediary should be provided but restricted the appointment to the defendant's testimony. The court considered that an 'intelligent observer would be puzzled' as to why the matching service provided a registered intermediary to a vulnerable witness while giving evidence, but not to a defendant in the same position (*R (OP) v Secretary of State for Justice* [2014] EWHC 1944 (Admin), para 47).

In the absence of access to the matching service for registered intermediaries, there is no standard way of finding a suitable defendant intermediary. Unpublished guidance to court staff provides a 'non-exhaustive' list of organisations as a starting point (HM Courts and Tribunals Service, undated); it does not include Triangle or Communicourt and none of the organisations that are listed provide this assistance routinely (Talbot, 2012). A clinical nurse specialist employed by the National Health Service and based at the Old Bailey screens expert reports on defendants. Where it appears that an intermediary appointment may be appropriate (for example, because the report identifies the defendant's learning disability), he raises this with defence solicitors and refers them to a list used by London Crown Courts of registered intermediaries who take defendant appointments. This list consists of those on the register because of their status with the Ministry of Justice and because private sector organisations' charges are higher. Most Old Bailey appointments are for the duration of the trial. A private discussion group on the website LinkedIn is used by registered and non-registered intermediaries to exchange information about solicitors seeking a defendant intermediary. Intermediaries for Justice, the intermediaries' professional organisation launched in December 2014, expects to provide a list of intermediaries undertaking defendant work.

Funding for a defendant intermediary is by no means automatic and arrangements to fund pre-trial and trial work differ. Defence solicitors seek prior approval from the Legal Aid Agency to cover costs of intermediary assessments and other pre-trial work, whereas the court covers the cost of intermediaries 'during court proceedings' with judicial authorisation (HM Courts and Tribunals Service, undated). We were unable to obtain details of the number of defendant intermediary appointments paid for by the Legal Aid Agency and courts.

Most young defendants appear in the youth court. As discussed in Chapter Ten, youth court advocacy is widely considered to be problematic. Court applications for intermediaries are likely to be approved for young defendants 'who need to be communicated with in developmentally appropriate ways and those with physical disabilities and mental disorders which adversely affect their communication' (*R v GP and 4 Others* (2012) T20120409, 'Guidance for future applications', para 66(3)). However, inability to obtain an intermediary is not a reason to stay (suspend) a trial where judges can adapt the trial process to help defendants follow proceedings, for example by setting ground rules requiring all witnesses to be asked simple questions and to give short answers (Criminal Practice Directions 3F.4-6, 2015).

Duration of appointment

Courts make most intermediary appointments for the duration of the trial, recognising 'a right, which might in certain circumstances amount to a duty', to appoint a registered intermediary to assist the defendant to follow the proceedings 'if without assistance he would not be able to have a fair trial' (*R (AS) v Great Yarmouth Youth Court* [2011] EWHC 2059 (Admin), para 6, involving a child with attention deficit hyperactivity disorder). More recently, however, the Divisional Court was 'not persuaded that it is essential a registered intermediary be available to all defendants for the duration of their trials' (*R (OP) v Secretary of State for Justice* [2014] EWHC 1944 (Admin), para 41). During the rest of the trial, the defendant's needs could be met by:

> general support, reassurance and calm interpretation of unfolding events ... a task readily achievable by an adult with experience of life and the cast of mind apt to facilitate comprehension by a worried individual on trial. In play are understandable emotions: uncertainty, perhaps a sense of territorial disadvantage, nervousness and agitation. (para 35)

However, 'Sympathy and compassion cannot compensate for the cognitive deficits of defendants with comprehension as well as communication difficulties' (Hoyano, 2015, p 82). We agree. The intermediary contributes to delivering such defendants' right to effective participation in the entire trial process as required by Article 6 of the European Convention of Human Rights (*SC v UK* [2005] 40 EHRR 10; *R v Jordan Dixon* [2013] EWCA Crim 465).

'Evidence only' intermediary appointments

Lorna, who has experience of 'evidence-only' appointments, explains why these make the intermediary's role more difficult:

> 'You present yourself at the most stressful time for defendants. They don't know you and vice versa. If involved throughout the trial, we pick up so much about their communication and level of understanding – and sometimes as a result we ask for another ground rules hearing just prior to cross-examination. Also, if you haven't had the chance to work alongside the defence lawyer taking instructions from the client, you may have to intervene during the defendant's evidence-in-chief. It is much better to get to know the defence representative who can then "model" the way you want questions to be

asked of the defendant before the prosecutor cross-examines him.'

Appointment for the whole trial generally enables intermediaries to assist in relevant pre-trial matters. Cameron finds it easier to make recommendations and be involved in the trial if he has attended lawyer conferences and pre-trial hearings:

'You have a much more in-depth knowledge of the case and the defendant's needs. You are familiar with the lawyers, have made them aware of a good communication style, and have had a chance to build rapport with the defendant as well as the legal teams. You can then implement your recommendations with them before the trial begins.'

Cameron was appointed as intermediary for H, a defendant with depression and anxiety:

'Spending a lot of time building rapport with H was essential to my role in this two-week trial. This in turn led him to tell the solicitor and barrister his full account of what had happened, which he had not shared with anyone before the trial began. If I had been requested only for evidence-giving I doubt that he would have shared his true account with his lawyers and he may have chosen not to give evidence.' (H was found not guilty.)

There is a practical difficulty in restricting intermediary assistance to the defendant's evidence: a decision as to whether the defendant will testify is often not made until the close of the prosecution case. The pilot registered intermediary scheme in Northern Ireland provides an intermediary matching service for defendants, but only while giving evidence; no defendants received this assistance in the first 18 months of the scheme (Department of Justice, 2015, para 31). For the rest of the trial, if necessary, the Northern Ireland Department of Justice will arrange for MindWise, a mental health charity which has the contract for the Appropriate Adult Scheme, to provide a supporter to accompany the defendant. The Department considers that appointing intermediaries for the entire trial potentially jeopardises their independence: 'Neutrality could surely be called in to question if a registered intermediary was writing notes to a defendant or using pictures/ diagrams to assist them to follow what was going on but these communication aids were not visible to the court, only the defendant' (2015, para 56). As described later in this chapter, English intermediaries active during the course of the trial acknowledge tensions surrounding the performance of their role, but their impartiality is generally accepted. Where communication aids are to be used, this is agreed with the court beforehand.

The police interview

> 'I'd be reluctant to use an intermediary for a client at a police interview because the position on legal privilege is so unclear.' (Defence solicitor)

Intermediaries are seldom asked to assess vulnerable suspects before a police interview. Police guidance on identifying vulnerability covers witnesses, not suspects (Ministry of Justice, 2011b; see however, toolkit 10, *Identifying vulnerability in witnesses and defendants*, www.theadvocatesgateway.org). Official guidance on questioning young or otherwise vulnerable suspects at the police station provides only for the presence of an 'appropriate adult' (Home Office, 2013, Code C). Their responsibilities include facilitating communication but they need not have specialist skills and are not the equivalent of professional intermediaries (O'Mahony, 2012).

On one of the rare occasions when the police requested intermediary assistance for a defendant, Melissa was asked to assess Q, a man with severely impaired understanding and speech following a stroke. The intermediary concluded that it seemed like a "waste of everyone's time and money" due to what she felt was a lack of understanding of her role:

'I assessed Q and recommended planning the questions to ensure we had the right props (words and pictures or symbols to which Q could point) in order to obtain a meaningful answer. This included how to give and explain the caution so that he would understand the implications of refusing to answer questions at interview. I was present at Q's initial interview with his lawyer who then excluded me while advising his client. The lawyer and custody sergeant were unfamiliar with the intermediary role and appeared to confuse it with that of an appropriate adult. The lawyer advised Q to say "no comment" to all questions. The interviewer ploughed through the questions as originally planned, even though by this time Q was almost falling off his chair with exhaustion. He got muddled trying to remember how and when to say "no comment", for example saying "yes, coming" or "no, can't", until I added "no comment" to his written "yes"/"no" cards. Then he just kept stabbing the "no comment" card, often before the officer had asked the next question. Q ended up crying and begging to go home.'

Defence solicitors have been reluctant to avail themselves of intermediaries on the few occasions when their presence was arranged by the police. Solicitors' requests for an intermediary to attend a police interview are often withdrawn when solicitors realise they will have to commit to paying for the service before knowing whether the Legal Aid Agency will authorise funding. (Triangle reports that some solicitors authorise funding themselves in advance of a legal aid decision.) Timing is especially crucial if the suspect is in custody. In Northern Ireland, where the registered intermediary pilot scheme covers defendants, no request has been received for a suspect in custody (Department of Justice, 2015). Where an intermediary has been appointed for the police interview, the suspect was either released on police bail or detained in hospital, allowing for the assessment and interview to be scheduled with less urgency (communication from the Department of Justice, October 2014).

While there is no direct authority governing intermediaries and legal privilege, it is suggested that anything said to the intermediary by the defendant about the offence should be disclosed to the defence solicitor but not to the prosecutor (Cooper and Wurtzel, 2014).

Assessment

'I watched the intermediary assess my client. It was fascinating. The help provided was excellent.' (Defence solicitor)

'Prison staff had no idea what we were doing during the assessment and were intrusive. It was with great difficulty that it was eventually reasonably complete.' (Intermediary)

Often the precise nature of a defendant's communication difficulties has not been recognised prior to their contact with the criminal justice system. Even if the defendant has previously received a formal diagnosis, this may not be known to the solicitor who may therefore lack sufficient information to seek an intermediary with the requisite skills, as when a solicitor requested an intermediary for a defendant who seemed 'odd'; the person had in fact been discharged from psychiatric services. A recommendation to seek an intermediary sometimes arises as the result of the defence commissioning a psychological or other expert report concerning the defendant's 'fitness to plead' (that is, ability to stand trial). In the absence of an expert report, intermediaries have identified previously undiagnosed problems such as autism spectrum disorder, mental illness and illiteracy.

Intermediary assessments are often arranged at short notice. They take place in solicitors' offices, secure hospitals and in court and prison cells and young offender institutions but less often in the defendant's home. (Triangle intermediaries do home assessments if defendants are young, unlikely to attend the solicitor's office or the time frame is short.) Carrying out assessments in custody settings is often problematic. Elena was unable to arrange an assessment in a secure training centre so the judge had the young man brought to court: "He was assessed there, even though he had no hearing that day. It solved a problem, but it felt like an extreme solution."

Policy requires that registered intermediaries are not left alone with a witness. There is no such constraint on the defendant intermediary. Recently, an intermediary was accompanied at an assessment in a secure hospital, by "an enlightened defence barrister", but this degree of involvement from defence lawyers is unusual. Most Communicourt and Triangle assessments are conducted without a third party's presence, though a parent is sometimes present at Triangle assessments. Registered intermediaries who are accustomed to being accompanied when working with witnesses often try to find someone to accompany them at a defendant assessment, even if this person is unconnected with the defence team. The position of an intermediary who is unaccompanied in the presence of a defendant could be compromised if the defendant discloses case sensitive information.

Intermediaries appointed after a witness's police interview are entitled to see the DVD or transcript of the interview as an automatic part of their assessment, but this is not the situation when working with a defendant. When given the opportunity to review the transcript of the police interview, intermediaries often identify officers' questions that they feel defendants would not have understood. Jane prepared a report for B, a defendant with severe expressive language difficulties. His legal team was aware that he had learning difficulties but had not realised the extent of his receptive language impairment until after her assessment: "On the first day of trial the case was dropped. Following my report, it was decided that he could not have correctly understood the officer's questions and the court considered his interview to be unreliable."

Confusion with an expert witness

Intermediary assessments for trial may reach one of three conclusions: that the defendant requires intermediary assistance (if the defendant's problem is one of expression rather than understanding, help may be needed only for giving evidence); that an intermediary is unnecessary provided that certain steps are taken to facilitate communication with the defendant (Criminal Practice Directions 3F.4–6, 2015); or that, even with the intermediary's assistance, the defendant may be unable to participate fully in his trial due to the severity of his communication difficulties. This third option is rare but has to be carefully phrased. The intermediary report should not express a view that the defendant's disability renders him 'unfit to plead'; only assessment by an expert witness, a role with different responsibilities, can draw this conclusion.

Defendant intermediaries express concern that they may be appointed for someone who is actually unfit to plead, or their role may be confused with that of an expert witness who will alert the court if the defendant becomes unfit to stand trial. Cameron was put in this position at a trial most of which was to be conducted in Welsh. The defendant Y was bilingual; he gave evidence in Welsh but this intermediary is not a Welsh speaker. Y listened to what was said in Welsh; the intermediary heard the English translation over headphones and simplified this for Y but concluded that this laborious process was overloading him. The translation was slow and the intermediary was not confident that the English translation was exactly what Y was hearing in Welsh:

> 'Although I made suggestions and continually flagged up my concerns, I wasn't listened to. There had been a concern about Y's "fitness to plead" and I'm convinced that I was only there so the court could say "Well, we had an intermediary present, so of course he understood." It was an extremely challenging week.'

A defence barrister in a different case confirmed the possibility of an intermediary being used in this way. He described expert evidence from both prosecution and defence as suggesting that the defendant was "almost fit to plead" and said that the prosecution expert "gave the impression" that appointment of an intermediary would make a fair trial possible.

While intermediaries try to resist being drawn into an expert witness role, the trial judge may nevertheless request a further assessment by the intermediary part-way through the trial and use the findings to conclude that the defendant is unfit to plead. Watson worked with F, who had suffered a head injury several years earlier and had severe difficulties of comprehension, expression and emotional management. The case was pending for two years and was scheduled for a four-week trial. As the first week went on it became clear that F was having significant difficulty in following the proceedings, recalling the events being discussed and understanding the evidence and how it fitted together. He struggled to give his version of events to his legal team. Watson raised these concerns with F's barrister, who relayed them to the judge. He halted the proceedings and asked Watson to 'assess F informally', report how much of the trial F had understood thus far and whether any additional recommendations would enable him to participate for the remainder of the trial:

> 'My assessment confirmed that F was not following the proceedings, although all my recommendations were being thoroughly adhered to. I wrote an addendum report overnight. The judge questioned me about my findings. I stated that I did not feel that F was going to be able to fully participate in the remainder of his trial, even with my assistance and any additional recommendations I could make. The judge decided that F was unfit to plead and that the trial would go ahead as a "finding of fact" case where F would not be required to be present or to give evidence.'

Facilitating the defendant's participation before trial

> 'It is incredibly hard as counsel to give advice or take instructions without occasionally forgetting that your audience may not process matters as easily or at the same speed as 95% of those that you converse with on a daily basis. I thought that I was more than capable of conversing with this defendant. However, when I over-thought "simplified" explanations, my advice often became even more difficult to digest. The intermediary provided an excellent guide and professionally

interjected only as and when she thought necessary; no more, no less. Both myself and my client's father were most grateful for her assistance.' (Barrister)

'The intermediary helped me take instructions from my client. He was able to put matters in simple terms thus enabling me to have worthwhile discussion about the nature and seriousness of the offences. His professionalism was beyond reproach and his report was of great assistance to the district judge by helping him to understand the client's difficulties.' (Defence solicitor)

The pre-trial process must be adapted 'so far as necessary' to facilitate the defendant's effective participation (Criminal Practice Direction 3D.2, 2015; Judicial College, 2013, chapter 5, para 8). Intermediaries assist by explaining the charges and the content of witness statements to defendants, helping defence lawyers take instructions and informing decisions about whether the defendant should testify. In addition, they explain court procedures, arrange court familiarisation visits (including enabling the defendant to practise speaking over the live link – an entitlement for vulnerable witnesses) and help the defendant practise 'rules' for answering questions at court. Crucially, they also help facilitate guilty pleas by ensuring defendants understand the advice of their legal representatives (for example, making a flow chart showing the consequences of plea and conviction) and by explaining legal terminology, such as 'duress' and 'joint enterprise'.

Watson spent a week helping a defence solicitor take instructions from M, a deaf man who was one of several defendants charged with murder. They worked with a British Sign Language interpreter, who advised that M did not use formal British Sign Language but spoke in 'broken' (non-standard) signs. Both the interpreter and intermediary had initial difficulty in communicating with him. Over the week, Watson helped explain the content of documents in the case to M as well as helping him to describe his version of events to his solicitor:

'Many of the witness statements contradicted each other. I had to employ different techniques to make the information accessible to him. For example, we used drawings and diagrams to discuss the scene where the incident took place and little figures to help M understand where all the individual people were and their positions in relation to each other. The most efficient way for him to explain to us what happened was to role-play parts of the scene. We asked him to demonstrate where he was and what he was doing by physically acting it out with us. It was good to be working alongside the British Sign Language interpreter, liaising with her about the best methods of communicating with M to help him tell his side of the story.'

Ground rules hearings

Ground rules hearings must now be scheduled where directions are necessary 'for appropriate treatment and questioning' of a witness or defendant; the intermediary must be present if one is appointed (Criminal Procedure Rule 3.9(7), 2015; Criminal Practice Directions 3E.2, 3E3, 2015). This new requirement may result in further development of good practice in ground rules hearings in vulnerable defendant cases. At the time of writing, practice in respect of ground rules for vulnerable defendants, as for witnesses, is uneven. Even when hearings are held, they are not always constructive. One barrister complained about the failure to "properly identify" ground rules at the hearing. Communicourt advised that although ground rules hearings feature in about 80% of its defendant cases, the intermediaries are not always invited to speak. A solicitor advocate observed that some judges do not know how to deal with defendant intermediaries and do not discuss how to explain their presence to the jury; trial counsel for the prosecution and defence "do not put themselves out to attend ground rules hearings, which makes the hearing unproductive. Those who attend do not have the conduct of the case or detailed knowledge of the defendant." As happens in respect of witness intermediaries, it is preferable for challenges to be ventilated and addressed at the ground rules hearing, yet a barrister reported that: "Any attempt to challenge an intermediary's assessment usually falls upon deaf judicial ears."

Judges vary in their approach to accommodations for vulnerable defendants. Some refuse applications for young defendants to give evidence over the live link, despite their apparent eligibility, or for the removal of wigs and gowns, even though Criminal Practice Direction 3G.12 (2015) states that the wishes of a vulnerable defendant should be taken into account. Recommendations to set limits on the overall length of cross-examination (good practice in respect of vulnerable witnesses) are not always well received, with one judge telling an intermediary: "Not in this court."

Intermediaries provided various examples of diverging judicial attitudes, sometimes between judges of the same court and occasionally in respect of the same judge's differing treatment of a vulnerable witness and a vulnerable defendant with similar needs. Eric contrasted two judges, the first of whom asked many questions about the needs of G, who had Asperger syndrome and severe anxiety. The judge established clear ground rules and explained the purpose of the intermediary role to the jury and why G was holding a stress ball. This judge agreed to the intermediary's request for a second ground rules hearing before G gave evidence (an increasingly common practice):

'He was open to me trying different approaches to reduce G's anxiety. He allowed the dock curtain [usually used to stop a vulnerable witness being seen by the defendant and the public gallery] to be drawn so that G could still be seen by the court but allowed him to feel comforted by the curtain being close to him, creating a small "room". The judge was happy for me to intervene in questioning by speaking directly to the advocates rather than going through him. When I flagged up that the prosecution barrister was not adhering to agreed ground rules, the judge supported me. It makes such a difference when the judge understands your role and what you are doing.'

The second judge conducted the trial of T, who had a learning disability and mental health issues. This judge declined Eric's request for a ground rules hearing:

> 'The judge appeared desperate to race through the trial. Breaks had to be persistently requested and I felt this irritated the judge. The jury bundle and other documentation were only given to me because I insisted; on occasion, there were not enough printouts for T and myself and we had to wait for these to be provided. It felt as if the judge did not understand T's needs or my role.'

Lawyer's receptiveness to intermediary advice

Lawyers differ in their response to intermediary advice about questioning the defendant. Resistance comes primarily from prosecutors, who may incorrectly regard an intermediary appointed for a defendant as part of the defence team. There may be a perception that the defence has requested an intermediary appointment to make a defendant look more vulnerable than he or she really is. A prosecutor commented to us that it was "apparent" that the intermediary was not needed at the Crown Court trial of a 17-year-old defendant with Asperger syndrome because "it was clear from his interview that he was an articulate young man from a supportive family".

A youth court prosecutor told Lorna, who had been appointed for V, a vulnerable adolescent, that he intended to ignore her recommendations "because in the interview V answered all the question types you say he will have problems with". Lorna explained that her duty was to the court, not the defence; that she was there to support everyone's communication with the defendant; and that her recommendations were based on her assessment. "We had a really good ground rules hearing and the judge backed me. In fact, this prosecutor later changed her approach."

Defendant intermediaries go out of their way to introduce themselves and explain their role to all the lawyers in the case. They may offer to review advocates' questions but this is never done as a collaborative exercise involving the intermediary, defence and prosecutor together, as sometimes occurs with a witness intermediary. Lorna finds that reviewing questions can be even more of a challenge in multi-defendant cases:

'When there are co-defendants, some advocates representing the other defendants may let you review their questions ahead of time [see Chapter Twelve]. In one such case, a defence lawyer with whom I had had to intervene said "I didn't get anyone to check my homework." Another said of my interventions: "I had to sit on the naughty chair."'

Facilitating the defendant's participation at trial

'It's a "Catch 22" situation. The judge may say we weren't needed because we didn't need to intervene during the trial, but that's only because of the amount of preparation done ahead of time.' (Intermediary)

'The intermediary sat with the defendant throughout the trial which meant that I did not have to spend any of my time explaining basic facts to the client. She noted down the defendant's legal questions and relayed them to us at a more convenient time.' (Defence solicitor)

The Court of Appeal takes the view that one of the intermediary's most useful functions is to assist judge and counsel in establishing the types of question likely to cause misunderstanding and thus avert it; the judge's overall responsibility for the fairness of the trial is unchanged (*R v Cox* [2012] EWCA Crim 549, paras 28–29). When defendants give evidence, intermediaries see their responsibilities as exactly the same as for witnesses: offering advice beforehand and intervening when questions are too complex or likely to be misunderstood (for example, when figures of speech such as 'caught red-handed' or 'giving someone a dose of their own medicine' are used with defendants whose understanding is literal). They ask for extra time for defendants to process questions and provide aids to support communication.

In the trial of Z, who was deaf and had learning difficulties, Bonnie recommended the use of figures so that he could show rather than tell:

> 'The sign language interpreters were initially resistant to their use but in the witness box, Z floundered and could not describe how a bottle was thrown or how he ran, and so on. When given the figures, he picked them up eagerly and could demonstrate what happened. The interpreters were converted.'

The defendant may require intermediary assistance if asked to look at witness statements or exhibits such as phone records. Bonnie flagged up concerns where F, a defendant with autism, was asked by prosecution counsel to look at a map of phone masts. F did not know what a mast or aerial was and could not read the map, which he described as all 'blurry'. She reminded counsel of reports about the nature of F's problems, at which point "the judge intervened and asked where the prosecutor was heading with this type of question. He was allowed to continue, even though I tried to demonstrate how difficult this was for F."

Despite their neutral status, intermediaries for defendants may not be invited to assist the court in quite the same way as those appointed for a witness. A judge told one intermediary at the start of the defendant's evidence not to intervene and not to take the intermediary declaration; she had to insist on doing so. When working with L, a defendant with a learning disability, George felt that the judge should have stepped in and sought his assistance, instead of which the intermediary was criticised for intervening too much. When George stepped back, the transcript shows that the questioning of L became nonsensical:

Prosecution counsel: 'Have you forgotten which is your left, now I am asking about it?'

Defendant: 'I forget. I have to think.'

Prosecution counsel: 'Imagine I am you and my back is to your front door, left is that way; do you follow?'

Defendant: 'Is it?'

Prosecution counsel:	'Just imagine; we will call it "blogging" direction, just think of it as "blog direction".'
Defendant:	'What does "blog" mean?'
Prosecution counsel:	'It is just an imaginary word because you can't understand the word left, so I have just taken an imaginary word. If you go in that direction from your house you would go down to the end of your street and go round to her back door, can't you?'

George notes that he had requested a break, as previously agreed at the ground rules hearing, when L became tired and confused. This was refused by the judge. The transcript showed that 26 questions were asked by counsel after the intermediary made this request. With hindsight, George felt that he should have requested a break again after a few more questions were asked, "but my resilience was probably low, having been admonished on more than one occasion for my interventions". He asked the court to convene a further ground rules hearing in which he restated that his function was to assist all parties to facilitate communication: "but I sensed that counsel would not consult me for assistance, and indeed they didn't".

People with a learning disability are likely to have difficulty in recognising when they do not understand. They may also be reluctant to say so through fear of looking stupid or because the questioner is an authority figure. When the person with the learning disability is a defendant – particularly someone with 'experience' of the system – courts sometimes misjudge their level of understanding. This is a classic example (O'Mahony, 2012):

Prosecutor:	'If you do not understand a word I use, please can you indicate it?'
Defendant:	'Yes.'
Prosecutor:	'If you don't indicate it, I am going to assume you understood the word; do you follow?'
Defendant:	'Yes.'

Intermediary:	'Your Honour, Miss X may not even understand the word "indicate".'
Judge:	'Hang on, let's keep a balance here. [To the defendant]: Miss X, if you don't understand Mr Y's questions, you say so. That is simple. If you don't say that you don't understand, we are entitled to assume that you do understand.'
Defendant:	'Okay, yeah.'
Judge:	'That is pretty simple with the problems you have. Either you tell us you understand or you don't. I don't see a problem with that.'
Prosecutor:	'Do you understand the word "indicate"?'
Defendant:	'No.'

'Every reasonable step': other intermediary recommendations

Adaptations recommended by intermediaries for a defendant with impaired vision include seating him near the jury box while jurors are empanelled, letting the intermediary explain to the defendant his right to 'object' to any jurors, and obtaining enlargements of evidential photos. Courts have allowed a police officer to read out questions from the defendant's police interview, with the intermediary reading the answers and prefacing each response by saying to the defendant: "You said ...". At the trial of R, a defendant with severe hearing loss and slight cognitive impairment, Roadrunner prepared explanatory information for him in large font. The judge agreed to this approach for other communications, including his opening remarks to the jury. The defence's questions were written in advance, adapted by the intermediary and judge, produced in large print and shown to the defendant at the same time as the defence advocate asked them aloud for the jury. The intermediary also wrote down in large print unplanned questions, often suggesting they be rephrased to keep the written form short and simple.

Cameron recommended that H, a defendant with significant depression and anxiety, use the live link to give evidence but also that he should be allowed to watch the DVD of the complainant's interview in the live link room so that explanations could be provided as necessary: "The judge was very on the ball regarding intermediaries. He really understood why I was there and that I was a communication specialist. He accepted all my recommendations, including those about breaks and the need to shorten the court day."

Assistance in following the proceedings

The defendant's ability to engage with proceedings is one of the criteria by which the fairness of the trial process is judged (*R v Cox* [2012] EWCA Crim 549). During the trial, intermediaries can play a vital role in helping defendants to follow proceedings. Techniques include cue cards ('time to listen/look', 'I can't hear' and 'I don't understand'); updating a visual timetable to help defendants know what is going to happen next; providing 'real-time' explanations (for example, some defendants are disconcerted when the jury leaves the courtroom); and alerting defence lawyers, with a note via the usher, to concerns that their client wishes to raise urgently during cross-examination of witnesses. This aspect of the intermediary's role appears to be highly valued by defence representatives.

Often, however, the trial process is simply too complex for a vulnerable defendant to follow in any detail. Lorna explains in her reports that "to ensure that some defendants understand their trial in real time, the whole court language and process would have to be simplified, and that's not possible". Elena agrees: "Some defendants do not want to listen to all the evidence and only pay attention to the summary at the end of each session."

Managing the defendant's stress and concentration levels

Helping to contain the defendant's stress levels has involved intermediaries in advising, and sometimes providing training for, custody staff. Sometimes intermediaries ask for defendants to be produced from custody a little earlier than usual to allow time to ensure the defendant is calm before the hearing starts. This is not always possible: one intermediary worked with a defendant on the autism spectrum whose journey to court took more than two hours at his first trial and over three hours at his re-trial.

During the second trial, he had to be prescribed medication to help manage his anxiety.

Activities such as doodling and breathing exercises are used to help concentration and manage a defendant's emotional state. Technology can also help: Bonnie recommended that W's behaviour would be improved if he was allowed to use an iPad in the dock with a relaxation programme such as the 'Breathing Zone' app, which can help control and slow down breathing: "After some initial judicial misunderstanding that the request related to an 'eye-pad', it was allowed. W used it while listening to me whisper the main aspects of what was being discussed in court."

Intermediaries often recommend the use of calming objects for the defendant to relieve stress while in the dock. A district judge told us: "Stress objects – yes, Blu-tack – no," after watching a young defendant in the dock make "a large phallic object". Other intermediary recommendations that have been accepted include allowing a volatile defendant to do "heavy muscle work" such as chair push-ups during breaks "to bring his anxiety and anger levels down" and familiarising an autistic defendant out of court hours with speaking from the witness box. He was allowed to practise walking towards the box while his favourite music was played, then answered 'Mastermind-type' questions from the box about his favourite subject. This relaxed him and enabled him to give evidence from the witness box at the trial.

Another key intermediary responsibility is assessing the need for breaks. Jane worked with R, a defendant with Asperger syndrome and post-traumatic stress disorder, who was under witness protection and therefore 'attended' the whole of his trial via a remote live link from a location away from the trial court. Jane built good rapport with R and was able to recognise when his anxiety was being triggered and to request a break to allow him time to recover. The judge allowed her to text the defence barrister in court when breaks were needed: "We also developed a system whereby I wrote notes and held them up to the camera so that they could be seen by the court."

Awareness of the defendant intermediary's contribution behind the scenes

Feedback about defendant intermediaries was mostly positive (see Chapter Fourteen). Several advocates commented on the usefulness of the defendant intermediary's wider role, for example observing that they "are more effective outside the courtroom". However, some judges and lawyers may be unaware of this aspect. A defence barrister who described the defendant intermediary as "very diligent" and noted that most of her recommendations were honoured, nevertheless concluded that he was unsure she "made much difference at all … save for a feeling that I can be assured by the intermediary's presence that I needn't do more than I was doing to feel satisfied that the defendant was following what I was saying to him". One judge observed that defendant intermediaries "did little that could not have been achieved by a solicitor's clerk assisting counsel, but legal aid no longer provides funding for such a person". Views are likely to be influenced in part by the perceived extent of the defendant's needs. Where a defendant was described as having a "severe" autism spectrum disorder, the judge saw the intermediary's involvement as "invaluable", whereas another described an intermediary for a "mildly autistic" defendant as having "played very little part".

Maria was appointed for D, a "difficult, volatile" 15-year-old boy with Asperger syndrome with a history of decamping from meetings with his lawyers and who had absconded from a previous trial. The intermediary's presence helped deter him from leaving the court on this occasion; she stayed with him through the trial up until the point when he finished giving evidence. Maria recalls the judge saying: "'I think we will let the intermediary go now and stop wasting the court's money.' I felt that the judge had no idea of all that went on behind the scenes to make sure that D was there to give evidence effectively."

It can be even more difficult to demonstrate the intermediary's contribution where the defendant does not give evidence. Alexa worked with S, a defendant with behavioural difficulties and a tendency to make frequent verbal outbursts. She found it a significant challenge to manage the S's behaviour in the dock and keep him focused. At the end of the trial the judge thanked her but commented "You weren't really needed after all." The intermediary concluded: "The background work I'd done throughout the trial had gone unnoticed."

A judge who is not fully alert to the extent of a defendant's needs may decide to dispense with an intermediary altogether. A district judge approved a pre-trial application for Melissa to act as intermediary for F, a 14-year-old defendant on the autism spectrum, and asked her to assist defence counsel consult with F. Melissa was then excluded from the youth court trial by a different judge who said: "I have many years of experience talking to young defendants and I don't need guidance." The judge was unaware that, while waiting to go into court, F was exhibiting disturbed behaviour: "He had been drawing people, stabbing them through the heart with a pen and then wearing the resulting 'corpses' as a bracelet." After Melissa left, F apparently became so stressed that "he started crawling round the courtroom floor at one point looking for a lost comfort object, oblivious to the judge's words of admonishment". Later, Melissa sat in on F's closing debrief with his solicitor: "It became evident that he was unaware of what had been said to him by the judge in court."

Working in the dock

> 'The judge explained to the jury why the intermediary was sitting in the dock with the defendant, and why we were going to have more breaks than normal.' (Defence barrister)

> 'Some judges interfere with where intermediaries stand or sit with the defendant, making their presence pointless.' (Solicitor advocate)

> 'When I'm in the dock I regularly signal that I cannot hear and counsel need to speak up, something which I doubt most defendants feel confident to do.' (Intermediary)

On occasion, intermediaries appointed for the trial are allowed to move with defendants to the body of the court. However, the norm is for them to sit with defendants in the dock, accompany them to the witness box and stay with them while they give evidence. Proximity allows the intermediary to monitor understanding, provide explanations and watch for signs of loss of concentration. Nevertheless, they describe being in the dock as a challenge, both physically and professionally. Seating is hard and immovable and the dock is one of the worst positions from which to hear what is said in court. Others in the courtroom may not appreciate the extent to which the dock impairs communication: the security screen reduces sound quality; lawyers have their backs to the dock, reducing their volume; and visual cues from the face of the speaker are lost. Alexa points out that exchanges between the judge and advocates can be particularly hard to hear: "When the barristers discuss points of law with each other and the judge, they speak less audibly than when they address the jury."

Being in the dock also disadvantages defendants and intermediaries who are deaf as they are reliant on communication from a sign language interpreter who is usually some distance away at the front of the courtroom. Not all docks are equipped with hearing loops or earphones (HM Courts and Tribunals Service could not provide details of the number of courts with this equipment: communication, August 2014).

Some courtrooms have microphones to improve audibility. Jeeves recalls a 'toe-curling moment' when she overheard the defence advocates joking together, forgetting that the microphones were still on:

> 'The barrister referred to me as "a scrubber with a scrubber" (my defendant was accused of scrubbing the victim with a scourer). I made him aware I'd heard by glaring at him from the dock. Thankfully, I don't think the defendant heard and the barrister apologised to me afterwards.'

Intermediaries are aware of distractions during the trial such as the movements of dock officers, who have no interest in the proceedings, and the noise of flushing toilets. To counter such difficulties, Poppy often asks for a schedule of 20-minute breaks, at least hourly: 10 minutes for a rest and 10 for the legal team to brief the defendant, clarify what has gone on during the previous hour and take instructions. These breaks also give the intermediary an opportunity to alert the defence lawyer to anything about which the defendant appeared unsure.

Up to half of Triangle and Communicourt appointments are for defendants who also have co-defendants. Intermediaries can find being in the dock alongside co-defendants "difficult and oppressive". The defendant for whom they have been appointed may not have the only, or even the most severe, communication need; it is common for other defendants in the dock to try to follow the intermediary's explanations about what is happening. Tension among co-defendants can have a significant impact on levels of stress and concentration. Elena worked with L, a defendant with autism, in a multi-defendant case:

> 'A guilty verdict was returned on one defendant before the jury had reached a decision about the others, including the one with autism whom I was supporting. This first defendant was involved in a scuffle with several dock officers in the dock and in the corridor outside. I worked with the other defendants encouraging them not to look, to use calming breathing techniques and essentially stopping them joining in to help their friend.'

In the case of S, managing his volatile behaviour was made more difficult by what Alexa felt were deliberate attempts to antagonise S by his co-defendant's barrister:

> 'Initially a joint defence was presented but after the first day it became a "cut-throat" defence [in which one defendant blames the other for the offence]. I quickly realised that in order to have the best chance of S remaining calm, I needed to sit between him and his co-defendant. The other counsel took every opportunity (in court but before the judge entered) to agitate S and provoke an angry outburst. He did this by making frequent references to recent verdicts and prison sentences and when this did not have the desired effect, he took to commenting directly to S

about the way he spoke to a family member who was the subject of many of his outbursts.'

Some vulnerable witnesses fear being seen by the defendant when they give evidence. The witness box can be curtained; if the witness is in the live link room, the defendant's live link screen can be turned off or he can be re-seated where he cannot see the courtroom screen. There is a balance to be struck with ensuring fairness to the defendant: Ashley acted as intermediary for a defendant with learning difficulties and hearing loss where a temporary screen was placed in front of the dock itself, blocking the view of the entire court and making it virtually impossible for the defendant and intermediary to follow what was happening.

The skills and status of the defendant intermediary

'It requires superhuman efforts not to be too much drawn into the defence "camp".' (Intermediary)

'The intermediary in the defence context carries a heavy burden in balancing on one hand the inevitable closeness over a period of time to the client and sympathy with the problems, with on the other the necessity to be scrupulous in observing responsibility to the court and to the administration of justice.' (Judge)

Intermediaries assisting defendants require a broader and more in-depth understanding of the legal process and terminology than when working with witnesses, as they must be able to give simple explanations throughout the trial. As Ramiro says: "It can be very risky to explain some legal point to a defendant only to find out you have not understood it yourself."

Defendant intermediaries not operating on behalf of the two private sector providers negotiate their own contracts and pay rates. Demands on the time of a defendant intermediary are even more uncertain than with witness work: a booking for a three-week trial may disappear without advance warning if the defendant pleads guilty on the first day.

Impact of defence work on the intermediary

Defendant intermediaries regard themselves as neutral and working for the court, not the defence team. This is stated in intermediary reports but is not always well understood by defence lawyers. George recalls "a frosty exchange" with defence counsel who asked for his views about the complainant's evidence, which he declined to give. Elena finds that: "Often the defence barrister will say to the defendant in my presence, 'We're all on your team,' and you have to find an appropriate time to reassert your neutrality." Private communications to anyone responsible for, or likely to be providing views on, the care of the defendant are beyond the intermediary's remit; permission must be sought from the court.

However, the nature of defence work can put a strain on the intermediary's impartiality (O'Mahony, 2013). Ramiro describes herself as needing to be more assertive in "fighting the defendant's corner with prison staff and others who may not be open to suggestions that the defendant has needs. You may also have to deal with the defendant being found guilty and facing a long prison sentence. This can be hard." Claire is conscious that "unless one is particularly watchful, it would be all too easy to cross the boundary into a support role. I've been intrigued to find myself being slightly inclined to stand up for a defendant who is being harangued, but I resisted."

Until recently, formal training on the defendant intermediary role has been available only to those working for the private sector organisations Triangle and Communicourt (in March 2015, the organisation Intermediaries for Justice devoted its first training event to the work of defendant intermediaries). Communicourt and Triangle also make a staff member available to provide advice to their intermediaries when at court. Elena finds that: "Working in teams helps us share experiences and think about ways and methods of working. This means that you can become comfortable with the role more quickly."

All defendant intermediaries operate in an unregulated environment. This requires professional confidence. Even experienced registered intermediaries feel the need for guidance to address the different challenges of defendant work. They feel that the lack of regulation and training is "totally wrong" and that courts are "justifiably confused" by the distinction between registered and non-registered status: "It's the Ministry of Justice's responsibility to plug this procedural gap and prevent further confusion and inequality of access to justice. The role of intermediary should be regulated for all." Eventually, the problems led Ashley to decline defendant appointments, even though she recognises there are benefits: "Working with defendants has enhanced my registered intermediary skills. It has helped me to see how the evidence of a witness fits into the big picture and to appreciate everyone's roles and pressures."

The response of defendants

> 'He felt humiliated by appearing to need assistance in understanding.' (Intermediary)

> 'He said he was "chuffed" that he had managed to say all that he wanted. He was proud that he hadn't sworn or walked away and had "done his best".' (Intermediary)

Defendants in the court system tend to place the professionals with whom they come into contact into one of two camps: those aiming to prove them guilty of offences with which they are charged and those trying to get them acquitted. It is therefore not surprising that defendants can be confused by intermediaries' neutrality and see them as part of the defence team: George is "careful to remind them frequently that I am not". K, a defendant with a mental disorder, thought that George and the defence barrister believed him "because we assisted him to give his account to the court. However hard I tried to explain that I was just facilitating his account and that it was not my role to believe or disbelieve, he did not seem to grasp it."

At the other end of the spectrum, some defendants resent the intermediary's appointment because of the personal implications. Roadrunner worked with H who felt it "lowered his 'street cred' to have someone help him understand what was going on". Sometimes intermediaries are able to overcome this resistance. T, a young man, was assessed by Claire while he lay on the solicitor's office floor, saying repeatedly "'I'm not fucking doing this,'" while actually cooperating "quite a bit, including during the final 10 minutes of my assessment via a mobile phone after he left, saying he'd had enough". At court, Claire persuaded the judge to let T give evidence by video link as he was so distractible and volatile: "T behaved really well once he realised every effort had been made to support him."

After the trial is over, or in the case of a guilty plea, defendants appear to appreciate intermediary assistance when lawyers explain the sentence (in one case, the judge came off the bench to assist in explaining detailed conditions). Intermediaries have also facilitated interviews with youth offending teams and probation officers; the language of the probation assessment questionnaire is complex. However, intermediaries are sometimes unable to follow through with post-sentence work because funding is not routinely available.

Intermezzo

Tag-teaming with Mike, a defendant at the Old Bailey

Bonnie and Ramiro (non-registered intermediaries; also on the Ministry of Justice register)

In the first joint intermediary appointment, we were asked to assist Mike, a young man with learning difficulties who was deaf, in a long multi-defendant murder trial at the Old Bailey. It was agreed at a pre-trial hearing that because of the expected length and complexity of the case, it was advisable for more than one intermediary to be involved. (British Sign Language interpreters were also appointed.) We assessed Mike together and both of us attended the ground rules hearing, sharing the witness box to discuss our report. We worked out a schedule of the trial days each would cover, enabling us to fulfil commitments in other cases. We met to produce symbols for visual support of counsel's explanations of legal terms, which helped Mike decide whether to give evidence.

Mike went into the witness box and managed extremely well, answering questions using picture symbols and signing. He used jointed figures that we supplied to show the jury what happened. Mike would have found this extremely difficult to convey using his limited signing ability. During his evidence both of us attended court. We assisted jointly: one stood next to Mike in the witness box while the other stood or sat just behind. We swapped over during frequent breaks. This worked well as we could speak at the breaks or communicate during the trial by passing written notes with ideas to assist. Intermediary assistance was important in building Mike's confidence, enabling him to make informed decisions. We also helped him to manage his fits of anxiety and depression. We both elected to attend the summing up and the verdict so that we could ensure Mike understood the outcome. He was acquitted of the murder charge but pleaded guilty to an offence of violent disorder.

It was our responsibility to ensure that Mike followed what was said in court. It is often assumed that if a defendant does not make of point of saying he is not following then all must be well. Indeed, if asked, a defendant may state that he has understood: in our experience this is often not the case. Sufficient time must be allocated to the intermediary to go over evidence given in court, using communication aids if necessary. One frustration was the difficulty of obtaining sufficient access to Mike in custody. He could not communicate with prison staff, none of whom used British Sign Language.

The whole experience of working from start to finish on a long, multi-defendant trial was good training in the whole court process. Every evening we debriefed, which proved invaluable in keeping up with the progress of the trial and allowed us to reflect and to discuss possible strategies. This joint thinking also formed a type of peer supervision which helped maintain our wellbeing in this distressing and lengthy case; working together felt less overwhelming than working alone. We both reflected that we felt more confident by the end and had learned a huge amount.

FOURTEEN

A new profession

Intermediaries have emerged as a new professional identity: there is surely potential now for a distinct professional qualification. (In South Africa, the Institute of Child Witness Research and Training plans to launch a university-level National Diploma for Intermediaries in 2015: communication from Karen Muller, November 2014.) Management structures have not kept pace: governance of registered intermediaries who work with witnesses is much as it was at the end of the pilot stage and intermediaries who work with defendants are not subject to regulation at all. The expanded intermediary role has not been evaluated but it seems evident that the system, in respect of services to both witnesses and defendants, is under enormous pressure. In relation to witness work alone, a shrinking pool of registered intermediaries has experienced a five-fold increase in demand over the last five years.

This chapter looks at feedback about the work of intermediaries. It also addresses concerns for future governance: for example, logic dictates that the same regulatory requirements should apply to intermediaries for witnesses and for defendants. It is anomalous for the Ministry of Justice to have oversight of an operational service. The viability of current arrangements must be in question because the Ministry is pulling back from active management of even the existing small pool of registered intermediaries. Key components of effective governance are considered, including monitoring, training, mentoring and supervision, quality assurance and capacity planning. Some possible reasons for the high turnover of intermediaries on the register are explored with a view to encouraging investment in retention. The chapter highlights problems relating to payment for intermediary services and concludes by discussing the potential for raising the profile of the role.

Feedback on intermediary performance

'The intermediary has an important function in the interests of justice.' (Judge)

'At trial, an intermediary is now considered a vital link in the chain to ensure that a witness or defendant is best placed to give evidence.' (Barrister)

This section summarises feedback in respect of intermediary work with witnesses and with defendants. Comments from criminal justice professionals are overwhelmingly favourable.

Positive police and CPS feedback about registered intermediaries

The police and CPS, which pay for intermediaries at the investigative and trial stages respectively, are routinely invited to submit comments to the National Crime Agency which manages the registered intermediary appointments process. Between August 2009 and June 2014 the Agency received over 2,000 comments; these related to only a small proportion of intermediary appointments in that period. However, 99% of the feedback received was positive. Additional information provided to us by police officers and Crown Prosecutors was also almost all favourable. For example, a Senior Crown Prosecutor who is a specialist in rape and sexual offences said:

> 'Having witnessed at first hand the impact that an intermediary can have in facilitating effective communication with a vulnerable witness and ensuring that a witness' communication difficulties are not used against them in a court's credibility assessment, I am undoubtedly more positive about the viability of these challenging prosecutions.'

Many officers acknowledge that their own practice had changed as a result of working with an intermediary: "There are lots of opportunities for the police to learn from intermediaries"; "As an experienced interviewer, it made me think of ways to address interviews which I would probably not have considered in the past." An officer with experience of the scheme since its inception concludes: "It has improved the confidence that people have in us and improved the confidence that we have in ourselves to deal with people who have communication difficulties."

Positive judicial and Bar feedback about registered intermediaries

We received feedback about registered intermediaries from 138 criminal justice professionals, including 77 judges, 37 barristers and one solicitor advocate. Nearly all comments from the judiciary and advocates acknowledge the professionalism, independence and helpfulness of intermediaries. Many commend their contribution both at the ground rules hearing and trial. Judges describe intermediaries as: "focused and appropriate", "cooperative, consensual and effective", "amenable to negotiation" and as having "a very different skill set". As a result: "There is now a much greater awareness of the needs of a vulnerable witness and this has led to simpler, swifter and more effective cross-examination." Individual intermediaries are widely praised, for example, being described as "a class act" and as "bringing light where there was darkness".

It is striking that two-thirds of judges say that working with intermediaries has changed their own practice. They refer to greater awareness that questioning needs to be "simple, short, with just one concept" and "to the point and no waffle". Intermediaries have helped them to "manage cross-examination more firmly"; "take the initiative"; "be more active with counsel, limiting their questions"; and "be more aware of the pitfalls of inappropriate questioning". In considering whether his practice had changed in this way, one judge responded: "My heart says no but my head says yes. We all assume that we can deal with vulnerability but it is very useful to have someone who knows pointing out where we go wrong."

Feedback from advocates (most of whom both prosecute and defend) is also largely positive: "fantastic, proactive and really helpful": "very efficient and sensible … In virtually all respects, intermediaries have shown great professionalism; they have refrained from taking over the examination process, a common fear of lawyers in the case." Advocates speak of intermediaries being "well-received by a less sceptical judiciary", "providing good evidential ammunition for an unenlightened judge to adapt a court" and providing "a useful way of meeting the challenge of difficult judges or opponents who see no need for special measures". Several commend the practice of taking intermediary advice on questions beforehand, thus minimising interventions at trial. Almost all agree that their experience of intermediaries has changed how they interact with vulnerable witnesses and defendants in other cases.

Many judges and lawyers praise the contribution of the intermediary's written report: "If it is authoritative, it makes the ground rules very easy to lay down and apply." This judge's observation is typical:

> 'The report and intermediary input provides detailed and helpful information about a witness that the judge would not know about and would have to ascertain. This saves judicial time and distress to the witness as questioning is more sensitive to their particular circumstances. There is no doubt that the additional information that they provide is of great assistance in the management of a vulnerable witness's evidence.'

Negative feedback about registered intermediaries

Negative comments accounted for only around 1% of police and CPS feedback on the National Crime Agency database. The small number of logged complaints mostly concern failure to attend police appointments, lateness or late delivery of reports; a few relate to assessments perceived to be inadequate. Some officers criticise intermediaries' lack of intervention to assist communication in the interview; others feel that they interrupt too much (both perspectives perhaps indicating a need for better planning).

Similarly, we received little adverse feedback from the judiciary and lawyers. The most sweeping complaint came from a barrister who felt that intermediaries "largely curtail the defendant's right to a fair trial". He queried their independence and criticised their "self-interest" in recommending that an intermediary is needed at trial, because he had never seen an assessment of a prosecution witness that concluded "that no intermediary was necessary".

This criticism seems misjudged: intermediaries assess only those already identified by other criminal justice professionals as likely to benefit from the special measure. While it is unusual for intermediaries to conclude that their assistance is not needed at trial, such reports do occur but would not be seen by defence counsel because no application for an intermediary would be made to the court. This barrister also seemed mistakenly to equate the intermediary role with that of an expert witness: "The defence should have an automatic right to have a separate assessment conducted of the witness's capacity to give evidence by a suitably qualified expert who can properly be described as 'independent'."

A small number of judges and advocates complain that intermediaries disrupt cross-examination by intervening too much but a similar number say they do not intervene enough (see also Henderson, 2015c, forthcoming). However, a small number of reports about differences in the 'quality' of intermediaries are a concern: "In half of the cases, the intermediary did nothing useful. In the other half, especially those involving very young children, they were magnificent" (judge); "Good ones are very good; the poor ones are awful. Those helping child witnesses in sex cases tend to be the best and most helpful" (judge); "I have found a variety of standards and that makes a difference. Some are fierce and will not budge at all, which is not constructive. Some forget that they are in fact independent" (barrister).

But even some critics acknowledge benefits. A barrister who complained about "the hardest and most troubling trial I have ever done" in which "the intermediary constantly interrupted my cross-examination, to the point where I was completely hampered in putting the defendant's case to the witness", ended by conceding that now "I am more cautious about asking tagged questions."

Feedback about defendant intermediaries

Thirteen judges commented specifically on their experience with a defendant intermediary: most were positive. One spoke of "commending publicly" defendant intermediaries who had assisted throughout the trial. Others said intermediaries had raised awareness of "the variety of forms of vulnerability" and described them as "thoroughly professional and of assistance to the court". Yet another observed that they were "most useful" to remedy poor questioning by "too many counsel". This judge cited a barrister for a defendant with an IQ "in the bottom 1%, who asked his client: 'Does that presuppose that you knew that already?'"

Feedback from barristers about intermediaries for defendants was also largely approving, as were comments by solicitors given to the National Crime Agency when it provided registered intermediaries for defendants (some of these comments are included in Chapter Thirteen). Barristers praised defendant intermediaries as "very effective … very helpful to ensure that the defendant understands what is going on whilst counsel is on their feet". Examples included "assistance given in explaining the evidence to a 13-year-old defendant with severe learning difficulties" and an intermediary who "made his position clear and stood his ground when he thought the defendant was not able to concentrate any more". Another found working with the intermediary "an extremely valuable experience. I have had many clients with serious problems who have been treated with sensitivity, but having an intermediary would have given them a much better chance of having a fair trial." In a case where the appointment was 'evidence only', defence counsel described this as "a tremendous help to the defendant and me, particularly in giving him the confidence to give his account".

Concerns focused on the lack of a legislative basis for defendant intermediary appointments. Only two judges were critical of defendant intermediary practice: one who thought that they were "more problematic when dealing with the defendant, especially in a long trial", and another who described a defendant intermediary as "over-protective, making the trial process difficult". The few complaints from lawyers were mostly from those who prosecuted, querying whether individual defendants needed an intermediary; a report that was "short of practical advice" from an intermediary whose "approach was over-interventionist and combative"; and an intermediary who "tried to suggest what she thought the defendant was trying to say thus, in effect, giving evidence [herself]. She did not ask for the question to be rephrased or suggest an alternative question." A defence lawyer criticised the practice where one intermediary conducted the assessment and others accompanied the defendant on consecutive days at trial.

Governance and accountability

> The Intermediaries Registration Board and Quality Assurance Board were created 'to ensure that intermediaries ... meet an acceptable standard nevertheless [they] have neither statutory basis nor coercive disciplinary powers'. (R (OP) v Secretary of State for Justice [2014] EWHC 1944 (Admin), para 31)

Responsibilities for registered intermediaries are divided between different bodies. The Ministry of Justice 'runs' the Witness Intermediary Scheme (R (OP) v Secretary of State for Justice [2014] EWHC 1944 (Admin), para 6). It contracts out the matching service to the National Crime Agency; it also convenes a Quality Assurance Board which is externally chaired. The Intermediaries Registration Board, chaired by the Ministry of Justice, 'focuses on [the scheme's] strategic direction, policy management and *operation*' (Ministry of Justice, 2012, p 48, our emphasis). Following an internal review in 2014, the 'operation' of the scheme was removed from the Board's remit and it is unclear where operational responsibility now lies. The relationship between the committees and the Ministry is ill-defined. Even where recommendations are made with a view to improving the service, there is no obligation on the Ministry of Justice to implement the changes.

Intermediaries are concerned about the lack of oversight. They see little evidence of strategic planning and feel that committees meeting only three times yearly are not equipped to manage a service under considerable pressure or to oversee its expansion. One indicator that the system is in crisis is the growing practice of seeking an available intermediary through Registered Intermediaries Online (RIO), a secure website operated by the National Crime Agency on which intermediaries can exchange information. If the matching service is unable to find an appropriate intermediary by phone, the case is offered to available intermediaries by 'posting' it on RIO. 'Matches' made this way fall outside agreed procedures.

Until recently, there was always a designated Home Office or Ministry of Justice staff member dealing with intermediary issues full-time and responding to their policy and administrative queries. Since the last incumbent left the post, the Ministry of Justice no longer provides this service. The implications have not been explained and so intermediaries are unclear to whom their operational and policy questions should be addressed.

The Witness Intermediary Scheme lacks a liaison point to address 'rubbing points' with other parts of the justice system. Intermediaries have a unique perspective to identify problems across the process: currently, these can only be addressed through informal channels. A major operational concern, at present unaddressed, relates to the inefficient way intermediary time is scheduled by the courts. Problems with court listing are a common cause of complaint across the criminal justice system but this has serious consequences when the number of intermediaries is small and under pressure. Trials involving vulnerable witnesses should be scheduled for a fixed day (Criminal Practice Direction XIII.F.3, 2015; Ministry of Justice, 2013b, Standard 9) but intermediary cases are often allocated to a 'trial week' or other period, requiring the intermediary to hold open in their diary more days than is strictly necessary. A further complication is that the CPS often fails to provide courts with the intermediary's availability dates. These problems have a knock-on effect on workforce planning, limiting the number of trial appointments intermediaries can accept and disrupting existing trial commitments at other courts. The problem is most severe for intermediaries who are also in employment: they say that they had not anticipated the difficulties of accommodating frequent changes to intermediary schedules within their fixed work commitments.

Training, mentoring and quality assurance

Induction training for registered intermediaries is currently delivered in small-group intensive courses led by two academic barristers. The courses have evolved over the scheme's first decade and now include contributions from intermediaries. The training continues to be well received but experienced intermediaries see the potential to draw more extensively on their knowledge to strengthen practice-based skills, for example in relation to tailoring assessments to the needs of the criminal justice process.

There is a clear need to support newly recruited intermediaries. Experienced intermediaries take the view that: "However good the classroom training might be, it can never be adequate preparation for the 'rough and tumble' of a real police interview or trial"; "You can only be taught the basics in a short space of time. So much of the learning is what you do once you come out and actually do the job." In 2014, an optional mentoring scheme was offered to the new cohort of recruits. While the provision was welcomed, it is limited to six half-hour sessions. In future, mentoring of new recruits will be compulsory but experienced intermediaries would like to see the arrangements monitored and extended, possibly along with introduction of a probationary period for those joining the register.

Longer term training needs should be addressed. There is a judicial view – voiced even by those who describe the current intermediary role as invaluable – that "the more experienced the courts become in dealing with child and vulnerable witnesses, the more the need for intermediaries will reduce". We do not agree, but intermediaries will need to improve and develop their skills if they are to continue to demonstrate the value of their unique contribution.

Intermediaries are required to keep a Continuing Professional Development (CPD) log. A process for evaluating a sample of these logs is now in place and there has been a marked improvement in the quality of the submissions. However, many intermediaries express surprise that the requirements for staying on the register are less rigorous than in the professions to which they belong. They are concerned that the CPD criteria do not adequately address what should be expected by way of professional intermediary competence. Strengthening the requirements would involve additional resources, for example for selectively reviewing intermediary reports; uneven quality of writing and lack of support for recommendations is a concern. In practice, intermediaries have seen a reduction in funding for professional development: for the first time since the scheme's inception, no CPD training day was scheduled for 2015.

There are opportunities to strengthen quality assurance procedures through regular feedback. Limited feedback from witnesses and carers was obtained during the intermediary pilot evaluation (see Chapter Two) but their views, which should be obtained as a matter of routine, have not been sought since that time. There is also a gap in respect of the views of legal professionals on intermediaries' court work. A standard annex in intermediary court reports invites the judiciary, lawyers and HM Courts and Tribunals Service to provide comments to the Ministry of Justice; apparently it is unused. (In this respect, the private sector organisations for defendant intermediaries do better, actively soliciting and obtaining feedback from those with experience of their services at court.)

Few complaints from the police and CPS are raised with the Quality Assurance Board. Those it has formally investigated have revealed some concerns about intermediary performance; others have illustrated that the complainant had insufficient understanding of the role and methods used by intermediaries. The Board also monitors negative feedback from the police and CPS that is not the subject of a formal complaint. It is important for confidence in the scheme that an effective way is found to obtain feedback from the judiciary and advocates.

The greatest disquiet about aspects of intermediary practice was expressed by registered intermediaries themselves:

'It's difficult to know what to do when it is clear that a fellow intermediary isn't fulfilling the role or following guidelines. As we are such a small profession and still relatively new, I hate the thought that a negative experience may influence whether someone uses the scheme in the future.'

Intermediaries flag at least three categories of concern. The first is problematic practice in individual cases. Those who have tried on occasion to raise concerns about the work of others express frustration. One intermediary who took over a case from someone else on the register 'blew the whistle' about the first intermediary's work to the Ministry of Justice. This led to an investigation and recommendations for change but "many of these remain unimplemented". The second concern is that some intermediaries accept appointment for witnesses whose needs lie outside their skill set. The third is that, given the increasing number of requests for intermediaries, some – particularly new recruits to the register – are taking on more cases at one time than is realistic to deal with in tight timescales, with the possible knock-on effect that cases will be returned for reassignment to other intermediaries as trial dates approach. These are issues where experienced intermediaries see a need for active monitoring because of the risks to the reputation and reliability of the scheme.

The need for support

> 'It's a lonely role, carried out in very "alien" environments for most of us.' (Intermediary)

Intermediaries are, by their nature, resilient but their role is performed in isolation and can be highly stressful. They are not supervised and have no access to a formal support service. They have created their own regional support groups which are greatly valued; membership is a CPD 'requirement' but some do not attend. The impact of the work can be severe and, in such instances, the lack of formal supervision and support may result in an intermediary leaving the register or taking a break from accepting cases, placing further pressure on capacity:

> 'The nature of the crimes and the impact on you cannot be overestimated. I spend far too much time crying in my car following harrowing interviews. The accounts of sexual and physical violence are horrifying and I often take time out after cases and come off the register for a period to try to come to terms with what I have heard.'

A highly anxious teenage witness with whom an intermediary was working committed suicide just days before he was due to give evidence; the intermediary had to give evidence to the coroner. Another experienced intermediary suffered extreme distress during the course of another case:

> 'It was only when I heard that the witness was not continuing with the case that I became fully aware about the strength of my own feelings and relief that I will no longer be involved. I have been an intermediary for seven years and nothing prepared me for the crimes described. After I completed the assessment, the witness consented to me contacting her psychologist, a potential witness. Due to the circumstances of the case, the psychologist said she had fears for the safety of the witness and her family, which was chilling. Of course I passed this information to the police. The officers involved, like myself, felt stunned and distressed by the witness's disclosures. The officers could share this with one another and with senior officers, and could also access counselling. In contrast, I work in isolation, not as part of a team. When intermediaries are exposed to extremely distressing disclosures, supervision and mentoring should be available; without it, there is a real risk of burnout.'

A few intermediaries have made formal alternative arrangements:

> 'I worked on a particularly horrible case of a
> paedophile ring within a family. I had to take this case
> to supervision and realised that the images had burned
> into my psyche. Thank goodness for supervision,
> which every intermediary should have but is not
> paid for by the Ministry of Justice.'

Stress can also result from the way intermediaries are treated
at trial. Criticism of how some intermediaries perform their
role will be justified on occasion but even when overruling or
disagreeing with intermediaries, most judges and lawyers treat
them as respected officers of the court. However, intermediaries
can come into conflict with those in the courtroom even when
carrying out their responsibilities appropriately. When advocates
are unresponsive to their interventions and judges fail to back
them up by enforcing ground rules, some intermediaries
persevere but others feel obliged to give up in the face of
"barristers who make it very clear they are not going to listen"
or when the judge and barrister are "obviously exasperated".

A hostile judge can make it difficult for intermediaries to
do their job. One ended a recent lengthy ground rules hearing
concerning very young witnesses by requiring the advocates to
submit their questions for his review but said he "had no interest"
in what the intermediary had to say. When cross-examination
started, the intermediary had to intervene after every question.
Advocates take their lead from judges, and are likely to disregard
the intermediary's advice if the judge does so.

Turnover is high across the intermediary scheme and it is
possible that some leave because they find the trial environment
too difficult to cope with. However, even experienced
intermediaries who are familiar with the rough and tumble of
the process describe having been made to feel "totally belittled
and undervalued", "inhibited", "dismissed", "muzzled", "less
free to intervene", "terribly uncomfortable", "brow-beaten" and
"bullied"; "I was not able to do my job properly and felt bad
about that." Melissa worked with E, a terminally ill woman who
gave evidence by remote live link. E had had a laryngectomy

so she was unable to speak aloud; although she could read and write a little, she chose not to as she was also dyslexic. Melissa had to sit with her back to the live link screen in order to try to lip-read answers from E, who faced the camera:

> 'Counsel asked complicated questions requiring complex answers, and also asked further questions while I was still trying to get E's meaning before I could relay her answers back to the court. I kept asking him to stop doing these things but he just talked louder and faster and continued to talk over her. Eventually he started saying sarcastically that he would make a better intermediary as he could lip-read what she was saying better than I could. E was very distressed and needed frequent help from the nurse accompanying her to assist her breathing. The judge did not intervene, not once. In hindsight, I should have asked to speak to the judge without the jury, but I was so concerned about E's poor health that I didn't want to delay proceedings any further. It was perhaps the most complex and upsetting case I have dealt with.'

Overall, these instances are relatively few in number and contrast markedly with the way intermediaries are normally treated, but their impact on the intermediary profession is profound.

While regular supervision paid for by the Ministry of Justice may not be economically feasible, intermediaries should nevertheless be consulted as a matter of priority about the type of support needed in cases with an extreme impact. This would be a small investment compared with the costs of training new intermediaries to replace those who leave the scheme or of losing the services of intermediaries who come off the register temporarily.

Requests for appointment and numbers on the register

'We would use intermediaries more often if there were more of them.' (Police officer)

Ministry of Justice and National Crime Agency figures reveal the growth in requests for registered intermediaries since national rollout: 511 (2009); 1,206 (2010); 1,230 (2011); 1,432 (2012); 1,793 (2013); and 3,332 (2014). The 2014 figure is an increase of 86% over the previous year; 'urgent' requests rose by 30%. Of the requests received since 2009, 75% have come from the police, 24% from the CPS and 1% from defence solicitors or the courts.

Intermediaries have been recruited on an ad hoc basis since the scheme was introduced; this has not kept pace with rising demand. The number of intermediaries on the register is declining (communication from the Ministry of Justice, October 2014). At any given time, only a proportion of registered intermediaries are 'active' – that is, accepting new cases; others are 'inactive', either having requested a temporary break from new appointments or not taking cases in the long term. In 2009 there were 93 intermediaries on the register, 60 of whom the Ministry of Justice described as active. In 2011, the number had risen to 148, of whom 112 were active. This was followed by a two-year moratorium on recruitment and a significant fall in numbers. Recruitment recommenced in 2014 and by December there were 98 registered intermediaries; of these, 77 were classed as active.

The fact that almost all requests result in the appointment of an intermediary is a tribute to the perseverance of the matching service. Nevertheless, it is of concern that the number of unmatched appointments is growing steadily: from 8 in 2010 to 20 in 2012 and 83 in 2014. At the end of 2014, even with the new recruits, the register had little spare capacity.

Early in 2015, the Ministry of Justice announced plans to recruit up to 100 new intermediaries (press release 23 February 2015, www.gov.uk/government/news/courtroom-communications-experts-to-double).

Addressing future growth

'I wish the CPS would consider using intermediaries more widely than they do.' (Barrister)

There are no published figures of vulnerable witness numbers on which to base plans for growth of the intermediary scheme: in these financially straitened times, there are inherent tensions between identifying need and saving money. It is nevertheless clear that intermediary use is uneven: the number of appointments in some of the smallest police force areas exceeds that of forces serving the most populous areas in the country. If the provision of intermediaries for defendants is put onto a formal footing (under consideration by the Law Commission as part of its work on fitness to plead) the numbers needed would certainly increase.

It is, however, possible to estimate projected need in respect of young witnesses, who are automatically eligible to be considered for special measures by virtue of their age. New policies have created a presumption of intermediary assessment for children aged under 11 (Criminal Practice Direction 3F.5, 2015) and for all children alleging sexual assault (Crown Prosecution Service, 2013, paras 37, 85, 86). *Measuring Up?* found that 9% of young witnesses are aged under 11 and that 35% give evidence in sexual offence cases (Plotnikoff and Woolfson, 2009a; this proportion may be increasing because reports of rape against children under the age of 16 have risen by over a third in the last five years: Criminal Justice Joint Inspection, 2014a, Foreword).

Between 25% and 60% of young witnesses have additional need to be assessed by an intermediary due to health or development issues, short attention span or stress symptoms (Plotnikoff and Woolfson, 2007b, 2009a). There is a presumption of intermediary assessment for children aged 11 and under (Criminal Practice Direction 3F.5, 2015) and for any child in sex abuse cases (CPS Guidelines on Prosecuting Cases of Child Sex Abuse 2013, paras 37, 85, 86). Even if only a quarter of the estimated 21,000 young witnesses attending court annually (Criminal Justice Joint Inspection, 2012) was assessed by an intermediary, this would require over 5,000 assessments a year. This is more than five times the current number of appointments for children (880 appointments in 2013: Hansard HC Col 385W, 26 February 2014) which accounts for only 4% of young witnesses attending court.

In a first-time exercise in late 2014, the Ministry of Justice surveyed the current registered intermediary workforce to enquire about capacity and future plans. This is a welcome exercise. The register loses around 10 intermediaries each year; up to a third of successful candidates complete training but fail to register, indicating weaknesses in the recruitment process. Exit interviews are not held but are essential to establish the reasons for turnover and failure to register. Recruiting and training intermediaries is costly and the degree of apparent 'wastage' over recent years is a serious concern. Planning for the future of the scheme should address potential savings achievable through improved retention.

Paying for intermediaries

'In these pressured economic times, it is crucial that the police and CPS recognise that using an intermediary in the right case always justifies the cost incurred.' (Senior Crown Prosecutor)

During the pilot period intermediary costs were met centrally by the Home Office, with the intention of delegating this to local areas at rollout. There was concern that a premature shift in costs would mean that areas that had not experienced the benefits that intermediaries can bring would be slow to request their services if costs had to be borne locally from the outset. The evaluation therefore recommended a two-year transitional phase, with national rollout completed by the end of the first year and the costs of intermediary appointments paid for centrally, at least until the end of the second year. As identification of eligible witnesses improved, a picture of demand based on need would have emerged. This proposal was rejected. At national rollout, the Ministry of Justice immediately transferred responsibility for payment to the police and CPS.

Cost should not be a factor in deciding whether to request intermediary appointments. However, in some parts of the country intermediaries report that frontline practitioners are discouraged from requesting an intermediary by budget-conscious managers. A Criminal Justice Joint Inspection (2014a, para 6.7) identified that police supervisors were required to authorise use of an intermediary; while funding would 'usually' be approved, 'officers indicated that covering the cost of intermediaries in lengthy child sexual exploitation cases, with multiple victims, could be very challenging for forces'.

In 2014, a registered intermediary's hourly rate for professional duties (not travel) was £36, £1 more than when the scheme was introduced a decade ago; in 2015, they received an 80p increase. Intermediaries advise that rates in their other professional work are often much higher. While some remain deeply committed to intermediary work, the government pay scale surely deters recruitment, makes retention more difficult and limits the amount of work that registered intermediaries take on. Unregulated intermediaries for defendants are free to set the charge for their services (see Chapter Thirteen). This is criticised by advocates, particularly in light of cuts to their own legal aid payments.

Correcting misconceptions and raising awareness

> ... the importance of the use of intermediaries to act as child 'buddies'. (Horvath et al, 2014, p 15)

> Intermediaries are 'experts qualified to provide support to vulnerable witnesses.' (Radio Four 'Today' programme, 5 October 2013)

> 'Victims and witnesses will be given more support than ever before with double the number of courtroom experts soon to be available to help them give evidence.' (Ministry of Justice press release, 23 February 2015, www.gov.uk/government/news/courtroom-communications-experts-to-double)

Intermediaries are neither 'buddies' nor, in the court context, 'experts' or 'supporters'. Their role is still misunderstood even within the legal community. Lord Hope, former Supreme Court Justice, spoke in a House of Lords debate against converting the existing policy presumption of intermediaries for children under 11 to a compulsory provision (Hansard, Col 757 HL, 22 October 2014), describing their role as providing 'some kind of protection' for the witness.

There is a specific problem relating to awareness in respect of vulnerable defence witnesses who are eligible for intermediary assistance on the same grounds as witnesses for the prosecution (Youth Justice and Criminal Evidence Act 1999, section 29). However, the defence team does not appear to have equal access to the register. Even given the lower numbers of defence witnesses overall, we are aware of only two requests for an intermediary for a vulnerable defence witness. Both found the Ministry of Justice unhelpful. One request was the subject of a complaint to the National Crime Agency in 2011:

> 'Nothing went well. The intermediary was appointed too late to carry out an assessment or even meet the witness, a child. This meant they could not be used. The system is skewed towards the prosecution and is unnecessarily obstructive in access for defence witnesses. This is clearly unjust as the point of using an intermediary is to achieve best evidence, whichever side this is for. In legally aided cases such as this, which will be the vast majority of cases where an intermediary is required, the system operates with a lack of transparency, is clumsy for defence utilisation and, even worse, requires two separate streams of funding, the Legal Services Commission [now the Legal Aid Agency] and the court [see chapter 13]. This does not make sense and is obstructive. The Ministry of Justice was unhelpful. Just finding out how to obtain an intermediary for the defence was an obstacle course requiring too much time and perseverance. The result is injustice due to an appalling inequality of arms in a country reputed to be fair and just.' ['Equality of arms' is a principle of the Article 6 'right to a fair hearing' in the European Convention on Human Rights.]

We received feedback from a solicitor in 2014 who found an intermediary for a defence witness, but only through a private sector source:

'Just by chance I was given a suggestion by a very helpful registered intermediary to contact an organisation that provided intermediaries for defence work. Funding was not a problem. I had to obtain authorisation from the court and then apply to the Legal Aid Agency for funding approval with two quotes. Once that was in place, I made arrangements for the intermediary to meet my defence witness. The meeting took place in a room at my office and the intermediary was very helpful and put my witness at ease. An assessment was done and assistance was provided at trial. The process on the whole went well. However, the Ministry of Justice was not very helpful in assisting me in finding a registered intermediary to carry out defence work. More needs to be done to assist defence advocates in securing intermediaries.'

Aside from the issue of defence witness eligibility, much could be done to raise the profile of intermediaries generally. The launch of the profession's website (www.Intermediaries-for-Justice.org) in December 2014, spanning the role for witnesses and defendants, is therefore especially welcome. The National Crime Agency website does not refer to the Witness Intermediary Scheme, even in its listing of 'What we do'; a search for 'intermediary' on the Ministry of Justice website is equally unproductive. The criminal justice system's report in this regard might read: 'could do better'.

Intermezzo

Abeni and the musical judge
Bonnie (registered intermediary)

The police requested my appointment after an unsuccessful attempted interview with Abeni, a young woman who had been treated in a psychiatric unit for post-traumatic stress disorder. She had a tendency to vomit when stressed and had been sick in the police interview. She also dissociated, which disrupted her ability to stay in the 'here and now'. I assisted at further police interviews concerning alleged childhood abuse in which she became selectively mute and wrote down her answers.

The ground rules hearing at court was very thorough. We discussed the impact of questioning on Abeni's emotional state. I explained to counsel that despite her normal intelligence, owing to her difficulties I would be monitoring her carefully throughout. Problematic forms of question for her included tags, assertions and 'why' questions; these have an adverse impact on the psyche of someone whose processing is compromised by trauma, triggering over-analysis and self-blaming thoughts such as 'Why doesn't he believe me?' I recommended that counsel focus on 'concrete' questions ('what', 'where' and 'when') and that Abeni be allowed to use figurines, symbol cards and a timeline if necessary. Again, I had to explain why this was appropriate for someone of normal intelligence; her condition meant that on occasion she was simply unable to talk. The judge directed counsel to send me their questions in advance of her evidence.

Abeni initially wanted to give evidence screened in court; the judge offered to have more effective screens borrowed from a local hospital. In the end, she decided to go into the live link room because she did not want to be in the same room as the defendant or to see the jury watching her. The lawyers thought that use of the live link was preferable because of their concern that Abeni might throw up in court. She had concerns about formal court clothing; it was agreed that wigs and gowns would be removed. The judge and lawyers considered whether to wear casual clothes when meeting Abeni; I thought this was unnecessary. The judge and counsel met her in chambers. The judge played music on his sound system in which she was interested; they chatted about favourite composers. He then arranged for the equipment to be taken to the live link room, which was very helpful as we spent a long time in there. At memory refreshing, Abeni found it too distressing to watch her police DVDs; I recommended and it was agreed that the officer could read out the transcripts to her instead.

Despite agreed ground rules, I had to intervene in cross-examination when Abeni was asked 'why' questions; I also requested a further discussion of ground rules when defence counsel's eyes kept going to the ceiling. Abeni was so upset by his facial expressions that she broke down and became mute. She wrote that she was having difficulty in talking about specific events. The judge told her that they could go at her pace. He suggested that she wrote down what she wanted to say and when she had finished she should give the note to the court. A Witness Service volunteer was in the room with us while this went on.

Abeni them proceeded to write down many points. Some were memories; some were flashbacks and others were hallucinations. I suggested that she use a colour coded key to distinguish the hallucinations, flashbacks and the points that were real. She did this. The process took an hour or more and then the clerk took the note to the judge. It was discussed with counsel and given to the jury. She was cross-examined about what she had written down and the judge allowed her to write her answers. Neither advocate was comfortable about this but when dealing with someone who has mental health problems you have to accommodate uncertainty.

I had recommended in my report that Abeni be cross-examined for no more than two hours per session. It took six days for her to say, write and sign all she wanted to say. I reassured her that she could stop but she insisted that she wanted to continue. This trial is not finished, but no matter what the outcome, Abeni was pleased that she had achieved something she really wanted to do – to say publicly things she alleged a relative had done during her childhood. I am not concerned whether it was true or not but I was pleased to see the process being adapted to her needs. The judge directed that I see Abeni after the verdict, whatever it was. (This trial ended in a conviction.)

FIFTEEN

Conclusion

Intermediaries have helped open the floodgates of change. They provide access to justice to witnesses who were previously excluded and contribute to the fairness of the trial process for both vulnerable witnesses and vulnerable defendants. In a raft of creative ways, intermediaries facilitate 'best evidence'. When necessary, they take on a coordinating role behind the scenes to ensure policy commitments are delivered. Their innovations have been enshrined in Criminal Procedure Rules, Criminal Practice Directions, the Equal Treatment Bench Book and *The Advocate's Gateway* toolkits.

Above all, intermediaries have helped rewrite the 'rules' of cross-examination. With the court's permission, they intervene in questioning as a third party – a dramatic departure from centuries of convention. Despite the adversarial nature of the trial process, they increasingly foster collaboration between the parties and the judge to ensure that questioning is developmentally appropriate. As one judge put it: "The first time I saw an intermediary intervene in cross-examination, I thought it was wondrous. But the miracle is what goes on if they don't have to intervene at all." The body of professional knowledge they have brought to the criminal justice system has informed Court of Appeal judgments, not least in relation to restricting the persuasive power of 'tag' questions, a term not previously used in a legal context. In the absence of compulsory training, many advocates are changing their practice as the result of exposure to intermediary guidance.

The intermediary contribution to justice and fairness

The overriding objective of the Criminal Procedure Rules is to deal with cases justly. In 2011, Lord Judge, then Lord Chief Justice, called on lawyers to abandon 'strait-jacketed ideas' about cross-examination of vulnerable witnesses and defendants, declaring that: 'The testing of the evidence – which is legitimate, whether of the defendant or the prosecution witnesses – must be fair in that broadest possible sense' (2011, p 11). This 'fair' approach to cross-examination does not impinge on a defendant's Article 6 rights to a fair trial.

Readers of this book will, we are confident, be persuaded that intermediaries can help the justice system deal with cases more justly and fairly. However, as the book also reveals, their effectiveness is predicated on the actions of others: the police, CPS, judges and lawyers. The empowerment of the intermediary to flag up actual or potential misunderstanding or witness distress is in the hands of the judge. The extent of intervention depends on lawyers' ability and willingness to adopt intermediary advice and abide by ground rules decisions.

None of these is a given. Intermediaries still encounter antagonism, ignorance of their role and disregard for their recommendations. Too often justice and fairness for a vulnerable witness appears to rest on 'the luck of the draw': the witness must be one of the fortunate few for whom an intermediary has been appointed; the judge must be sufficiently case management minded; and the advocates must be both skilled and amenable to modifying their approach. Most intermediaries come to the role without prior knowledge of the criminal justice system and their experience has made them cynical about "game-playing", "entrenched attitudes and behaviours" and questioning that is "unnatural, intimidating and coercive". But they are also encouraged by recent changes in approach.

Intermediaries are the great untold 'good news' story of the criminal justice system. The achievements of the first 10 years are due in large part to the skills and determination of a small group – for most of the decade fewer than 100 – who have truly 'punched above their weight'. The senior judiciary describe access to justice as 'a fundamental feature of any society committed to the rule of law' (Judiciary of England and Wales, 2014b, para 1). Very often, access to an intermediary literally *is* access to justice.

Challenges for advocacy

Recent Court of Appeal decisions provide clear guidance for the questioning of vulnerable witnesses and defendants. The force of this guidance is less clear: even if the advocate is aware of the guidance, he is not obliged to follow it. A recent review of criminal advocacy concluded there was no reason why the requirement of ticketing should apply to the judiciary and prosecution but not to the defence: the profession should 'consider its early adoption' (Jeffrey, 2014, p 32). The Quality Assurance Scheme for Advocates is intended to set a minimum level of competence: even this will be difficult to achieve while the legal professions' written codes and standards differ. There is a need for a single set of advocacy standards in respect of questioning witnesses, whether vulnerable or not (*R v Farooqi and Others* [2013] EWCA Crim 1649, Lord Chief Justice, para 109).

Since intermediaries were introduced, the tendency to overestimate professional competence in questioning vulnerable witnesses and defendants has reduced but still exists. Awareness of what constitutes developmentally inappropriate questioning has improved but the old ways continue to be widely tolerated. Judges do not use professional complaints procedures to deal with recalcitrant counsel. Without a departure from the collegiate courtroom culture, the new duty requiring barristers to report serious misconduct by others (see Chapter Ten) will be honoured only in the breach.

Traditionally, Court of Appeal judgments focus any criticism on the questioning, not the questioner – for example: 'We want to make it clear that we are quite sure that neither counsel cross-examined this child inappropriately' (*R v W and M* [2010] EWCA Crim 1926), although the judgment goes on to make clear that much of the questioning was inappropriate. Aggressive cross-examination of a 16-year-old with mental health problems was described as 'robust and combative ... notwithstanding her obvious vulnerability and fragility ... without characterising it as improper' (*H v R* [2014] EWCA Crim 1555, paras 69–70). This courteous convention to withhold direct criticism from advocates may have coloured the response of a QC who dismissed the change of approach signalled by *Barker* and other key decisions with the words: "It's *only* the Court of Appeal." Judicial case management efforts to address poor advocacy performance would be strengthened if the Court of Appeal's approach to advocates who defy good practice was not quite so gentlemanly.

Cross-examination aims to create doubt about the witness's testimony in order to undermine the other side's case. Until quite recently, it was acceptable to do this by exploiting a vulnerable person's developmental limitations. The changes now taking place are therefore quite extraordinary. The judiciary and professions have been exposed to research-based intermediary recommendations which discredit traditional cross-examination methods. As a result many judges and at least some lawyers now accept that such questioning of a vulnerable witness is no longer appropriate.

These messages are powerfully addressed in new judicial training. The much-delayed requirement of relevant advocacy training is welcome but it is still in the planning stages; it is unclear whether it can deliver the change of culture called for in 2009 by Lord Justice Thomas, now Lord Chief Justice (Plotnikoff and Woolfson, 2009a, Introduction).

The criminal justice system automatically provides the services of an interpreter to someone who does not speak English. The same does not apply to the provision of an intermediary to a vulnerable person whose communication needs may be just as profound. The significant increase in registered intermediaries announced in 2015 is very welcome, but it will only address a small proportion of all those eligible for their assistance. There is a risk that practice will not change, or not change sufficiently, in cases without an intermediary – namely, in the vast majority of cases involving a vulnerable person. In the brave new world of advocacy, the criminal justice system must avoid a two-tier approach and ensure that standards are consistently applied whenever vulnerable people are questioned.

Lord Judge describes the adversarial system as dependent on the proposition that it will produce justice:

> But we have to face the reality that if the adversarial system does not produce justice, that is justice to everyone involved in the process, it will have to be re-examined, and it should be re-examined. If it fails to do justice then the system requires to be changed. (2013a, pp 10–11)

The experience of working with intermediaries has led many in the criminal justice system to reflect on how cross-examination of vulnerable people is conducted. There is a growing acceptance that ways to test evidence must be found that do not rely on leading, confusing or distressing the witness. It is a serious concern that intermediaries report a wish on the part of some advocates to avoid putting their case to the witness, even where it could be done simply and directly and be readily understood. This is unfair and runs counter to the principle of best evidence.

Several years ago, a senior member of the judiciary said to us with a twinkle in his eye, "If we start to pull at the thread of cross-examination, the fabric will unravel." Research findings about the adverse effects of conventional cross-examination on witness accuracy are not confined to children and vulnerable adults. They apply to 'ordinary' witnesses too. There is a need for formal scrutiny of assumptions about cross-examination, perhaps through a new 'Pigot initiative': a quarter of a century on, it is time for a fresh vision.

References

Advocacy Training Council, 2011, *Raising the Bar: The Handling of Vulnerable Witnesses, Victims and Defendants at Court,* http://advocacytrainingcouncil.org/vulnerable-witnesses/raising-the-bar

Advocacy Training Council, 2013, *The Advocate's Gateway,* www.theadvocatesgateway.org

Association of Chief Police Officers and Office for Criminal Justice Reform, 2005, *Intermediaries Pilot Scheme: Giving Witnesses a Voice*

Association of Chief Police Officers, Crown Prosecution Service and HM Courts and Tribunals Service, 2015, *A Protocol between the Association of Chief Police Officers, the Crown Prosecution Service and Her Majesty's Courts and Tribunals Service to Expedite Cases Involving Witnesses Under 10 Years,* www.judiciary.gov.uk/wp-content/uploads/2015/03/police-cps-hmcts-ywi-protocol.pdf

Ayling, T, April 2014, Practise what we preach, *Counsel,* 31–32, http://counselmagazine.co.uk/articles/practise-what-we-preach

Baird, G, Simonoff, E, Pickles, A, Chandler, S, Loucas, T, Meldrum, D and Charman, T, 2006, Prevalence of disorders of the autistic spectrum in a population cohort of children in South Thames, *The Lancet,* 368 (9531), 210–215

Bar Council, 2013, *A Guide to Representing Yourself In Court,* www.barcouncil.org.uk/media/203109/srl_guide_final_for_online_use.pdf

Bar Standards Board, 2012, *Perceptions of Criminal Advocacy,* ORC International, www.barstandardsboard.org.uk/media/1402386/orc_international_-_perceptions_of_advocacy_report.pdf

Bar Standards Board, 2013, *Barristers' Working Lives: A Second Biennial Survey of the Bar*, www.barstandardsboard.org.uk/media/1597662/biennial_survey_report_2013.pdf

Bar Standards Board Handbook, 2014, www.barstandardsboard.org.uk/regulatory-requirements/bsb-handbook/

Blackstone, W, 1769, *Commentaries on the Laws of England*, Oxford: Clarendon Press, www.gutenberg.org/files/30802/30802-h/30802-h.htm

Brown, H, April 2014, *The Death of Mrs A: A Serious Case Review*, Surrey Safeguarding Adults Board, www.surreycc.gov.uk/__data/assets/pdf_file/0011/815384/FINAL-Mrs-A-full-report-26.03.14.pdf

Bryan, K, Maxim, J, McIntosh, J, McClelland, A, Wirz, S, Edmundson, A and Snowling, M, 1991, The facts behind the figures: A reply to Enderby and Davies (1989), *The British Journal of Disorders of Communication*, 26 (2), 253–261; discussion 262–267.

Burton, M, Evans, B and Sanders, A, 2006, *Are Special Measures for Vulnerable and Intimidated Witnesses Working? Evidence from the Criminal Justice Agencies*, London: Home Office, http://collection.europarchive.org/tna/20080205132101/homeoffice.gov.uk/rds/pdfs06/rdsolr0106.pdf

Carlile, Lord, 2014, *Independent Parliamentarians' Inquiry into the Operation and Effectiveness of the Youth Court*, www.ncb.org.uk/media/1148432/independent_parliamentarians__inquiry_into_the_operation_and_effectiveness_of_the_youth_court.pdf

Cashmore, J and De Haas, N, 1992, *The Use of Closed Circuit Television for Child Witnesses in the ACT*, Sydney: Australian Law Reform Commission

Cashmore, J and Trimboli, L, 2005, *An Evaluation of the NSW Child Sexual Assault Specialist Jurisdiction Pilot,* Sydney: New South Wales Bureau of Crime Statistics and Research, www.bocsar.nsw.gov.au/agdbasev7wr/bocsar/documents/pdf/r57.pdf

Communication Matters, 2013, *Shining a Light on Augmentative and Alternative Communication*, www.communicationmatters.org.uk/shining-a-light-on-aac

Cooper, D and Roberts, R, 2006, *Special Measures for Vulnerable and Intimidated Witnesses: An Analysis of Crown Prosecution Service Monitoring Data*, London: Crown Prosecution Service, www.cps.gov.uk/legal/assets/uploads/files/monitoring%20data.pdf

Cooper, P, 2012, *Tell Me What's Happening 3: Registered Intermediary Survey 2011*, The City Law School, www.city.ac.uk/__data/assets/pdf_file/0008/126593/30-April-FINAL-Tell-Me-Whats-Happening-3.pdf

Cooper, P, 2014, Speaking when they are spoken to: Hearing vulnerable witnesses in care proceedings, *Child and Family Law Quarterly*, 26 (2), 132–151

Cooper, P and Wurtzel, D, 2013, A day late and a dollar short: In search of an intermediary scheme for vulnerable defendants in England and Wales, *Criminal Law Review*, 1, 4–22

Cooper, P and Wurtzel, D, 2014, Better the second time around? Department of Justice registered intermediaries schemes and lessons from England and Wales, *Northern Ireland Legal Quarterly*, 65 (1): 39–61

Cossins, A, 2012, Cross-examining the child complainant: rights, innovations and unfounded fears in the Australian context, in J Spencer and M Lamb (eds) *Children and Cross-Examination: Time to Change the Rules?*, Oxford: Hart, 95–112

Crane, P, 1999, Child abuse procedures in practice, *Judicial Studies Board Journal,* 7

Criminal Justice Joint Inspection, 2012, *Joint Inspection Report on the Experience of Young Victims and Witnesses in the Criminal Justice System*, HM Crown Prosecution Service Inspectorate and HM Inspectorate of Constabulary, www.hmcpsi.gov.uk/documents/reports/CJJI_THM/VWEX/CJJI_YVW_Jan12_rpt.pdf

Criminal Justice Joint Inspection, 2014a, *Achieving Best Evidence in Child Sexual Abuse Cases*, HM Crown Prosecution Service Inspectorate and HM Inspectorate of Constabulary, www.justiceinspectorates.gov.uk/cjji/wp-content/uploads/sites/2/2014/12/CJJI_ABE_Dec14_rpt.pdf

Criminal Justice Joint Inspection, 2014b, *A Joint Inspection of the Treatment of Offenders with Learning Disabilities within the Criminal Justice System – phase 1 from arrest to sentence*, HM Inspectorate of Probation, HM Inspectorate of Constabulary, HM Crown Prosecution Service Inspectorate and the Care Quality Commission, www.justice.gov.uk/downloads/publications/inspectorate-reports/hmiprobation/learning-disabilities-thematic-report.pdf

Crown Prosecution Service, 2013, *Guidelines on Prosecuting Cases of Child Sex Abuse*, www.cps.gov.uk/legal/a_to_c/child_sexual_abuse/

Cutts, J, 9 February 2011, presentation, Registered Intermediary Continuing Professional Development day

Darbyshire, P, 2014, Judicial case management in ten crown courts, A Nuffield-funded study of diverse judicial pre-trial case management regimes, *Criminal Law Review*, 1, 30–50

Department for Children, Schools and Families, 2008, *The Bercow Report: A Review of Services for Children and Young People (0–19) with Speech, Language and Communication Needs*, London: Department for Children, Schools and Families, http://dera.ioe.ac.uk/8405/1/7771-dcsf-bercow.pdf

Department of Justice Northern Ireland, 2015, *Northern Ireland Registered Intermediary Schemes Pilot Project: Post-Project Review*, www.dojni.gov.uk/index/publications/publication-categories/pubs-criminal-justice/ri-post-project-reviewfeb15.pdf

Ellison, L, 2001, *The Adversarial Process and the Vulnerable Witness*, Oxford University Press

Ellison, L and Munro, V, 2014, A 'special' delivery? Exploring the impact of screens, live-links and video-recorded evidence on mock juror deliberation in rape trials, *Social & Legal Studies*, 23:1, 3-29, http://sls.sagepub.com/content/23/1/3.full.pdf+html

Ellison, L and Wheatcroft, J, 2010, "Could you ask me that in a different way please?" Exploring the influence of courtroom questioning and pre-trial preparation on adult witness accuracy, *Criminal Law Review*, 11, 823–839

Enderby, P and Davies, P, 1989, Communication disorders: Planning a service to meet the needs, *British Journal of Disorders of Communication*, 24, 301–331

European Commission for the Efficiency of Justice, 2014, *Report on 'European Judicial Systems – Edition 2014 (2012 Data): Efficiency and Quality of Justice'*, www.coe.int/t/dghl/cooperation/cepej/evaluation/2014/Rapport_2014_en.pdf

European Union, 2012, *European Directive Establishing Minimum Standards on the Rights, Support and Victims of Crime*, directive 2012/29/EU of the European Parliament and of the Council, http://eur-lex.europa.eu/legal-content/en/TXT/?uri=CELEX:32012L0029

Family Justice Council, 2011, Guidelines on children giving evidence in family proceedings, [2012] *Family Law* 79, www.judiciary.gov.uk/wp-content/uploads/2014/10/fjc_guidelines_-in_relation_children_-giving_evidence_-in_-family_-proceedings_dec2011.pdf

Family Justice Council, 31 July 2014, 'Interim Report of the Children and Vulnerable Witnesses Working Group', www.judiciary.gov.uk/wp-content/uploads/2014/08/pfd-consultation-interim-report-of-children-vulnerable-witnesses-working-group.pdf

Gawande, A, 2011, *The Checklist Manifesto*, Profile Books Limited

Gerety, C and Kauffman, B, 2014, *Summary of Empirical Research on the Civil Justice Process 2008–2013*, Institute for the Advancement of the American Legal System, University of Denver http://iaals.du.edu/images/wygwam/documents/publications/Summary_of_Empirical_Research_on_the_Civil_Justice_Process_2008-2013.pdf

Graffam Walker, A, 2013, *Handbook on Questioning Children: A Linguistic Perspective*, Washington, DC: ABA Center on Children and the Law

Green, N, 28 June 2014, *Advocacy in Peril?*, Keynote address for the International Advocacy Teaching Conference, Nottingham Trent University, www.judiciary.gov.uk/wp-content/uploads/2014/11/nottingham-speech.pdf

Grove, T, 2000, *The Juryman's Tale*, London: Bloomsbury

Hampel, G, Brimer, E and Kune, R, 2008, *Advocacy Manual: The Complete Guide to Persuasive Advocacy*, Australian Advocacy Institute

Hanmer, O, 2013, Assessment and Assurance, *Magistrate*, October 2013 4-5, issue available at www.magistrates-assocation.org.uk

Hanna, K, Davies, E, Henderson, E, Crothers, C and Rotherham, C, 2010, *Child Witnesses in the New Zealand Criminal Courts: A Review of Practice and Implications for Policy*, Institute of Public Policy, AUT University, www.ipp.aut.ac.nz/__data/assets/pdf_file/0020/119702/Child-Witnesses-in-the-NZ-Criminal-Courts-full-report.pdf

Henderson, E, 2002, Persuading and controlling: The theory of cross-examination in relation to children, in H Westcott, G Davies and R Bull (eds) *Children's Testimony: A Handbook of Psychological Research and Forensic Practice*, Chichester: Wiley, 279–293

Henderson, E, 2012, Alternative routes: Accusatorial jurisdictions on the slow road to best evidence, in J Spencer and M Lamb (eds) *Children and Cross-Examination: Time to Change the Rules?*, Oxford: Hart, 43–74

Henderson, E, 2014, All the proper protections: the Court of Appeal rewrites the rules for the cross-examination of vulnerable witnesses, *Criminal Law Review*, 2, 93–108

Henderson, E, 2015a, Taking control of cross-examination: judges, advocates and intermediaries discuss judicial management of the cross-examination of vulnerable people, *Criminal Law Review*, 9 (forthcoming)

Henderson, E, 2015b, Theoretically speaking: English judges and advocates discuss the changing theory of cross-examination, *Criminal Law Review*, 12 (forthcoming)

Henderson, E, 2015c, "A very valuable tool": judges, advocates and intermediaries discuss the intermediary system in England and Wales, *International Journal of Evidence and Proof*, 19 (3) (forthcoming)

Henderson, E, 2015d, Bigger fish to fry: Should we expand the reform of cross-examination beyond vulnerable witnesses?, *International Journal of Evidence and Proof*, 19 (2), 83–99

Henderson, E, 2016, Communicative competence? Judges, advocates and intermediaries discuss communication issues in the cross-examination of vulnerable witnesses, *Criminal Law Review* (forthcoming)

Henderson, E, Heffer, C, and Kebbell, M, 2015, Courtroom Questioning and Discourse, in G Oxburgh, T Myklebust, T Grant and B Milne, (eds) *Communication in Investigative and Legal Contexts: Integrated Approaches from Forensic Psychology, Linguistics and Law Enforcement,* Wiley (forthcoming)

HM Courts and Tribunals Service, undated, *Registered and Non-registered Intermediaries for Vulnerable Defendants and Vulnerable Defence and Prosecution Witnesses: Guidance for HMCTS Staff*

HM Courts and Tribunals Service, March 2014, *Section 28 Pilot Newsletter*

HM Courts and Tribunals Service, November 2014, *Section 28 Pilot Newsletter*

Hobbs, P, 2002, Tipping the scales of justice: Deconstructing an expert's testimony on cross-examination, *International Journal for the Semiotics of Law* 15 (4), 411–424

Hobbs, P, 2003, You must say it for him: Reformulating a witness testimony on cross-examination at trial, *Interdisciplinary Journal for the Study of Discourse,* 23 (4), 477–511

Home Office, 1989, *Report of the Advisory Group on Video Evidence (The Pigot Report),* London: Home Office, www.law.cam.ac.uk/faculty-resources/download/pigot-report/8979

Home Office, 1998, *Speaking up for Justice: Report of the Interdepartmental Working Group on the Treatment of Vulnerable or Intimidated Witnesses in the Criminal Justice System,* London: Home Office

Home Office, 2002, *Achieving Best Evidence in Criminal Proceedings,* London: Home Office

Home Office, 2003, *Intermediaries: A Voice for Vulnerable Witnesses – Frequently Asked Questions,* London: Home Office

Home Office, 2013, *Code C, Revised Code of Practice for the Detention Treatment and Questioning of Persons by Police Officers,* London: Home Office, www.gov.uk/government/uploads/system/uploads/attachment_data/file/364680/2013_PACE_Code_C.pdf

Hope, T and Walters R, 2008, *Critical Thinking about the Uses of Research,* Centre for Crime and Justice Studies, www.crimeandjustice.org.uk/sites/crimeandjustice.org.uk/files/Evidencebasedpolicyfinal.pdf

Horvath, M, Davidson, C, Grove-Hills, J, Gekoski, A and Choak, C, 2014, *"It's a Lonely Journey": A Rapid Evidence Assessment on Intrafamilial Child Sexual Abuse*, London: Office of the Children's Commissioner, www.childrenscommissioner. gov.uk/content/publications/content_822

House of Commons Home Affairs Committee, 2013, *Inquiry into Child Sexual Exploitation and the Response to Localised Grooming*, HC 68-1

Hoyano, L, 2015, Commentary on R (on the application of OP) v Secretary of State for Justice, *Criminal Law Review*, 1, 79–83

Hoyano, L and Keenan, C, 2010, *Child Abuse: Law and Policy across Boundaries*, Oxford University Press

Jackson, H, 2012, Children's evidence in legal proceedings: The position in Western Australia, in J Spencer and M Lamb (eds) *Children and Cross-Examination: Time to Change the Rules?* Oxford: Hart, 75–94

Jeffrey, W, 2014, *Independent Criminal Advocacy in England and Wales*, Ministry of Justice, www.gov.uk/government/ publications/independent-criminal-advocacy-in-england- and-wales

Joint Advocacy Group, 2011, *analysis of responses to Joint Advocacy Group consultation paper on proposals for a quality assurance scheme for criminal advocates*, Solicitors Regulation Authority, ILEX Professional Standards and Bar Standards Board, www.jag- consultation-response-quality-assurance-3.pdf

Judge, Lord, 2011, *Vulnerable Witnesses in the Administration of Criminal Justice*, Australian Institute of Judicial Administration, www.judiciary.gov.uk/wp-content/uploads/JCO/ Documents/Speeches/lcj-speech-vulnerable-witnesses-in- admin-of-criminal-justice-29092011.pdf

Judge, Lord, 2013a, *The Evidence of Child Victims: The Next Stage*, Bar Council Annual Law Reform Lecture, www.barcouncil. org.uk/media/241783/annual_law_reform_lecture_rt_hon_ the_lord_judge_speech_2013.pdf

Judge, Lord, 2013b, Toulmin Lecture in Law and Psychiatry, *Half a Century of Change: The Evidence of Child Victims*, www. judiciary.gov.uk/wp-content/uploads/JCO/Documents/ Speeches/lcj-speech-law-and-psychiatry.pdf

Judicial College, 2013, *Equal Treatment Bench Book,* www.judiciary.gov.uk/wp-content/uploads/JCO/Documents/judicial-college/ETBB_all_chapters_final.pdf

Judicial Studies Board, 2004, *Equal Treatment Bench Book*

Judicial Studies Board, 2009, Serious Sexual Offences Seminar, DVD

Judicial Studies Board, 2010, *Crown Court Bench Book – Directing the Jury,* www.judiciary.gov.uk/wp-content/uploads/JCO/Documents/Training/benchbook_criminal_2010.pdf

Judicial Studies Board, 2012, *Fairness in Courts and Tribunals*

Judiciary of England and Wales, 2014a, *Section 28 of the Youth Justice and Criminal Evidence Act 1999: Pre-recording of Cross-examination and Re-examination*

Judiciary of England and Wales, 2014b, *The Response of the Senior Judiciary to the Ministry of Justice Consultation Paper Court Fees: Proposals for Reform, Cm 8751,* www.judiciary.gov.uk/wp-content/uploads/JCO/Documents/Consultations/senior-judiciary-response-court-fees-proposals-for-reform.pdf

Judiciary of England and Wales, 2015, *Report of the Vulnerable Witnesses and Children Witness Group,* www.judiciary.gov.uk/wp-content/uploads/2015/03/vwcwg-report-march-2015.pdf

Judiciary Diversity Statistics, 2014, Judiciary website, www.judiciary.gov.uk/publications/judicial-diversity-statistics-2014

Kebbell, M, Hatton, C and Johnson, S, 2004, Witnesses with intellectual disabilities in court: What questions are asked and what influence do they have? *Legal and Criminal Psychology,* 9, 23–35

Kelly, L, Temkin, J and Griffiths, S, 2006, *Section 41: An Evaluation of New Legislation Limiting Sexual History Evidence in Rape Trials,* Home Office Online Report 20/06, http://collection.europarchive.org/tna/20090120202659/homeoffice.gov.uk/rds/pdfs06/rdsolr2006.pdf

Klemfuss, J, Quas, J and Lyon, T, 2014, Attorneys' questions and children's productivity in child sexual abuse criminal trials, *Applied Cognitive Psychology,* (28)5, 780-788, http://onlinelibrary.wiley.com/doi/10.1002/acp.3048/abstract

Krähenbühl, S, 2011, Effective and appropriate communication with children in legal proceedings according to lawyers and intermediaries, *Child Abuse Review,* 20, 407–420

Lamb, M, Hershkowitz, I and Lyon, T, 2013, Interviewing victims and suspected victims who are reluctant to talk, *APSAC (American Professional Society on the Abuse of Children) Advisor*, 25 (4) 16–19

Law, J, Lindsay, G, Peacey, N, Gascoigne, M, Soloff, N, Radford, J, Band, S and Fitzgerald, L, 2000, *Provision for Children with Speech and Language Needs in England and Wales: Facilitating Communication between Education and Health Services*, Department for Education and Employment research report 239, http://dera.ioe.ac.uk/4475/1/RR239.pdf

Leveson, B, 2015, *Review of Efficiency in Criminal Proceedings*, Judiciary of England and Wales www.judiciary.gov.uk/wp-content/uploads/2015/01/review-of-efficiency-in-criminal-proceedings-20151.pdf

Libai, D, 1969, The Protection of the Child Victim of a Sexual Offence in the Criminal Justice System, *Wayne Law Review*, 15, 977–1032

Liverpool Crown Court (2014) *Guidance Note for section 28 ground rules hearings*

Lodder, P, 2011, Why fear the assessment of advocacy?, *The Middle Templar*, 50, 20

Lord Chief Justice, 2015, *Criminal Practice Directions (Amendment No 3)*, [2015] EWCA Crim 430 www.justice.gov.uk/courts/procedure-rules/criminal/rulesmenu

Marchant, R, 2013a, How young is too young? The evidence of children under five in the English criminal justice system, *Child Abuse Review*, (22)6, 432-445, DOI: 10,1002/car, 2273

Marchant, R, 2013b, *New ways to explore understanding of truth and lies with children,* Presentation at International Investigative interviewing Conference, Maastricht

Maybin, J, Mercer, N and Stierer, B, 1992, 'Scaffolding' learning in the classroom, in K Norman (ed) *Thinking Voices: The Work of the National Curriculum Project,* 186-195, London: Hodder & Stoughton

Meehan, R, posted June 1, 2011, *Cross-examination: The Real Truth Serum,* http://blog.ctnews.com/meehan/2011/06/01/cross-examination-the-real-truth-serum

Mendelle, P, 27 September 2014, *Pre-recording questioning of vulnerable witnesses under section 28, Youth Justice and Criminal Evidence Act 1999,* Presentation to the London Criminal Courts Solicitors' Association http://newsletter.v11.the-vx.com/pdfs/vulnerable-witnesses--s-28-alicante-september-2014-final4.pdf

Ministry of Justice, 2009, *Government Response to the Improving the Criminal Trial Process for Young Witnesses Consultation,* London: Ministry of Justice

Ministry of Justice, 2011a, *Achieving Best Evidence in Criminal Proceedings: Guidance on Interviewing Victims and Witnesses and Guidance on Using Special Measures,* London: Ministry of Justice, www.justice.gov.uk/downloads/victims-and-witnesses/vulnerable-witnesses/achieving-best-evidence-criminal-proceedings.pdf

Ministry of Justice, 2011b, *Vulnerable and Intimidated Witnesses: A Police Service Guide,* London: Ministry of Justice, www.justice.gov.uk/downloads/victims-and-witnesses/vulnerable-witnesses/vulnerable-intimidated-witnesses.pdf

Ministry of Justice, 2012, *Registered Intermediary Procedural Guidance Manual,* London: Ministry of Justice, www.cps.gov.uk/publications/docs/RI_ProceduralGuidanceManual_2012.pdf

Ministry of Justice, 2013a, *Code of Practice for Victims of Crime,* London: Ministry of Justice, www.gov.uk/government/uploads/system/uploads/attachment_data/file/254459/code-of-practice-victims-of-crime.pdf

Ministry of Justice, 2013b, *Witness Charter: Standards of Care for Witnesses in the Criminal Justice System,* London: Ministry of Justice, www.cps.gov.uk/victims_witnesses/witness_charter.pdf

Ministry of Justice, 2014a, *Report on Review of Ways to Reduce Distress of Victims in Trials of Sexual Violence,* London: Ministry of Justice, www.gov.uk/government/uploads/system/uploads/attachment_data/file/299341/report-on-review-of-ways-to-reduce-distress-of-victims-in-trials-of-sexual-violence.pdf

Ministry of Justice, 2014b, *Our Commitment to Victims,* London: Ministry of Justice, www.gov.uk/government/uploads/system/uploads/attachment_data/file/354723/commitment-to-victims.pdf

Ministry of Justice, 2015, *Criminal Procedure (Amendment No 2) Rules 2015* www.justice.gov.uk/courts/procedure-rules/criminal/rulesmenu

Office for National Statistics, 2005, *Survey of the Mental Health of Children and Young People in Great Britain*, London: Office for National Statistics, www.hscic.gov.uk/catalogue/PUB06116

O'Kelly, C, Kebbell, M, Hatton, C and Johnson, S, 2003, When do judges intervene in cases involving people with learning disabilities?, *Legal and Criminal Psychology*, 8, 229–240

O'Mahony, B, 2012, Accused of murder: Supporting the communication needs of a vulnerable defendant at court and at the police station, *Journal of Learning Disabilities and Offending Behaviour*, 3 (2), 77–84

O'Mahony, B, 2013, *How do Intermediaries Experience their Role in Facilitating Communication for Vulnerable Defendants?*, Professional doctorate, DPharm thesis, University of Portsmouth (available under resources on www.theadvocatesgateway.org)

Plotnikoff, J and Woolfson, R, 1993, Replacing the judge's pen? Evaluation of a real-time transcription system, *International Journal of Law and Information Technology*, 1 (1), 90–106

Plotnikoff, J and Woolfson, R, 1995, *Prosecuting Child Abuse*, London: Blackstone Press

Plotnikoff, J and Woolfson, R, 2002, *Judges' Case Management Perspectives: The Views of Opinion Formers and Case Managers*, London: Lord Chancellor's Department, http://lexiconlimited.co.uk/wp-content/uploads/2013/01/Judgescasemanagement.pdf

Plotnikoff, J and Woolfson, R, 2004, *In Their Own Words: The Experiences of 50 Young Witnesses in Criminal Proceedings*, London: NSPCC, http://lexiconlimited.co.uk/wp-content/uploads/2013/01/InTheirOwnWords.pdf

Plotnikoff, J and Woolfson, R, 2007a, *The 'Go-Between': Evaluating in six pathfinder areas the use of intermediaries to assist vulnerable witnesses to communicate with the court when giving evidence*, http://lexiconlimited.co.uk/wp-content/uploads/2013/01/Intermediaries_study_report.pdf

Plotnikoff, J and Woolfson, R, 2007b, *Evaluation of Young Witness Support: Examining the impact on witnesses and the criminal justice system,* http://lexiconlimited.co.uk/wp-content/uploads/2013/01/Young_Witness_Study_Report.pdf

Plotnikoff, J and Woolfson, R, 2008, Making best use of the intermediary special measure at trial, *Criminal Law Review,* 2, 291–104

Plotnikoff, J and Woolfson, R, 2009a, *Measuring Up? Evaluating Implementation of Government Commitments to Young Witnesses in Criminal Proceedings,* NSPCC and Nuffield Foundation, http://bit.ly/1u16QE9

Plotnikoff, J and Woolfson, R, 2009b, *Good Practice Guidance in Managing Young Witness Cases and Questioning Children,* NSPCC and Nuffield Foundation, http://bit.ly/1um8UYT

Plotnikoff, J and Woolfson, R, 2011, Young witnesses in criminal proceedings: A progress report on *Measuring Up?,* Nuffield Foundation, www.nuffieldfoundation.org/sites/default/files/files/Young%20witnesses%20in%20criminal%20proceedings_a%20progress%20report%20on%20Measuring%20up_v_FINAL.pdf

Plotnikoff, J and Woolfson, R, 2012, 'Kicking and screaming' – The slow road to best evidence, in J Spencer and M Lamb (eds) *Children and Cross-Examination: Time to Change the Rules?,* Oxford: Hart, 21–41

QASA, 2013, *Handbook for criminal advocates,* Bar Standards Board, ILEX Professional Standards, Solicitors Regulation Authority, www.qasa.org.uk/QASA-Handbook.pdf

Righarts, S, Jack, F, Zajac, R and Hayne, F, 2014, Young children's responses to cross-examination-style questioning: The effects of delay and subsequent questioning, *Psychology, Crime & Law,* 21(3), 274-296, http://dx.doi.org/10.1080/1068316X.2014.951650

Russell, A, 2006, Best practices in child forensic interviews: Interview instructions and truth-lie discussions, *Hamline Journal of Public Law and Policy,* 28, 99–130

Sanders, A, Creaton, J, Bird, S and Weber, L, 1997, *Victims with Learning Disabilities,* Occasional Paper No 17, Oxford: University of Oxford Centre for Criminological Research

Saywitz, K, 2002a, Developmental underpinnings of children's testimony, in H Westcott, G Davies and R Bull (eds) *Children's Testimony: A Handbook of Psychological Research and Forensic Practice*, Chichester: Wiley

Saywitz, K, 2002b, *Child Victim Witness Bench Handbook*, California Center for Judicial Education and Research

Schalling, E, 2009, Accessibility to health-care services: The need to build more 'communication ramps', *International Journal of Therapy and Rehabilitation*, 16 (3), 126–127

Schuman, J, Bala, N and Lee, K, 1999, Developmentally appropriate questions for child witnesses, *Queen's Law Journal*, 25, 251–304

Solicitors Regulation Authority, 2010, *Statement of Standards for Solicitor Higher Court Advocates*, www.sra.org.uk/solicitors/accreditation/higher-rights/competence-standards.page

Spencer, J, 2012, Introduction, in J Spencer and M Lamb (eds) *Children and Cross-Examination: Time to Change the Rules?*, Oxford: Hart, 1–20

Stevenson, M and Valley, H, 23 May 2014, Pre-recorded cross-examination, *Criminal Law and Justice Weekly*, www.criminallawandjustice.co.uk/features/Pre-recorded-Cross-Examination

Talbot, J, 2010, *Seen and Heard: supporting Vulnerable Children in the Youth Justice System*, Prison Reform Trust, www.prisonreformtrust.org.uk/Portals/0/Documents/SeenandHeardFinal%20.pdf

Talbot, J, 2012, *Fair Access to Justice? Support for Vulnerable Defendants in the Criminal Courts*, Prison Reform Trust, www.prisonreformtrust.org.uk/portals/0/documents/fairaccesstojustice.pdf

Wigmore, J, 1974, *Evidence in Trials at Common Law*, Boston, MA: Little, Brown & Company

Williams, G, 1987a, Videotaping children's evidence, *New Law Journal*, 108, 351

Williams, G, 1987b, Child witnesses, in P Smith (ed) Criminal Law: Essays in Honour of J.C. Smith, *Cambridge Law Journal*, 46, No. 3, 539–541

Wurtzel, D, January 2011, Advocacy focus: David Wurtzel believes that the guidance given by the Court of Appeal in *R v M and W* on questioning young witnesses has muddied its own message, *Counsel*, 40–42

Wurtzel, D, November 2012, Time to change the rules?, *Counsel*, 33–34, www.counselmagazine.co.uk/articles/time-change-the-rules

Wurtzel, D, 2014, The youngest witness in a murder trial: Making it possible for very young children to give evidence, *Criminal Law Review*, 12, 893–902

Yamamoto, K, Solman, A, Parsons, J and Davies, O, 1987, Voices in unison: Stressful events in the lives of children in six countries, *Journal of Child Psychology and Psychiatry*, 28, 855–864

Zajac, R, O'Neill, S and Hayne, H, 2012, Disorder in the courtroom? Child witnesses under cross-examination, *Developmental Review*, 32 (3), 181–204, www.sciencedirect.com/science/article/pii/S0273229712000275

Index

Index

Table of cases